PRECARIOUS BALANCE

STUDIES IN RELIGION AND CULTURE

John D. Barbour and
Gary L. Ebersole, Editors

PRECARIOUS BALANCE

Sinhala Buddhism and the Forces of Pluralism

Bardwell L. Smith

University of Virginia Press • *Charlottesville and London*

University of Virginia Press

Printed in the United States of America on acid-free paper

First published 2022

1 3 5 7 9 8 6 4 2

Library of Congress Cataloging-in-Publication Data

Names: Smith, Bardwell L., author.
Title: Precarious balance : Sinhala Buddhism and the forces of pluralism / Bardwell L. Smith.
Description: Charlottesville : University of Virginia Press, 2022. | Series: Studies in religion and culture | Includes bibliographical references and index.
Identifiers: LCCN 2022012101 (print) | LCCN 2022012102 (ebook) | ISBN 9780813945378 (hardcover) | ISBN 9780813945385 (paperback) | ISBN 9780813945392 (ebook)
Subjects: LCSH: Buddhism—Sri Lanka—History. | Sinhalese (Sri Lankan people)—Religion. | Social conflict—Sri Lanka. | Social conflict—Religious aspects—Buddhism. | LCGFT: Essays.
Classification: LCC BQ359 .S65 2022 (print) | LCC BQ359 (ebook) | DDC 294.3095493—dc23/eng/20220524
LC record available at https://lccn.loc.gov/2022012101
LC ebook record available at https://lccn.loc.gov/2022012102

Cover art: PrinceOfLove/Breaking The Walls/Shutterstock

CONTENTS

Preface vii

Note on Transliteration xvii

Introduction 1

1 Concepts of an Ideal Social Order as Portrayed in the Chronicles of Ceylon 5

2 Kingship, the Sangha, and the Process of Legitimation in the Anurādhapura Period, Third Century BCE to Tenth Century CE 31

3 Varieties of Religious Assimilation in Early Medieval Sri Lanka 53

4 The Pursuit of Equilibrium: Polonnaruva as a Ceremonial Center, 993–1293 75

5 Sinhalese Buddhism and Its Modern Quests for Identity: The Dilemmas of a Pluralistic Society 101

6 Identity Issues of Sinhalas and Tamils: Dilemmas of Identity in the Throes of Social Conflict 125

Epilogue: A Vision of Pluralism Enacted 135
JERRI HURLBUTT

Notes 139

Selected Bibliography 165

Index 177

PREFACE

Visiting Sri Lanka frequently (seven times) since 1965, I have considerable appreciation for its people, history, and culture. Friendship and scholarly ties in that country remain important to my professional and personal life. Years of studying Sri Lankan society also provide a healthy respect for the nation's conflictive forms of ethnic, cultural, economic, and religious identity. Seeking to understand the protracted tensions between the Liberation Tigers of Tamil Eelam (LTTE) and successive governments of Sri Lanka, and the increasing communalism that surfaced after independence more than seven decades ago, one heeds historian Kingsley de Silva's words that "the country is haunted by a history which is agonizing to recall but hazardous to forget." This preface is about one of my visits, in 1998, which exemplifies the importance of understanding the present through its history.

I came to Sri Lanka at that time to make arrangements for American undergraduate students on the consortial Intercollegiate Sri Lanka Education (ISLE) program, founded in 1983, to study with faculty at the University of Peradeniya, near Kandy. Preparing myself for a two-month visit, I was influenced by a clinical psychologist friend whose concerns are centered on issues of peace and justice. Having gathered a basket of stones from Lake Superior, she discovered, to her surprise, that by placing one of these at locations that cry out for reconciliation she became better able to address situations that appeared to be intractable. Moved by this simple practice, I packed six small gneiss rocks for our trip to India and Sri Lanka. In this case, the rocks were even more special, as they were gauged to be 3.6 billion years old, among the oldest in the world.

Because of the complex relationship over two millennia between India and Sri Lanka, I selected a few sites in each country. Within India I chose Odisha and Tamil Nadu, as these were already on my wife Charlotte's and my itinerary. They were examples of places manifesting cultural beliefs in mythic powers that once channeled human energy for constructive purposes. In no way did I expect that these acts of placement would have any social impact. Rather, they represented my conviction and experience that transforming energy is latent, if not obvious, even in the heart of destructive circumstances.

Site number one was Dhaulī (five miles south of Bhubaneswar in Odisha), the location of Aśoka's 13th Rock Edict, which, based on Buddhist principles, contains a central document of Aśokan history. According to Romila Thapar, in *Aśoka and the Decline of the Mauryas* (1961), this edict is regarded by Buddhists as evidence of destructive power being transmuted into alternative means of exercising dominion. The choice of "conquest by Dhamma" rather than by violence arose out of Aśoka's remorse upon seeing the slaughter of the Kāliṅgas on the battlefield before him. The transformation of this celebrated ruler from Candāśoka (the cruel Aśoka) to a paradigm of responsible power—Dharmāśoka—has exerted considerable influence on many Asian models of kingship. On the other hand, the use of this story for ideological purposes by various Buddhist monk scholars and political figures in Sri Lanka over the centuries is well chronicled. The contrast with Aśoka's counsel of tolerance among different religious communities could not be more striking.

It seemed appropriate to insert a stone inside the cage surrounding this edict carved in Brāhmī script (translated into Odia, Hindi, and English) at Dhaulī. Juxtaposed against the original site of battle from the third century BCE is the interesting addition atop a nearby hill of a white peace pagoda, built by Japanese Buddhists in the 1970s. To these latter-day Buddhists, Dhaulī remains a symbol for the possibility of peace in the present time, not just a remembrance of an ancient king's decision.

In the temple city of Kānchipuram (Conjeeveram), forty miles southwest of Madras (Chennai) in Tamil Nadu, is a large Shaivite complex, the Sri Ekambaranātha Temple, with its 190-foot-high gopura, five large separate enclosures, and a huge multipillared hall. Kānchi, one of India's great sacred cities, was for centuries the capital city of the Pallava, Chola, and Vijayanagar kingdoms. It remained in a tense relationship with its island neighbor to the south, allying at times with certain factions in Sri Lanka, frequently at war with others, but typically perceived as a threat from the mid-Anurādhapura period through the Polonnaruva period that followed. Over this long period there were migrations as well as invasions into Sri Lanka, with a steady flow of Hindu influences, especially Shaivite. Out of this mixed history emerged a chronic ambivalence in the Sinhala psyche about South India's hovering presence. The ambivalence was politically reasonable, but its more paranoid form still colors Tamil and Sinhala perceptions and behavior, especially within Sri Lanka, adding to a climate of suspicion.

As one of many great temples in Tamil Nadu, this temple to Shiva, located in the region's capital with its vast patronage from successive dynasties, possessed symbolic and worldly importance. Kānchipuram was sacred to Vishnu as well and was once a noted center for both Buddhists and Jains. With this confluence of religious traditions, with the region's extended political predominance, and with its impact on Sri Lankan history and culture, this particular temple seemed an apt place for stone number two. Because peaceful relations had sometimes existed between communities of different persuasions, might not Kānchipuram or other South Indian centers of influence play this role again? Despite skepticism over such an outcome, I communicated my request to Sri Ekambaranātha's senior priest, who personally placed the stone on the central altar. Invoking Shiva's blessing for a peaceful resolution to the ongoing tensions between Tamils and Sinhalas in Sri Lanka, he understood my motive and was not offended by the request. Hopes of transforming violent interaction, however, do not survive without strong doses of realism. The escalations of violence from both sides are well documented.

After several days in Tamil Nadu we flew to Sri Lanka for our two-month stay. What I sought in this two-month period was greater clarity of understanding about the complexity of forces composing Sri Lanka and how these were in tension with counterparts in India. My project was thus related to my own decades of research on Sinhalese Buddhism and the social order in this part of South Asia.

This particular time (January and February 1998) was an eventful one. It was not only the occasion for celebrating the ISLE program's fifteenth anniversary; it was also the fiftieth year of Ceylon's independence from Great Britain and of its entry into the British Commonwealth, an event about to be attended by Prince Charles and other dignitaries. Kandy, the former Sinhala capital in the central highlands, had been selected as the focal point of this celebration. Administrators from our program's participating colleges in America spent four days early in January in this part of the country. Among the places we visited was the Temple of the Tooth in Kandy, where I placed the first of my remaining four stones.

The Temple of the Tooth (Dālada Māligāwa) is well known for housing the sacred Tooth Relic of the Buddha that, as tradition reports, was brought from India in the early fourth century CE, hidden in the hair of an Odishan princess. The Buddha's eyetooth symbolizes the strength and independence of the Sinhala nation. Over centuries it was kept in successive centers of power, finally reposing in Kandy in 1590. In the Esala Perahera festival, celebrated every midsummer, the parading of this relic in the central district of Kandy occasions an intermingling of Buddhist and Hindu beliefs and practices. Thus the Dālada Māligāwa is revered not only by Buddhists but also, in various ways, by other religious communities, including Hindus. As sponsors of a program whose students study local beliefs and customs, it was natural for us to visit this site. The security outside and inside the temple was palpably tense, but once inside, one's focal length switched to the beauty of the colors, the symbolism, and the sense of history. It was in a white lotus flower on the altar in the "Hall of Beatific Vision" that I placed another small rock.

Three weeks later, in stark juxtaposition to this ritualized visit, a powerful bomb exploded at 6:00 a.m. on Sunday, January 25, outside the entrance to the Dālada Māligāwa. As the crow flies it was a mile from where we were living. Jolted out of bed by this explosion, we could see smoke, in the darkness of early morning, rising from the temple area. Over the next two hours we learned that the bomb had been delivered in a truck driven by a suicide squad of the LTTE. Crashing the security gates alongside the area in which the shrines to the deities Nātha and Pattinī are located, the truck raced down the pathway toward the Māligāwa, only to be stopped short of its goal to enter the temple. News reports indicated that thirteen persons had been killed, among them security people, several civilians, and three Tamil Tigers. Many others were injured. The extent of damage to various religious buildings was considerable, but the inner chamber had not been impaired. A number of nearby structures (the Queen's Hotel, several banks, and stores) had windows blown out, some suffering worse damage. Even the Devon Hotel across the lake had extensive breakage of glass.

In the hours following the explosion, time passed as if in slow motion. It was impressive to see how people, in Kandy especially, were stunned by the lengths to which Tamil extremists had gone in this attack. Thousands of people lined the south side of the lake, looking in disbelief at the temple across the way. Sinhala and Tamil alike were incredulous at what had taken place. Over the preceding two decades, violence against one ethnic or religious group had often resulted in retaliation by members of other groups. On this rare occasion, the worst attack symbolically, it was different. Not only had President Kumaratunga acted promptly by urging calm on TV and by visiting the bombing site and the injured in the hospital, but uncharacteristic restraint was displayed by most people in every religious community. In fact, the bomb attack had backfired, bringing condemnation by Tamils as much as by Sinhalas, generating again the prospect that communalism could be transcended.

I felt like a CNN reporter communicating by email to the agent institution of our program as to whether the fall semester should be canceled. Since no further incident occurred in the Kandy-Peradeniya area, we continued as planned. Throughout the country the situation remained uncertain, as it had been since the early 1980s. Threads of hope continued within a climate of sustained mistrust.

The fourth site at which I placed a stone is, aside from the Temple of the Tooth, the most holy spot to Buddhists on the island. A sapling from the original Bodhi Tree in Bodhgaya had supposedly been brought by Aśoka's daughter, Samghamitta, in the third century BCE. Known as the Śri Mahā Bodhi, this ancient vestige of the original enlightenment is located in

Anurādhapura, a place we had visited many times. Beginning in 1965, by foot and on superannuated rented bicycles, I had leisurely traversed for two or three days at a time this remarkable city, the island's capital for a thousand years. By mid-February 1998, however, portions of Anurādhapura, with its vast sweep of partially reconstructed dagobas, monasteries, palaces, and other ruins, had become heavily guarded, fenced off, and protected by elaborate security measures.

We were startled by the military presence, though the reasons for caution were obvious. It was also a reminder that over this city's long history there were numerous times when it had become a besieged capital and the target of invasions from South India, as recorded in inscriptions, documents, and art history. While Anurādhapura is well acquainted with sorrow and grief, the present threats seemed more determined. The site of the sacred Bodhi Tree, by its location near the railway station and by its symbolic significance, is often the starting point for visiting other features of this large area. One is immediately aware of the caged condition of this venerable tree, sometimes considered the "oldest historically authenticated tree in the world." Its appearance at that moment was like a patriarchal lion confined in a large but shabby compound for its own safety, protected from a threatening world. The area, once open to access, had been a symbol of freedom from suffering caused by attachment to greed, violence, and ignorance. While ancient symbolism persisted, its altered appearance was strikingly incongruous.

Entering the compound, we were drawn up the steps toward the base of the tree. The three of us, my wife and I accompanied by a Sinhala-speaking close friend, were alone except for the slender figure of a woman quietly engaged in chanting, seated on the sand-covered hard surface near the railing a few yards from the tree. When she had finished, our friend, recognizing that she was a type of Buddhist nun, spoke to her about the heavily guarded nature of this place. As it turned out, she had been there with a sizable group of pilgrims on that day, May 14, 1985, when a segment of Tamil Tigers forced their way into the compound and began shooting randomly with automatic rifles at everyone in sight. Somehow, she escaped the rain of bullets that killed 146 people and wounded many others. Those killed included twenty-five women, one bhikkhu, and four Buddhist nuns. Her account was grimly specific, told without animus, but was eloquent in its portrayal of a society locked in self-contradiction.

As one hears about Tamil terrorism, one recalls repeated atrocities committed by government troops and local police, as well as the rioting, especially since 1983, instigated by Sinhala groups against innocent Tamils throughout the country. To place a stone at the Bodhi Tree, having listened to this woman's story, intensified my understanding of why efforts in conflict resolution had come to nothing. It is clear that no lasting antidote to cynicism is possible except through nonviolent and nonideologically driven means. Placing this fourth stone in the tree's enclosure, we were brought full circle to where we started two months before at Dhaulī, a place whose meaning lies in reminding others of how unrelieved atrocity is self-perpetuating but also how violence can, so say the edicts of Aśoka, be transformed into responsible power. This private act of placing a stone reinforced one's hope for such a possibility, however unlikely it seemed at that time.

Two weeks after the event at the Dālada Māligāwa, my wife and I, with two former students and a colleague from the University of Peradeniya, decided to make the ascent to Adam's Peak, which provides a commanding view of the surrounding area. Even more interesting is its significance to the major religious traditions on the island: at the top is a large, stone footprint, which is said to be that of the Buddha by Buddhists; the locus of Shiva's creative dance (Shivan Adipatham) by every Hindu; the footprint of Adam (the primeval human) by both Muslims and Christians; and by Roman Catholics the footprint of the Apostle St. Thomas, who had preached the gospel in South India. Before the arrival of these traditions, the mountain was called "Sumanala Kanda" (Saman's Hill), the sacred lodging of the region's protective deity, whose residence here imbues other traditions with a presence free from communal struggle, though it, too, is a tradition reconstructed over time.

The coexistence of diverse spiritual paths up the mountain is a harbinger of resolvable conflict. To destroy one person's sacred meaning at this site would be to destroy one's own. The higher one climbs, the further one seems to leave behind the violent turmoil below. Ascending in the darkness of night, one has a sense of rising above the stars on the horizon. It is a heady feeling, different from what one ordinarily experiences. Even if one has climbed this mountain before, one does not know what lies ahead, up the infinite steps, around each twisting corner. One climbs above the forested jungle below and knows that in a few hours one will return to a world that cannot be escaped. Because of this double awareness, one of aspiration, the other of sobriety, the climb provides clearer recognition that what we see day after day we seldom see in its own terms. One's vision of ordinary life is distorted, not just limited. Yet the climb itself, not just the view from the top, triggers one's imagination to see beyond communalism.

The hours spent at the summit waiting for the sunrise is a time of quiescence following the steep, five-hour 7,300-foot climb. It is a pause before the most awesome of creation's miracles. One is deeply moved by the sight of this returning source of energy. As one mother expressed it, seeing the golden orb rise out of the distant ocean is like watching the head of a child emerging from a contracting uterus. It is literally a rebirthing of life. In all religions there is celebration of nature's prime miracle. Impressive forms of this awareness are found in early Vedic and later Hindu rituals known as *saṃdhyā,* chanted by a priest who welcomes the dawn, the noon, and the close of each new day. At the first glimpse of the sun that day, the pilgrims gathered on Adam's Peak and in one voice gasped in amazement.

Before descending, I asked my colleague, a scholar of Sinhala literature, if he would inquire of the Buddhist monk, supervising the pilgrims queued up to venerate the sculpted footprint of the Buddha, whether I might place a stone along with my donation at this shrine. Informing the monk that this was an act of devotion on behalf of reconciliation and peace, my friend vouched for my goodwill and my familiarity with Sinhala Buddhism. The monk was clearly moved by this request and motioned us to enter a door leading to where he stood and allowed me to place a stone directly on the "footprint." I was not prepared for my own feelings of gratitude toward his receptivity to my request.

Why had I been so moved? In part because this time and place were a tangible instance of how people, sometimes suspicious of each other, were in this shared sacred space transported beyond their normal prejudices and separated destinies. To believe, however briefly, in the possibility of reconciliation among warring groups is to experience a glimmer of regenerated vision. It is to become a pilgrim in the midst of conflicting evidence. The damage we do to each other by our fears and hatred is damage we inflict upon ourselves. Given the oft violent social order in Sri Lanka, one descends the mountain and reenters the ordinary world where suffering and ambiguity flourish. But in the meantime, one's skepticism has been chastened.

I began writing this preface after learning that Neelan Tiruchelvam (1944–99), a scholar who had worked to bring warring sides together, had been assassinated. Because his whole adult life had been devoted to advocacy of pluralism and diversity as intrinsic to healthy political structures and process, the loss was incalculable. That is precisely why he was such a threat to extremists: his efforts toward justice and peace were based on the vision of an inclusive society. Such a vision is never promoted by ideologues, let alone by terrorists on either side. One is equally aware that judgments rendered by outsiders, such as myself, may only exacerbate what is already tragic.

As for my final stone, I carried it home as a reminder that violence and the need for reconciliation are everywhere. Each stone was, after all, a testimony to a twin truth—about the omnipresence of suffering and about belief in a path to the overcoming of suffering. In this period of ten weeks, which was never intended to be a pilgrimage but became one of sorts, the realization had grown that the casting of blame across political, ethnic, and religious lines is constant, making it unlikely but clearly possible for either side to recognize its complicity in this unfolding self-destruction.

The preface is a revision of an article previously published as "Talismans of Hope in Worn-Torn Sri Lanka." *Dharma World: For Living Buddhism and Interfaith Dialogue* 29 (November/December 2002): 21–25.

Chapter 1 is revised from "The Ideal Social Order as Portrayed in the Chronicles of Ceylon," in *The Two Wheels of Dhamma: Essays on the Theravada Tradition in India and Ceylon,* by Bardwell L. Smith, Frank Reynolds, and Gananath Obeyesekere, 31–57, AAR Studies in Religion 3 (Chambersburg, PA: American Academy of Religion, 1972). Reprinted earlier, with permission, in *Religion and Legitimation of Power in Sri Lanka,* edited by Bardwell L. Smith, 48–72 (Chambersburg, PA: Anima Books, 1978), with permission from Columbia University Press.

Chapter 2 is revised from "Kingship, the Sangha, and the Process of Legitimation in Anurādhapura Ceylon: An Interpretive Essay," in *Religion and Legitimation of Power in Sri Lanka,* edited by Bardwell L. Smith, 73–95 (Chambersburg, PA: Anima Books, 1978), with permission from Columbia University Press; revised from an essay originally published in *Buddhism in Ceylon and Studies on Religious Syncretism in Buddhist Countries: Report on a Symposium in Goettingen* (Goettingen: Akademic der Wissenschaften, 1978), a volume edited by Heinz Bechert and included in the series of the Abhandlungen der Akademic der Wissenschaften in Goettingen. The conference took place in Goettingen in July 1974.

Chapter 3 is revised from "Varieties of Religious Assimilation in Early Medieval Sri Lanka," in *Buddhist Philosophy and Culture: Essays in Honour of Nicholas J. Jayawickreme,* edited by David J. Kalupahana and W. G. Weeraratne, 259–78 (Kelaniya, Sri Lanka: Vidyalankara University, 1987).

Chapter 4 is revised from "In Pursuit of Equilibrium: Polonnaruva as a Ceremonial Center," in *The City as a Sacred Center: Essays on Six Asian Contexts,* edited by Bardwell L. Smith and Holly Reynolds, 60–87 (Leiden: E. J. Brill, 1987), with permission from E. J. Brill. Also published in the *Journal of Developing Societies* 2 (1986): 208–35.

Chapter 5 is revised from "Sinhalese Buddhism and the Dilemmas of Reinterpretation," in *The Two Wheels of Dhamma: Essays on the Theravada Tradition in India and Ceylon,* by Bardwell L. Smith, Frank Reynolds, and Gananath Obeyesekere, 79–106, AAR Studies in Religion 3 (Chambersburg, PA: American Academy of Religion, 1972). Reprinted earlier, with permission, in *Contributions to Asian Studies,* edited by K. Ishwaran, 3:1–25 (Leiden: E. J. Brill, 1973).

Portions of chapter 6 appeared in "Identity Issues of Sinhalas and Tamils," in *Buddhism, Conflict and Violence in Modern Sri Lanka,* edited by Mahinda Deegalle (New York: Routledge, 2006).

I wish to thank John D. Barbour for his help in the long process of guiding this manuscript to publication. I thank Jerri Hurlbutt for her careful editing of my writing and for writing the epilogue, based on our conversations. I am grateful to Roger Jackson for making the chapter abstracts and keywords and for a final careful editing.

NOTE ON TRANSLITERATION

Following the lead of A. L. Basham, editor, *A Cultural History of India* (Oxford: Clarendon, 1975), a simplified system is used in these essays. For the most part, only five letters with diacritical marks appear here (ā, ī, ū, ṃ, ṅ, and ś), except in quotations and in the index (where the standard system used by Indologists is employed). Terms that have become familiar ones in the West (e.g., Theravāda, Mahāyāna, Brāhmanism, Tantrayāna, etc.) are used without long marks. Likewise, Śrī Laṅkā (Sri Lanka) is transliterated without diacritical marks.

PRECARIOUS BALANCE

INTRODUCTION

What follows in this collection of six essays is a re-presentation of my earlier studies in Sri Lankan history as a way of assessing how they may help to shed light on contemporary issues. The six essays in this book were written over a long period of time—from 1972 to 2012—and in most cases have been published previously but never in one collection, and not at all in a manner that accents the various themes that have existed in their different forms over centuries in Sri Lanka's history. This latter-day process has revised and deepened my own recognition of how the present, while not a mirror of the past, remains, in Kingsley de Silva's words, *haunted* by its long and rich history. The central task in these essays is to discuss a number of themes that have been present throughout this history. They are presented as points of focus to highlight the many issues that have, in my estimation, considerable implications for understanding many features of modern and contemporary Sri Lanka.

I am well aware that many important events have transpired in Sri Lanka since most of these essays were written, including the end, in 2009, of the long ethnic conflict that overshadowed so much of Sri Lankan life in the late twentieth and early twenty-first centuries. Yet the issues bedeviling the island three or four decades ago can hardly be said to have reached a full resolution. I also am well aware that many scholarly works of significance have been published on issues addressed here since the publication of my original essays. I have not been able to incorporate references to more recent scholarship into my essays or the notes to them, but have added a handful of relevant sources to the bibliography. While certain elements of my historical accounts and bibliographic references might require updating, I hope that the research and perspectives presented in my essays still speak to the concerns of scholars of Sri Lankan history, religion, and society, and to those interested in Theravada Buddhism more broadly.

The intent of chapter 1 is to examine concepts of an *ideal social order* as found in the earliest chronicles of the Sinhalese people, the *Dīpavaṃsa* and the *Mahāvaṃsa*. These portrayals deal with images of an ideal, not with historical facts in some independent or objective sense. The focus here is on the classical period of Sinhalese Buddhism from its inception in the third century BCE to the fall of its early capital Anurādhapura in 1029 CE and on how Sri Lanka came to regard itself as the *dhammadīpa,* the "island citadel" of Buddhism in its purest form. In sketching out the ingredients of an ideal social order the chapter discusses four elements: (1) the sense of continuity—of Indian tradition with Sinhalese tradition and of earliest Buddhism with later emerging forms; (2) the threat of disorder, particularly in relation to kingship; (3) the symbiotic relationship between monarchy and Sangha; and (4) the interconnection between what happens in society and what occurs in the cosmos at large.

The purpose of chapter 2 is to explore the process of legitimation with specific reference to the relationship between the monarchy and the Buddhist Sangha within the long Anurādhapura period (third century BCE to tenth century CE). The precariousness of social and cosmic order is addressed first, as this connection is sensed by tradition and attempts are made to fashion forms of existence that are less vulnerable to chaos or anarchy. The affirming of both historical and cosmic dimensions of legitimation that provide the structures and values of a particular society within some transcending authority is also discussed. Important here are the tensions that exist between varied claimants to legitimized power within any community and thus the resultant balancing of power, as well as the manner in which legitimation of authority is reinforced in symbolic, ritualistic, and doctrinal modes. The chapter ends with an examination of the validation of power in the midst of pluralistic perceptions of reality and in the face of crises threatening personal and communal existence alike.

In chapter 3, various modes and features of assimilation within Sinhala Buddhism in early Medieval Sri Lanka are discussed. They are viewed as comprising a spectrum—a model—not as isolated phenomena. These modes are sixfold: (1) resistance to assimilation, (2) proneness to assimilation, (3) the process of assimilation leading to synthesis, (4) limited assimilation within a hierarchical structure, (5) the tensions of polarity in the process of assimilation, and (6) the potential for a transformative process, from form to formlessness. In particular, the chapter looks at the process of assimilation in ways that indicate how Sinhala Buddhists became skilled yet sometimes threatened in relationships with other religious traditions.

Chapter 4 examines the principal forces at work in the Polonnaruva period (993–1293 CE), with a focus on the premodern capital city and how it related to other centers of power and influence within Sri Lankan society. Three approaches are employed here. The first is to investigate the political and socioeconomic developments of this period and the implications these had for Polonnaruva and other regions of the country. In this context, forms of pluralism were in ongoing tension with a centripetal process, generated from the capital, that sought to maintain equilibrium and to resist threats to the prevailing social and cosmic order. The second approach is to assess the process of legitimizing authority within this era. The last approach focuses on Polonnaruva as a ceremonial complex and the roles of ritual, symbolism, and cosmology as part of Sri Lankan society's overall response to cultural and social pluralism.

In chapter 5, the role of Sinhalese Buddhism is examined within the modernizing process in Sri Lanka and in the context of pluralizing forces. Five topics are addressed here. The first is the nature of sacro-political authority as perceivable from the classical to the modern period in India and Sri Lanka. The second involves the nature and impact of Sinhalese Buddhist identity in ancient and current forms, in relationship to the perceived essence of the early community and to the continuing quest for national self-consciousness. Third, the Buddhist Sangha, its genius for creativity as well as endurance, its patterns of decay and reform, and its present organizational crisis are examined. The fourth topic addresses the ongoing search for unity in the midst of pluralistic forces within Buddhist communities and within diverse local, national, and wider settings. The chapter concludes with a discussion of the primary vocation of Buddhism of keeping distinct, yet continually relating, the two domains labeled "sacred" and "profane."

Chapter 6 addresses the contemporary and complex issues revolving around identity for Sinhalas and Tamils in Sri Lanka and the role these issues play in the country's social conflict. The chapter begins with a broader discussion of the various elements of personal, communal, and national identity. In Sri Lanka, ethnic, class, religious, and other indicators of identity, in particular the differing interpretations of past and present grievances, have led to stalemate, violence, a culture of disarray and mistrust, and a neglect of the country's political and economic needs. These various aspects of the complexity of identity, each of which constitutes a significant part of the interplay between religious and social change in contemporary Sri Lanka, need to be understood. The chapter argues that the narrowness with which social identity is often defined and defended impairs efforts to imagine new possibilities. Such possibilities require coping with traditional and newly created definitions of self, community, and nation side by side. The chapter continues with a discussion of fundamentalism's failures and a summary of some of the primary points of Tamil and Sinhala self-interest. It concludes with a call for a vision of an inclusive society, as articulated by the words of Aśoka.

This text is bookended by two personal essays. The preface is an account of the author's decades-long history with Sri Lanka and of his witnessing the precarious balance of conflict and reconciliation, made more poignant on a pilgrimage in Sri Lanka in 1998. This experience can be described as practicing the vision of inclusive identity, one that acknowledges both the omnipresence of suffering and the belief in a path to the overcoming of suffering. At the end of the book, the epilogue offers a realized vision of a pluralistic community grounded in inclusion, as experienced by the author at the Asian Rural Institute in Japan. Here participants from around the globe and of different religions and ethnicities take part in learning and practicing sustainable agricultural measures and community leadership. This book tries to imagine the grounds for vision and hope, encompassing both clear-eyed realism and hard-won, fragile optimism.

1

Concepts of an Ideal Social Order as Portrayed in the Chronicles of Ceylon

> [*Sunātha me, Sunātha me.*] Listen to me, I shall relate the Chronicle of the Buddha's coming to the island, the arrival of the relic and the Bo-Tree and the advent of the Buddha's religion in the island and of the doctrine of the teachers who made the collection as well as of the advent of the chief of men. . . . Listen to the eulogy of the island, incomparable, that which deals with the lineage of the best dwellers, original, unrivalled and well-narrated, handed down by the elect, described by the noblest and adorned by the righteous.
>
> —*Dīpavaṃsa* (129–30 CE)

So begins the earliest Pāli chronicle of Sri Lanka (Ceylon), an authoritative historical poem, written in the late fourth or early fifth century CE by an unknown author. It is the aim of this chapter to discern the image or concept of an ideal social order that may be found within the pages of the two primary chronicles of the Sinhalese people, the *Dīpavaṃsa* and the *Mahāvaṃsa.* Together, these documents trace the history of Lanka, beginning with the advent of Vijaya from India in 483 BCE through to modern times. It must be stressed that this essay deals with the *images of an ideal,* not with historical facts in some independent or objective sense. In line with the chronicles themselves, the focus here is on the classical period of Sinhalese Buddhism, from its inception in the third century BCE to the fall of its early capital Anurādhapura in 1029 CE. For primary material the essay focuses largely upon these chronicles, though examination of other sources has helped to fill out the picture.[1]

Immediately, the question of historiography arises: how is one to treat source material such as the *Dīpavaṃsa* and the *Mahāvaṃsa,* material that is more normative than descriptive, more poetic than the writing of history as we now know it? It is difficult enough knowing how the chroniclers imagined the history of Buddhism, let alone discovering what the facts were during this period. B. C. Law may not be wrong in saying about the chronicles that "just as the religious motive cannot be divorced from the cultural achievement, so the patriotic motive cannot be separated from the promotion of the general cause of piety."[2] Clearly, this is history written with a motive. It is *heilsgeschichte.* It is the sacred history of a people who regarded themselves as destined with a sacred mission, namely, to maintain the purity of the Dhamma in a world of impermanence and self-seeking.[3] As one enters the world of these chronicles, one enters a world not unlike that of the Hebrew Bible (Old Testament), a world in which bare fact was less important than what the fact signified. In any case, this is interpreted history. It is didactic by nature, sometimes moralistic. By definition, it is ethnocentric; history itself revolves around the perceived history of this people. At its worst, it becomes fiercely judgmental, condoning savagery if done in the cause of mission. But, in all of this, one walks on familiar ground, as no people recording their ancient past (or their present, for that matter) are free of self-justification. As with wisdom literature in general, whether in the *Jātakas* or as found within the Sinhalese chronicles, the primary intent is twofold: to provide paradigmatic models for the present and the future and to engage in anamnesis or cultic reawakening of a people to the high points in its sense of past and present destiny.

Any piece of literature can be judged by what it excludes as well as by the bias it reveals. Clearly, the interests of the chroniclers acted as a sieve that ignored much that we would like to know. As Walpola Rahula stressed about these writings, "Secular history is subservient to religious history."[4] In no sense is this a history of Sri Lanka. It is at most source material for the history of Buddhism in Sri Lanka, especially for the Mahāvihāra bhikkhus, material composed of myth, fable, legend, and history interpreted through tradition. B. C. Law is right in saying that "germs of historical truth" are "buried deep under a mesh of absurd fables and marvelous tales."[5] Or, as put differently, by E. F. C. Ludowyk: "The garb in which these fantasies appear says more perhaps of the cultural and social circumstances of a people than its recorded history. To discard legend, and myth, and fairy tale would just as much rob one of one's most valuable sources of information about a people as to reject its art and literature as unimportant."[6]

With these comments in mind, this chapter proceeds to sketch out the central ingredients of an *ideal social order* as this emerges from the richly varied stories, accounts, and interpretations that comprise the chronicles in question. In the process, four categories are explored. First is the sense of continuity that is present throughout—continuity of Indian tradition with Sinhalese tradition, of earliest Buddhism with later emerging forms, of popular religious expression with the Buddha Sāsana itself. The second category is the awareness of evil and the ever-present sensed threat of disorder, in relationship to which the concept of kingship becomes an ambiguous reality.

Third is the concept of *Dharma-vijaya* (of conquest through righteousness, not force) as developed originally by Aśoka and as reaffirmed by the Sangha in Sri Lanka, providing the basis for a complex, ever-changing symbiosis between monarch and Sangha and between monarch and people, establishing the normative pattern for Sinhalese kings from the earliest days. And finally, the chapter addresses the assumed interconnection between what happens in society and what occurs in the cosmos at large, alongside the depiction of an ideal king and the configurations of the City of Righteousness, as these in some sense presage, and in some sense prepare people for, the ultimate goal of Nibbāna.

The Sense of Continuity

From start to finish in the chronicles one is kept aware of historic continuities, whether those of royal clans and families, apostolic succession (*ācariyaparamparā*) within the early Sangha, the lineage of the Buddha himself, or those stemming from cultural contact and productive of new forms.[7] Only a detailed study could do justice to Sri Lanka's cultural indebtedness to both Aryan and Dravidian India. The basic social and political institutions, the vast majority of literary and art forms, the gift of the Dharma itself all passed from the subcontinent over centuries to Sri Lanka.[8] The story is a complex and fascinating one in its own right; only certain highlights can be touched on here. This will be explored further in chapter 3, in which the ongoing process of religious assimilation is discussed.

One thread that provides both meaning and threat to Sinhalese self-consciousness is the ever-recurring pressure of Tamil invasion and occupation. Neither the present scene in Sri Lanka nor its lengthy history can be understood without a vivid awareness of the ambivalent relationship between these two peoples, now one of alliance and reciprocity, now of embittered hostility. Over the centuries it was essentially the latter that prevailed, reaching epic proportions in the chronicles and draining the economy and human resources seriously at many points in time. The "myth had been cultivated under Duttugemunu [Dutthagāmanī 101–77 BCE] and was writ into Sinhalese political tradition" that the Tamils were Lanka's natural enemy.[9] Whether from the Pāndyans, the Cholas, or the Pallavas, the threat never disappeared. By invasion, by infiltration, by being used increasingly as mercenaries, and through intermarriage, the Tamils made their presence felt until finally in 1325 they had established an independent kingdom in the north of Sri Lanka.

Far more important for our present subject, however, were the Brahmanic influences on Sinhalese culture and religion. Following the model of Aśoka in his reputed tolerance of other religions, Buddhism displayed openness toward many Hindu institutional forms and devotional practices, absorbing or converting them in the process. Wilhelm Geiger underscores the fallacy of separating too radically Buddhism from Brahmanism.[10] Brahmanism was regarded more as preparatory to Buddhism than antagonistic. The Hindu gods, Indra (Sakka) especially, are invoked throughout as guardian and protective figures who further the Buddha's cause in Lanka. As Theravada Buddhists typically indicate, the gods play no role in the attainment of Nibbāna.[11] In the Buddha's words, one must remain a refuge or island unto oneself; no one can cross over for another.[12] If this qualification is maintained, then orthodoxy has no quarrel with divine assistance. In the *Mahāvaṃsa* the Buddha himself speaks to Sakka prior to entering *parinibbāna,* recording in his last will and testament his wish that Vijaya, his followers, and Lanka be protected by the gods.[13]

Throughout the establishing and maintaining of the Dhamma in Sri Lanka, the path is facilitated for the Buddha's followers by the heavenly hosts, whether in the consecration of the nation's rulers, the arrival of the relics, the coming of the Bodhi Tree, or the wars against enemies. To put this into perspective with the Buddha's teaching, one may posit a correspondence between assistance rendered by the gods and that afforded by Sinhalese kings. While different in substance and degree, both serve to create the climate in which the Dhamma may thrive. In essence, then, the gods are converted to the Buddha's cause, revealing the cosmic nature of its scope.

With respect to Brahmanical influences on the Sinhalese concept of kingship and the political order, an entire study would be profitable.[14] Suffice it to indicate here the continuity that is apparent, without elaborating on its configurations. Of symbolic importance is the fact that Sinhalese kings retained both the central ingredients of the Hindu coronation ceremony (*abhiśeka*) and the institution of the *purohita,* or domestic chaplain to the throne. While partly ceremonial or cultic in form, these provided a perspective that conveyed extensive Brahmanical culture in the process. While it is possible to make too much of this channel, as discontinuities in the transformation of the caste system and in other areas are also important, the tie with Aryan tradition that this provided is unmistakable. Linguistic, religious, familial, economic, and political elements passed regularly from Indian to Sinhalese soil, inadvertently contributing to a partial "Sanskritization" of this culture and to an increasing, almost dominant Hindu influence in the Gupta period (ca. 320–550 CE) and beyond.

One aspect of the *purohita*-monarch relationship that needs further exploration is how this helped to introduce and institutionalize realpolitik procedures and policies. In what ways, for instance, whether through the king's chaplain or not, were policies shaped by the stratagems of Kautilya's

Arthaśāstra, the Machiavellian manual of Indian regents? Paul Mus, in commenting on the Theravada scene as a whole, raises this same question: "Even in ancient history has not State Politics in the area derived its inspiration more from the pragmatic tradition of power developed in neighboring Hindu Kingdoms, than from so aloof and retiring a Church?"[15] While somewhat rhetorical in nature, for he is equally concerned to show how Buddhism has expressed itself politically, Mus's question suggests the impact that Indian statecraft had on policy making in Theravada-influenced societies generally, an impact that is prominent in the Sinhalese chronicles. The teaching of *nīti,* or statecraft, to the future King Dhātusena by his uncle is one case in point.[16] While not at the hands of a royal chaplain—in fact, the uncle was a bhikkhu—the explicit mentioning of a ruler's need for such knowledge and training is both symptomatic of the internecine and foreign adversaries each king faced *and* symbolic of the Sangha's recognition that, this side of the coming of Metteyya (Maitreya, the future Buddha), heads of state do not rule by righteousness alone.

The final continuity to be mentioned is, for our purposes, the most important one. It is that which links the Buddha and early Buddhism in India to the advent and confirmation of the Dhamma in Sri Lanka. The *Dīpavaṃsa* and the *Mahāvaṃsa* both open with an account of the Tathāgata's three visits to Lanka in the first eight years of his enlightenment. These events are not recorded in the Pāli canon but, alongside the Buddha's invoking of divine protection for Lanka, set the stage in Sinhalese self-consciousness for its efforts to preserve the purity of the master's doctrine. Even this continuity is set in a Brahmanic context, for it is an astute Brahmana, the youngest of 108 consulted to interpret the meaning of the thirty-two "distinctive marks" (*lakkhanāni*) on the infant Siddhattha, who predicts that he is to become a Buddha, not a universal monarch (Cakkavatti).[17] And it is a converted Brahmana, Dasaka, who inherits the apostolic mantle from Upāli as the chain of succession proceeds from the Buddha, over two centuries, to Mahinda (Aśoka's purported bhikkhu son) and from him to the Sangha as it roots itself in Sri Lanka. Coupled with the placing of Gotama in the lineage of Mahāsammata, the Great Sage-King "in the beginning of this age of the world,"[18] one is given a distinct sense of the new doctrine and religion being presented as "a repetition of the ancient archetype."[19] The present is vividly connected with the past, providing for legitimacy and a continuing remembrance of the tradition's roots. One has a clear sense of how the Mahāvihāra chroniclers, writing several centuries later in a time of political and sectarian turmoil, are engaged in the task of re-creating their own tradition.[20]

Aside from the cosmic and existential significance of tracing its origins to the Buddha, the key ingredients in the Sangha's authentication of its mission were doctrinal, devotional, and political. With respect to *doctrine*, the history of Sinhalese Buddhism could be written from the standpoint of the interplay between the Theravadins and the whole Acariyavāda (or heterodox) movement with its many sects, beginning with the Vaiśālī monks at the time of the Second Council and continuing to the present. Early in the chronicles one is exposed to the conciliar movement, arising in Buddhism upon the Tathāgata's passing and reaching its peak at the time of Aśoka with the "compilation of the true Dhamma."[21] In contrast, throughout the *Mahāvaṃsa* one is aware not only of serious tensions existing between the Mahāvihāra bhikkhus and those in various sects coexisting with them in Anurādhapura but also of the subtle influences these sects, especially those affected by Mahayana ideas, had on the Theriya Nikāya, or orthodox strain. Some of these influences will be examined later. It only needs indicating here that Buddhism, like all great religious traditions, has dealt unevenly with the problems of schism, sectarianism, and heresy. While tolerant of other faiths, whether popular or sophisticated, and while able to incorporate and transform indigenous elements, Sinhalese Buddhism has persistently felt threatened by the specter of heretical movements from within. In the words of G. P. Malalasekera: "To the assaults of open opponents the Buddhist displays the calmest indifference, convinced that in its undiminished strength his faith is firm and inexpungable; his vigilance is only excited by the alarm of internal dissent, and all his passions are aroused to stifle the symptoms of schism."[22]

The *devotional* ingredients continuous with earliest Buddhism likewise play a major part in the chronicler's saga. If continuity of doctrine can be traced through the councils, the apostolic succession, and the safeguarding of the Dhamma's purity by the Sangha, the sense of wonder released through awareness of the Buddha's gift is enlivened through *anamnesis* and celebration. While images of the Buddha came only after centuries, his presence was (in the testimony of the chronicles) sensed from the beginning. The words voiced by Mahinda, as he yearns for his homeland and the holy places associated with Gotama, are the words of tradition: "If we behold the relics we behold the Conqueror."[23] As the story of Sinhalese Buddhism could be told through the interplay between orthodoxy and sectarianism, it could also be told by discussing the Buddhist sense of adoration. Without question, the high points during the reigns of Sri Lanka's two greatest kings in the Anurādhapura period, a period that spanned fourteen centuries, were the arrival and enshrinement of the relics from India.[24] Devānampiya Tissa and Dutthagāmanī are remembered as epic figures for many reasons, but the coming of the relics confirmed and consecrated not only their reigns but the nation itself in the judgment of the Sinhalese chronicles. As the planting of the Bodhi Tree symbolized the spreading of the doctrine from its land of origin, the receiving of the relics confirmed the Buddha's authority in the land. With both gifts, the results were seen to be miraculous and enduring. The chronicles spare no words in telling of the wonder: "When the prince [Dutthagāmanī] saw the celestial parasol, the celestial perfumes, and the rest, and heard the sound of celestial instruments of music and so forth, albeit he did not see the Brahma-gods he, rejoicing and amazed at the miracle, worshipped the relics, with the offering of a parasol and investing them with the kingship of Laṅkā."[25]

The problem of true authority and kingship leads directly to the third ingredient of continuity established by the Sangha in the doctrine's spread to Sri Lanka, namely, the *political*. This was preeminently crystallized in the reconsecration of Devānampiya Tissa by envoys from Aśoka. The *Mahāvaṃsa* records that at the first consecration of King Tissa "many wonders came to pass . . . treasures and jewels that had been buried deep rose to the surface," and that "all this was the effect of Devānampiya Tissa's merit."[26] Out of gratitude he sends these treasures to King Aśoka, a friend, though they had never met. In return, Aśoka sends "all that was needful for consecrating a king" and with these the message of his having taken refuge in the Three Jewels (*triratna*), urging his friend: "Seek then even thou, O best of men converting thy mind with believing heart refuge in these best of gems!"[27] It is a delightful passage, punctuated by directions to his envoys: "Consecrate my friend yet again as king."[28]

In these words and actions are symbolized the line of continuity from the imperial majesty of Aśoka to the small island of Lanka *and that* from where the doctrine arose to where it was destined to flourish. In time, Anurādhapura became the Sinhalese counterpart of Pataliputta, the great capital of Aśoka. In a sense, when Mahinda came to Sri Lanka, he brought not simply a religion but "a whole civilization at the height of its glory," its concepts of art and architecture, its language and literature, even its very alphabet.[29] But from the standpoint of establishing Buddhism's legitimacy there could have been no greater safeguard than imperial sanction. As more than one commentator has said, and as the chroniclers themselves frequently imply, royal support is a two-edged sword. Established religion is not always, if ever, true religion. In any case, while it cannot be proven that the Buddha's doctrine entered Sri Lanka for the first time with Aśoka's envoys or even with Mahinda, it can be dated as a state or court religion with the second consecration of Tissa. At this juncture and in what unfolded with Aśoka's follow-up mission through Mahinda two lines of succession merged, and Sinhalese Buddhism came into being. These lines were those of *rāja-paramparā* and *thera-paramparā*, of royal and ecclesiastical legitimacy. In the process two central realities were brought into fundamental relationship within the

Sāsana, both essential historically to Theravada at large, that of the patron-monarch, and that of the bhikkhu-Sangha.

The image of Aśoka loomed larger with time. Legends about the great king were circulated soon after his death (later collected in the Sanskrit *Aśokāvadāna*), but their full impact only hit Sri Lanka about the time the chronicles were being written. In his excellent translation and study of the *Aśokāvadāna,* John Strong has demonstrated that the legends about Aśoka as collected in this important second-century CE text portray this figure in a paradoxical fashion: "Not only is Aśoka revered as an ideal king; he is also feared, maligned, and ridiculed as an all-too-real figure who sometimes does not live up to the ideal."[30] It is significant that this paradoxical presentation is exactly what one finds in the Sinhalese chronicles in its depiction of certain great figures such as Dutthagāmanī (101–77 BCE) and Parākramabāhu I (1153–86 CE). On the other hand, Strong is correct in distinguishing the portrayal of Aśoka found in the chronicles, in which this figure emerges after his conversion to Buddhism as an unflawed paradigm, from the more "balanced" presentation found in the *Aśokāvadāna.*

It is evident not only from the prominence given to Aśoka in the early part of the scenario but, as one reads further, it becomes even clearer that the Sinhalese model for kingship, as well as for the upāsaka (lay-follower) in general, is based on the ideal image these legends afford of the great king. A major feature of what is to be sensed in the figure of Aśoka in the chronicles is the tradition's superimposing of the two great kings: the Buddha and the universal monarch. This becomes manifest only as one perceives the emergence of the Cakkavatti figure in later centuries. But suggestions of it are apparent in the first part of the *Mahāvaṃsa* (i.e., by the early sixth century). It was this image that, however variously construed, became the paradigm for each king of Lanka. As noted by Ludowyk, it was the image both of the universal monarch (the Cakkavatti) and of the great man (the *mahāpurisa,* the Buddha himself) fused into one. "It is in this light that the emblem of the sacred footprint should be considered. It could be taken as the symbol of the imprint of the civilization of the mainland on its island neighbor. It is more, it is the token of the Great Man. Incomprehensible though the devotion shown to it may be, its real value lies in [how] . . . Indian civilization has always paid to the great human being, the sage who through his wisdom enables humankind to free itself from ignorance."[31]

The Threat of Disorder

If there was a tendency for the image of Aśoka to assume Cakkavatti proportions, there was also the insistence that this flower had emerged from the mud of human rapacity. Injustice is done to Aśoka himself, the tradition insists, if one forgets what preceded his transformation. Indeed, this is central to his appeal as an ideal monarch; it is what makes identification with him by ruler after ruler more potent. It is not simply the majesty of his imperial power that appeals; it is the attraction of power tamed and made righteous. We have then in the chronicles as well as in the *Aśokāvadāna* an *ideal* of righteous and benevolent power in tension with self-seeking power as most people know it. The total image of Aśoka contains both; "his cruelty and his piety"[32] must each be seen in order to comprehend his paradigmatic attraction and to discern what Buddhism is indicating about the human condition. Aśoka, therefore, is cast not only as the great man (the *mahāpurisa*); he is also everyman. Aśoka the wicked and cruel (Candāśoka), becomes Aśoka the just and righteous (Dharmāśoka).[33] In one human life we have the crystallization of two contrasting images, that of classical brutality and that of classical tolerance. As is well known, what unites these two images is the sense of horror and repentance that were said to be Aśoka's following the carnage of the Kālingas by his troops. It was this decisive event and its aftermath that, as tradition reports, impelled him toward Dharma-vijaya, conquest through righteousness rather than by force. Here is not the renunciation of power but its transformation. It is this perceived *metanoia* that makes him a compelling model throughout the Buddhist world.

That this is seen to be roughly analogous with the experience of Prince Siddhartha makes the model all the more authentic. Siddhartha's exposure to the existence of suffering was transmuted upon enlightenment into insight regarding its causes. The Buddha's vision of human nature in the grips of self-aggrandizement was profoundly realistic. This insight is intrinsic to Buddhism, sparing it from naivete about the human capacity for evil. While the Buddha's teachings added new depth to this vision, it may be seen as continuous with the overall Indian analysis of humanity's plight. This is made graphic in the *Cakkavatti-Sīhanāda Sutta* within the Pāli canon, which presents two apocalyptic images: of life under the rule of evil and of life ruled by Dhamma.[34] The one is a picture of injustice, disorder, and confusion; the other portrays liberation and reciprocity. Both are extended images of the human potential. From the Buddhist standpoint, neither can be fully appreciated except in relationship to the other. It does little good trying to make sense of the ideal king concept or that of the City of Righteousness (as portrayed in *The Questions of King Milinda*), even of the king-Sangha relationship, unless one takes seriously the note of realism sounded by the tradition. This note is repeatedly implicit within the Sinhalese chronicles, even if the image of Aśoka after his conversion is idealized.

The opening words of the *Mahāvaṃsa* state the chronicler's intent throughout, namely, that these passages awaken in the reader "serene joy and emotion" (*pasāda* and *samvega*): joy, blissfulness, and satisfaction in the doctrine of the Buddha and emotion, horror, and recoil from the world and its misery.[35] Similarly, each chapter ends with the same refrain: "compiled for the serene joy and emotion of the pious." If one is encouraged toward ecstatic euphoria by some passages and events, one is brought into sharp confrontation with somber reality by others. Sobriety alternates with the sense of wonder in powerful juxtaposition. One is never led too far in either direction. If one is tempted to place evil outside one's community, it springs up in one's midst. Though stylized and moralistic at times, the language of the chronicles does not romanticize the human predicament. Sinhalese humanity, like humanity in the Hebrew Bible, is portrayed with candor.

At the very times one expects the picture to leave out the darker hues, they suddenly appear. Indeed, profane history portrayed in this manner becomes a subject for meditation (*kammatthāna*), showing not only life's impermanence but also humanity's anxiety in the face of it.[36] In the words of one commentator: "What better theme for meditation than the crimes and follies of mankind. If history had no other lesson to teach, scanning its pages or rather hearing its sad stories of the death of its kings, was to fortify oneself anew in the knowledge of the transiency of all things, and to savour, by contrast, the joy of the mind directed towards the Four Noble Truths."[37]

Basic to the Buddhist understanding of evil is apprehension about the consequences of disorder. The threat of anarchy and chaos is ever-present in the chronicler's mind. While the identity of the yakkhas has often been debated, whether demons or nonhuman tutelary deities or ancestors of the present-day Veddās, it would seem that tradition has invested them with more profound symbolism. If aborigines in some sense, they represent the endemic spirit of humans that lurks close beneath the surface, the protean font of fear and self-enslavement that, unless stilled, infects all of one's acts and colors every thought. While on one level the Buddha's coming to Lanka can be interpreted as freeing it from yakkha control, making it ready for the Sinhalese worldview, on another level it becomes exorcism of the demonic from humans themselves. As with the Marcan account in the New Testament of the Gerasene demoniac, one senses here the removal of that which can be lodged in any person.[38] When confronted by the Buddha, the yakkhas, "overwhelmed by fear," beseech "the fearless Vanquisher to release them from terrors."[39]

Hypostasized into imaginary figures, the yakkhas may represent tradition's own realistic fear of humanity's proclivity toward disorder and evil. In any case, sensitivity toward the demonic remains a permanent ingredient of Sinhalese consciousness. Though the yakkhas are released from their distress when converted to the Buddha's cause, the chronicles record the ongoing turmoil within and between people. Three centuries after the master's visit, Mahinda, in the *Dīpavaṃsa* account, reflects on his own mission to Lanka in conversation with Sakka (the lord of the gods) and makes a statement that history proves to be double-edged: "Tambapanni [Ceylon] is covered and closed with the overclouding darkness of ignorance and of worldly existence, it is destroyed by jealousy and selfishness. . . . It has obtained the wrong path, it has gone astray, it is entangled like a ball of string and covered with blight."[40] Such a statement can be double-edged, for to Sinhalese nationalism the liberation from fear and ignorance can seem to be a *fait accompli,* an unrepeatable act making Lanka for all time "fit for human habitation,"[41] while to more honest self-reflection it may appear as but the start of what must keep occurring throughout time.

The evidence is overwhelming in the chronicles that the latter appraisal is more basic. Consistent with the tension found even in the image of Aśoka, the image of the island kingdom presented in these pages is twofold—as the archetype of delusion and as the paragon of enlightenment. What one finds in the nation's history is a mixture of both. If the forces of evil are stilled in some, they are rampant in others. In all, however, they are realities acknowledged and underscored. As Vijaya, forebear of the Sinhalese people, was wild in his conduct before taming, so each person needs continuing separation from ignorance and self-possession. The centuries of Sinhalese history, like those of each people, are written in blood. Intrigue follows intrigue. Parricides appear continually. Subversion, treason, infamy, and unrest unfold with ritualistic regularity. The threat of disorder is constant, stayed only by strong monarchs who contain their adversaries. Whether viewed on the level of society or within the realm of the human spirit, the confrontation with disorder looms as a permanent vocation. On both levels the final destiny is soteriological; it is ultimate freedom. The stabilizing of order by the king and the exorcism of the demonic by religious incantation are both requisite to the ultimate goal of Nibbāna.[42] The establishment of the sacred boundaries (*sīmā*) of the Sangha as coterminous with the sacred city of Anurādhapura by Mahinda Thera and King Devānampiya Tissa symbolizes the inclusion of social and political order within the larger order of the Dhamma, which is the source of freedom from disorder itself.

The symbiotic ideal suggested here is seen to have repercussions that incorporate not only society but the natural world as well. It is in this perspective that one can comprehend the urgency to maintain both the purity of the doctrine and the unity of the Sangha. With the continuum between the "secular" and the "sacred" so conceived, any threat to order in the latter was automatically construed as disruptive of the former. It is to the politically relevant dimensions of Dhamma that we now turn.

The Monarchy-Sangha Relationship

In the long history of Sinhalese Buddhism there is no relationship more complex or more crucial than that existing between the monarchy and the Sangha. Of all the pithy sayings concluding each chapter of the *Mahāvaṃsa*, none perhaps is more telling in this respect than the following: "Thus, reflecting that sovereignty, being the source of manifold works of merit, is at the same time the source of many an injustice, a [person] of pious heart will never enjoy it as if it were sweet food mixed with poison."[43] The Sangha's historic dependence on the monarchy for support, protection, and confirmation of the faith has not been an unmixed blessing. At the core of the issue is the understanding of Dhamma and the role each institution had in its furtherance. Not unrelated are the problems caused by a religion's becoming established, problems that can be devastating for the religion as for the society in general, raising the very question of what the "establishment" of Buddhism (as of any religious faith) means.

Ironically, the most extreme instance of fanatical religious and national sentiment recorded in Sinhalese history was in the kingship of its classical hero, Dutthagāmanī, who, after the pattern of Aśoka, lamented the carnage his victories had wrought.[44] While similar in outward form, resemblance to the Aśokan *ideal* stops there. In the vanguard of a crusade, Dutthagāmanī, with a relic linked to his spear and accompanied by five hundred bhikkhus, marched into battle with the Tamils, declaring solemnly: "Not for the joy of sovereignty is this toil of mine, my striving (has been) ever to establish the doctrine of the Sambuddha."[45] And even his remorse following the slaughter is short-lived, for the Sangha, knowing his thoughts, sends eight arahants to comfort him: "'From this deed arises no hindrance in thy way to heaven. Only one and a half human beings have been slain here by thee, O lord of men. . . . Unbelievers and men of evil life were the rest, not more to be esteemed than beasts. But as for thee, thou wilt bring glory to the doctrine of the Buddha in manifold ways; therefore cast away care from thy heart.' Thus exhorted by them the great king took comfort."[46]

The very inclusion of this passage in the chronicles of Sri Lanka, while ironic, is of immense import. While neither monarch nor Sangha in this guise could be a model, the tradition's refusal to gloss over murder and self-justification becomes instructive for history. As the conscience of the nation, the Sangha, sobered by unending warfare and intrigue, is here recording its alarm. Though in a style different than the Hebrew prophets, one detects in the Buddhist monks a comparable judgment, upon themselves as upon those directly responsible.

Again and again, the bhikkhu community through these chronicles records its own need for purification, alongside that of the nation. Part of the solemn charge given to the king is that of helping to maintain a strong and united Order: "It was his right to see that the religion was kept pure [*sodhesi sāsanam*] and in its pristine condition. Consecrated in the ceremonial of the *abhiśeka* or 'anointing' with rites at which in time the *sangha* assisted, the king was head of the state with power to purify the *sāsana*, as he often did."[47] The monarch, in turn, was kept responsible by the Sangha, his meritorious works duly registered in the royal annals, his violations no less noted.[48] That there was friction between them one would expect, but that the *ideal* of reciprocity endured cannot be questioned. In essence, it was a symbiosis rooted in tradition with consequences for what it meant to be a Buddhist community in the best sense of the word, a *sāvaka-saṅgha*, or ideal social order.

As in every other way, the prototype for this relationship may be found in reports of the Buddha's life, here in his associations with monarchs. The sovereignty of political power is subsumed under the sovereignty of the Dhamma in the *Dīpavaṃsa* account of King Bimbisāra's vision at the age of eight: "A Khattiya is in need of sovereignty; he, the Enlightened one, the bull among men, should arise in my kingdom; the Tathāgata should approach to show himself first to me, he should preach the everlasting norm, I should penetrate (into) the excellent (norm)."[49] Tradition cements the fealty of king to Dhamma in the appealing story of Aśoka's attraction to and conversion by the young bhikkhu Nigrodha. Searching for "truth and untruth," "for the virtuous and skillful," Aśoka tests person after person in vain and in discouragement asks: "When should I approach to have a sight of good men? Listening to this good saying I shall give my sovereignty along with the kingdom."[50] At one point he sees Nigrodha and addresses an aide: "Behold, quickly conduct that monk, the young man moving on the road like an elephant, graceful and peaceful by nature, fearless and possessed of the quality of tranquility."[51] Nigrodha is brought in and, "like the fearless king of gods, Sakka," mounts the imperial throne, to Aśoka's amazement and delight. The king then utters the word that depicts the Sangha's vocation to instruct monarch and people alike: "Teach me the Norm which you have learnt. You will be my teacher and I shall be taught by you. Oh great sage, I will act according to your word. Instruct me, I will listen to your instruction."[52] The monk speaks; the king listens; and the teachings of the Buddha come alive. Aśoka then takes refuge in the Three Gems, bestowing upon the bhikkhu community his loyalty and his larder, saying, "As much as the monks desire I give them whatever they choose."[53] While a figment of later imagination, it takes root within the tradition.

What follows becomes the model of royal patronage to the Sangha in recognition of the Dhamma's true majesty. The needs of the monks are met, vihāras without number are built, and in the Third Council the true Dhamma is compiled and preserved. One further test put to Aśoka in response to his question "Whose generosity toward the doctrine of the Blessed One was ever (so) great (as mine)?" shows even more the king's responsibility toward the Sangha and seals the eventual tie with Lanka. When told there was no one more generous than he, Aśoka presses his luck and asks, "Is there a kinsman of Buddha's religion like unto me?" The reply of Moggaliputta Thera has implications not only for Aśoka and succeeding monarchs but for all people: "[Only] he who lets son or daughter enter the religious order is a kinsman of the religion and withal a giver of gifts."[54]

Much more could be said about the king's protection and support of the Sangha. The chronicles are replete with accounts of royal patronage to both Sangha and society; they are no less specific about lack of patronage.[55] Ideally, too, the ruler was expected to be the defender of the faith, protecting the Dhamma from heretical incursions, settling disputes among the bhikkhus, encouraging the teaching and spread of the doctrine. In actuality, however, kings were seen to support now one vihāra, now another, promoting "orthodoxy" at certain points in history, "heretical sects" at others. As with the misuse of power in general, the chronicles are candid about the infidelity of certain kings who fell into the clutches of wayward and lawless monks. One must remember, however, that the story is being told from the Mahāvihāra point of view. In any case, our concern here is for the *image* of ideal reciprocity.

On this score, the picture is unambiguous; it is a division of labor, with both parties dedicated to the same goal. This is seen in the frequent offering of the kingdom to the Sāsana by the monarch, symbolizing his own recognition of the state's purpose. While always returned to him, it was a gesture of acknowledgment that his authority is both delegated and responsible.[56] The division of labor is seen also in the fact that while it was the king's right and duty to ensure that the doctrine be taught, it was in fact the Sangha's task to provide the instruction. The most poignant example may be noted in Dutthagāmanī's attempt to propagate the faith himself. "He seated himself in the preacher's chair in the centre of the spacious hall and made ready to give the august assembly a discourse on some religious topic from the *Maṅgala Sutta.* But, although he was quite familiar with the Sacred Scriptures, he could not proceed; he descended from the pulpit 'perspiring profusely'; he had realized how difficult was the task of the teachers, and his munificence towards them was made greater."[57]

It would be a serious mistake, on the other hand, to view the monarch's relationship to the Sangha independently of his relationship to society and the body politic as a whole. It would be more true to say that the ideal of symbiosis between thera and king was symbolic of the ideal reciprocity between all persons in the society. As the monarch can be portrayed as a Cakkavatti at one end of the spectrum and as everyman at the other, so he can be in search of the Dhamma's meaning at the same time that he is its protector. It is this dual portrayal of each king that, as in the case of Aśoka, commends him as an illustration of each person's striving toward "greater merit" in the short run and Nibbāna ultimately. The concept of reciprocity is paramount to the Buddhist notion of an ideal society. This is conceived in the *Sigālovāda Sutta,* sometimes regarded as the "Whole Duty" or Vinaya of the Buddhist layperson. In it are depicted the ideal relationships between people in various roles or circumstances (e.g., husband-wife, parents-children, employers-servants, etc.). Though deceptively simple in presentation, it is a part of the Pāli canon that has exercised immense influence because it catches the rhythm of authentic association. We shall explore this further in the final section. At this point we examine the king's sociopolitical task in helping to make this reciprocity possible. It is in this regard that the idea of Dhamma has decidedly relevant social implications. This was put succinctly in the following statement, by B. G. Gokhale: "The early Buddhist philosophy of kingship is a compound of three distinct attitudes. Although the early Buddhists betray feelings of disquiet, bordering on fear, about the nature and functions of kingship as it existed in their times, they see no alternative to it and declare it to be absolutely essential to prevent humanity from lapsing into a state of anarchy. Finally, confronted with the fact of kingship and the absolute necessity for it for orderly human existence, they attempt to tame absolute political power by infusing into it a spirit of higher morality."[58]

Such a statement could have been affirmed either by Aśoka or by the Sinhalese chroniclers as the essence of the political task under Dhamma. The same ambivalence toward worldly power, the same acceptance of its inevitability, and the same striving to make it responsible are as evident throughout Buddhist history as in its early days. The frequent assumption by Westerners that Theravada lacks a social ethic cannot be maintained in light of overwhelming evidence to the contrary. As with all social philosophy, we are presenting here an ideal, but it is an ideal with policy repercussions. Again, the prime, but by no means the only, paradigm is that of Aśoka. If Aśoka provides the norm, it was emulated in countless versions within Sinhalese, Burmese, and Thai history.

In these and other cultural contexts we can see a repeated clash of historic cruelty with the Aśokan ideal. This should surprise no one; the chronicles themselves document this, reign after reign. Were this not so, the Dhamma would be fulfilled, not only preached. The carnage that supposedly brought Aśoka's conscience into sensitivity was but a ripple in the world's history of slaughter, but the paradigm that his reported response provided continued to affect Buddhist communities. It was finally this that became the model and norm, and not the political ideals of Kautilya.[59] In essence, this was to assert that the state is not an end in itself but a means toward a higher end of which it is the servant. This is always the more difficult task than that of absolutism, for the higher end is inevitably obscure and is never permanently reached within the political order.

It was acceptance of this lesser but crucial task of creating a just order that constitutes the crux of the Buddhist ideal of kingship. Acknowledging the limitations of its role makes the monarchy's reciprocity with the Sangha a viable one. The purpose of one was to create and maintain an ordered society within which people might pursue freely the greater goal beyond order. The purpose of the other was to discover this greater goal for themselves and to reveal to all persons the path to it. These two purposes were not at odds, only in tension. Order precedes liberation; liberation requires order. Besides, the type of order envisaged was one in which all basic human needs were met; it was order at the heart of which was justice. It was the latter that reputedly prompted Aśoka and later Buddhists to dig wells, provide rest houses, construct tanks, have mercy on animals, feed the poor, and a host of other manifestations. But it was the reason for taking these and other steps that reveals the character of their concerns. "These are trifling comforts," the *Edicts of Aśoka* confess. "For the people have received various facilities from previous kings as well as from me. But I have done what I have primarily in order that the people may follow the path of Dharma with faith and devotion."[60]

It was both the stated motive for his actions and the belief that Nibbāna cannot be pursued when human needs are ignored that made this political ethic a new entry into history. It created in the process a Buddhist ethos sometimes called *lokka-nibbāna* (or Nibbāna in this world), which is a potentially confusing term that connotes the compatibility, even interdependence, between social concern on the one hand and the quest for tranquility or equanimity (*upekkhā*) on the other. Far from being indifferent to the world, it is only through *upekkhā* that Buddhism sees genuine concern arising. Coupled with this view was the pragmatic realization that the pursuit of Nibbāna necessitates leisured meditation and that this requires both economic sufficiency and a stable sociopolitical order.[61] The king's task, therefore, was to "stabilize" this order. The odyssey of the human spirit was viewed within a cosmological and historical pattern where there is no progress, only order and disorder, both relative, both ambiguous yet filled with potential. Authentic progress comes only to the inner spirit—achieved by each person anew, moments building upon moments, each person, as the chronicles put it, going "according to his [or her] *kamma*" (*yathākammam*). Over this, no state, nor established religion, holds sway. It acts only as prelude, to facilitate or to obstruct. Like all worldly sovereignty, it is "sweet food mixed with poison."

The Society-Cosmos Relationship

The Aśokan concept of Dharma-vijaya (conquest through righteousness) pertained, in Buddhist thinking, not only to the present age but to the enduring future. If this eschatological note was not developed until later centuries, it was clearly struck in the emperor's hopes that his newly established pattern of conquest would become normative. One clue to this lies in his words that "whatever effort King Priyadarśī makes is for the sake of the life hereafter and in order that men may be saved from enslavement."[62] Like the chronicles of Sri Lanka, the Edicts of Aśoka betray no illusion about the difficulty of the task, a task that "rich and poor alike will find . . . difficult to do . . . unless they make a great effort and renounce all other aims."[63] It remains for this final section to look at the *eschatological* dimensions of Dharma-vijaya, to see how these came increasingly over time to be united with certain cosmological assumptions about the nature of reality, certain emerging visions of the ideal king, and certain growing expectations about the City of Righteousness.

While it is risky trying to date the emergence of these ideas, it is equally true that they were prominent in the time of the *Mahāvaṃsa* and that, in relatively undeveloped form, they can be found in the Pāli canon. Tradition, indeed, ascribes them to the time of the Buddha himself, with the insistence by Mahayana that they represent the core of his teaching. Without stopping to argue these points, it is pertinent to the chapter to observe their manifestations within the Sinhalese chronicles, especially within the *Mahāvaṃsa,* for the basic ingredients of an ideal order as perceived by Theravada Buddhists depend on these concepts. To reflect on their meaning within this context affords a clearer understanding not only of what Buddhism construes by Dhamma but of the relationship among the Three Jewels in which Buddhists take refuge.

The first of these concepts to be explored here stems from the sustained conviction within the Buddhist community about the essential oneness or interrelatedness of all reality, a concept having both temporal and spatial dimensions.[64] The most seminal idea at this point is that of *paticca-samuppāda,* a notion central to all Buddhism that has been translated in various ways, though most frequently as "dependent origination." Basically, it suggests that, while there is no *original* causative agent or event, all reality is a network of causes and effects, producing various degrees of good and evil, order and disorder, and within it human beings can discover, through discipline and eventually enlightenment, the ability to cause or bring about their own liberation.

In personal terms, it conveys the conviction that each person can come to realize the essential nonduality of "self" and "others," the fundamental union of all life, and the folly of clinging to the self-defeating notions of "me" and "mine." Fundamental to this realization is the awakening to the fact of impermanence (*anicca*) and to one's own capacity not simply to live tranquilly within it but to embody joy, harmony, and compassion. In social terms, it conveys the sense in which the actions, words, and desires of each person fit into a framework of interrelationship whereby what one does affects all others. And, in cosmic terms, it conveys the more immense awareness that the entire universe is a fabric with parts dependent on each other, a tissue of entities making up one whole.[65] It is intrinsic to Buddhist social concern that authentic community comes only through the unfolding consciousness of persons that their basic identity cannot be known in isolation from others. The most characteristic term for compassion, *karunā,* suggests a widening self-identification with all that lives.[66]

While this notion is common to all Buddhist testimony, its configurations in the Sinhalese chronicles are vivid and unique. One could do an entire study of the *Mahāvaṃsa* focusing on the personal, social, and cosmic aspects of *paticca-samuppāda,* as these are manifold. Each chapter of this book makes an assessment of the whys and wherefores of circumstances and events, interpreting them in light of actions taken or ignored, tracing the destinies of kings, in particular, "according to their *kamma.*" We shall focus here on the sense of cosmic consciousness that the chroniclers portray as they weave together the events of history with tradition's interpretation.

As might be expected, one finds the delineation of cosmic awareness peculiarly expressive in the accounts of royal consecrations, for at times like these relationships are made most explicit: those of monarch to Sangha and people to each other, those of time past to time present to time future, those of this place to all places. This is true with the kingly prototype, Aśoka. "Straightaway after his consecration his command spread so far as a yojana (upward) into the air and downward into the (depths of the) earth."[67] "The sense of this passage, not rightly understood up to the present time," Wilhelm Geiger quaintly suggests in a note to the text, "is evidently this: not only men upon the earth but also the spirits of the air and the earth heard and obeyed Aśoka's command."[68] Following this more general statement, the chronicle elaborates on the organic harmony that comprised Aśoka's rule: "From the Himalaya did the devas bring for cleansing the teeth twigs of nāga-creeper. . . . The spirits of the air brought garments of five colours. . . . Out of the nāga-kingdom the nāgas (brought) stuff, coloured like the jasmine-blossom and without a seam . . . ; parrots brought daily . . . wagon-loads of rice. Mice converted this rice, unbroken, into grains without husk or powder. . . . Perpetually did honey-bees prepare honey for him. . . . Karavīka-birds, graceful and sweet of voice, came and made delightful music for the king."[69] Reference was made earlier to what happened at Devānampiya Tissa's consecration, as a result of his merit: "In the whole isle of Laṅkā treasures and jewels that had been buried deep rose to the surface of the earth."[70] An even greater tumultuous display of rhythmic harmony, uniting humans and beasts, is found in the depiction of the consecration festival of Parākramabāhu the Great in 1154 CE.[71] While more tailored to the local setting, it is no less cosmic in orientation.

Each of these instances carries the conviction that the monarch's role in relationship to society and the cosmos is to sustain or to reestablish the living harmony underlying all existence. Royal power is the instrument of cosmic power. As with the classic Chinese understanding of the emperor as the "Son of Heaven," the character of whose rule affected not only society but nature, one finds here the assumed correspondence between an evil monarch and disasters in nature, or between goodness and harmony. It is assumed throughout the *Mahāvaṃsa* that men of power can do much, providing they have good understanding.[72] Sovereignty, when purged of poison, causes works that are sweet. Present in this view is both a "high" and a "low" estimate of royal power, estimates that are cautious yet hopeful at the same time. It is essentially a view of human nature that is realistic yet sensitive to humankind's potential. Above all, it stands awed before the power of the Dhamma. In commenting on Elara the Tamil, who for forty-five years ruled justly over Lanka, the chronicler speculates: if a nonbeliever can be so good, how much more so a believer![73]

It is again at this point that one sees the impact of the Sangha's relationship to the monarchy and why the latter remained pledged to the welfare of the Order. The ideal symbiosis between these institutions was the primal instance, the archetype, of what personal, social, and cosmic symbiosis involved. As an ideal, whether approximated in reality or not, it was the model of what genuine reciprocity entails. When the Dhamma is protected, the monarchy thrives, the Sangha becomes a blessing, and the people flourish. With any break in the continuum, disorder prevails. The most symbolic presentation of this in the chronicles may be the chapter in the *Mahāvaṃsa* entitled "The Acceptance of the Mahāvihāra," in which Mahinda marks off locations in Anurādhapura, the sacred city, upon which various buildings of the Great Vihāra will be constructed in future years. At each announcement there is a quaking of the earth. As with the account of the building of the Mahāthūpa later under Dutthagāmanī, the tradition is underscoring the connection between heaven and earth, between the present moment and all moments, between the sacrality of the Dhamma and all else.

Ironically, the establishing of the boundaries (*sīmā*) is the removal of all boundaries. It is humanity's way of saying that in order to see continuity, to experience reciprocity, one must establish distinctions where in reality none exist. The planting of the Bodhi Tree and the bringing of the relics are ways of making visible, and therefore present, what was never absent, though it was essentially invisible. At two points in the chronicles, both in relationship to the arrival or the enshrining of relics, the same words are used: "Thus are the Buddhas incomprehensible, and incomprehensible is the nature of the Buddhas, and incomprehensible is the reward of those who have faith in the incomprehensible."[74]

It is only in such a vein that *samsāra* is Nibbāna,[75] for it is through the attaining of enlightenment that *samsāra*'s potential may be imagined, a potential that otherwise remains obscure because of the enslavement it typically manifests. Expressed devotionally within the chronicles is the faith that ignorance may be transformed into wisdom, that self-preoccupation may become compassion for others. The profusion of festivals that color the pages of these documents and the seeming preoccupation with stūpa building, image making, and celebration in general depict a community mindful of blessings received. To adorn is to be adoring; to bestow gifts is to acknowledge the worthiness of what has been received. In the words of the *Mahāvaṃsa:* "Commanded by the lord of men, they, filled with deep reverence for the Sage (Buddha), adorned the place in manifold ways."[76] It was a community that had received a foretaste of what was possible for all people, of what society could become, and of what cosmic harmony would entail. The tension between the promise of a reconciled universe and the experience of a world in suffering made each more vivid. If the age of the Buddha (*buddhavassa*) had begun, its consummation occurred only in the imagination. The Wheel of the Law had been turned, but Dharma-vijaya's fulfillment remains alive only in anticipation.

Of one piece with this vision of unity and this continued experience of distress and enmity was the unfolding anticipation of an ideal king, a monarch whose rule by righteousness would occasion and cement the reality of the universe's intrinsic oneness. At the heart of any apocalyptic vision is the awareness of a soteriological necessity. To the tradition's sensitivity to suffering was added the gradual acknowledgment of the king's role as bodhisatta (Sanskrit, *bodhisattva*) and of the appearance in new guise of the Cakkavatti figure. Unquestionably, this development reflects the influence of Mahayana sects on Sinhalese consciousness, but it unfolded in ways that reinforced the orthodox insistence that human beings were the agents of their own release. This point has not been stressed enough in discussions of the interplay between the two major paths within Buddhist tradition. It is in part the intent of this section to highlight the compatibility of "taking refuge in oneself" with "taking refuge in Buddha, Dhamma, and Sangha," both of which are essential to Buddhist soteriological understanding.

Many scholars have traced the appearance and increasing effect of the bodhisatta concept in India, Sri Lanka, and elsewhere. It is the task here to perceive its emergence within the Sinhalese chronicles, for the part it plays in Theravada generally stems from these developments, influenced by Indian concepts as they were. While one can read back into discussions of earlier reigns the same intent, the earliest explicit reference in the chronicles to the bodhisatta-like nature of any monarch is to Buddhadāsa, who ruled in the mid-fourth century CE. The reference here, to be sure, is almost in passing, but it is unmistakable: "The Ruler lived openly before the people the life that bodhisattas lead and had pity for [all] beings as a father [has pity for] his children."[77] The significance of this comment can be minimized as a mere figure of speech and as one that may be found earlier in the Pāli canon itself. It is, however, in the impression one gets of the nature and character of Buddhadāsa, who "shone like the Perfectly Enlightened One," and of his reign that one detects the beginning of a new theoretical phenomenon, a savior-king, one whose meritorious action heals the sick, woos people out of enmity, and creates happiness for all his subjects.[78] Even earlier, in the person of Sirisamghabodhi in the mid-third century, we are put in the presence of one who, though not called a bodhisatta in the account, makes a self-oblation of his life in order that his realm may be freed from famine and drought.[79]

It is possible to discover at least four elements in the chronicler's judgment of what constituted a righteous monarch that contributed to, or at least were part of, the emerging Cakkavatti image. The first relates to the personal qualities such a king should possess. While these may be found attributed to many rulers in various ways, the most succinct attributions are to Buddhadāsa and to his eldest son, Upatissa: "Endowed with the ten qualities of kings (*dasa rājadhammā*), while avoiding the four wrong paths, practising justice, [Buddhadāsa] won over his subjects by the four heart-winning qualities (*cattāri samghavatthuni*)."[80] Even more was ascribed to the son: "Shunning the ten sinful actions, he practiced the ten meritorious works (*punnakiriyā*); the King fulfilled the ten royal duties and the ten *pāramitās*. By the four heart-winning qualities he won over the four regions of the world."[81] Geiger's notes in his translation of the *Cūlavaṃsa* detail these qualities, though, of course, these were familiar to all readers in ancient Lanka, indeed, to all bhikkhus and upāsakas, let alone to each monarch. The cataloging of the qualities was intended more as a focus for meditation than as a description of certain kings. But there can be no questioning the lofty concept of kingship that these revealed.

The second element present throughout portrayals of a righteous ruler is one to which we referred earlier, namely, his role as patron and supporter of the Sangha. One need not elaborate here except to say that one finds more explicit reference to social welfare measures appearing in the fourth and fifth centuries and beyond than earlier. The giving of alms, the concern for wages, the digging of wells, the planting of trees, and especially the construction of tanks and canals are frequently mentioned. While all of these actions had occurred before, their increased mention says much about the king's function not only as an establisher of order but as a creator and maintainer of a just and thriving society, which was held to be an intrinsic part of the ideal. The most graphic figure of the monarch at this point is one assigned to Udaya II, who was "like to a wishing tree, a dispenser of blessings for all the needy," an image often used in Indian mythology to depict the bounty of heaven.[82] This corroborates Geiger's comment that "the greatest virtue of a king was considered to be charitableness" (*mahākarunā*), a quality stemming from identification with one's subjects, not simply from feelings of kindness.[83]

The third element in the chronicler's judgment of what constituted a righteous monarch is that the ideal monarch is seen as a paragon of what it means to be a human being, not just a patron of society or of the Sangha. As the king takes on the proportions of a Cakkavatti, with all its soteriological connotations, this depiction of him as a paragon for all persons becomes increasingly important. There are a number of kings in the chronicles who are portrayed in this fashion, but two are especially intriguing, for different reasons: one, Sena II, seems almost the epitome of perfection and is therefore somewhat abstract, albeit no less a model of manhood; the other, Aggabodhi VII, is portrayed in very concrete and human terms, albeit no less an image of perfection. To juxtapose comments about these persons helps to create the impression of the tension, yet continuity, between the ideal as it was imagined and the reality that sometimes took flesh. As stated in the *Cūlavaṃsa:* "Showing conduct like that of the kings of the first age of the world, pious, wealthy, heroic, generous, impartial, succouring the needy . . . [Sena] represented in his spotless fame and his splendid ability, as it were a union of the sun and the moon: richly gifted with unblemished qualities, practising every kind of virtue, devoid of all sin, weary of the cycle of births, his gaze fixed on the highest."[84] This statement is replete with connotations, religious and political, that might profitably be explored. Suffice it to say here that there could hardly be a more unstinted accolade of what Buddhist humanity should comprise than this. While beyond the reach of ordinary laypeople, it would at least portray the upāsaka vocation as well as engender a deeper sense of the ideal king's paradigmatic nature.

Side by side with this we may place the portrayal of Aggabodhi VIII, with whom identification is more possible but who still embodies traits no less uncommon:

> The King found pleasure in the serving of his mother day and night. He went to wait on her already early in the morning, rubbed her head with

> oil, perfumed the parts moist with sweat, cleaned her nails and bathed her carefully. He clad her himself in a new garment, pleasant to the touch, and the castoff raiment he took and cleaned it himself. . . . After making obeisance before her three times, and walking, with right side facing, round her . . . he offered her delicious food with his own hand. . . . [Then] when he had put in order her chamber, fragrant with sweet odours, he carefully prepared there with his own hand her couch, washed her feet, rubbed her gently with fragrant oil, sat by her rubbing her limbs and sought to make her sleep. . . . Then happy at his action, and ever thinking of her, he went home. As long as she lived he served her in this way.[85]

The inclusion of this passage in the chronicles is hardly for reader interest alone. It bespeaks not only of filial respect but of the essence of bodhisatta-like tenderness, the sort of reciprocity counseled in the *Sigālovāda Sutta,* to which we pointed earlier. It bespeaks a sense of fittingness that sees and responds to the needs of all creation. As was said about one king, "For the bhikkhu community, for the laity, for fishes, game and birds, for his kinsfolk and for the troops he did everything that was mete for them."[86] Lastly, it is one with the reverence shown toward the Buddha by pious followers, in token of blessings received. It is at the core of purity, which manifests itself in compassion, service, and self-oblation.

The fourth and crowning attribute of the ideal king is the catalytic effect his meritorious actions have on other people. We are dealing here not simply with a paragon whose qualities are worthy of emulation but with a charisma and power that are said to call into existence traits dormant and unrealized in the lives of others. It is in this respect that the soteriological efficacy of the Cakkavatti takes on a dimension present but untapped in earlier tradition. As is true about the chronicler's judgment both of power and of human nature, the charisma of the ruler has demonic as well as beneficent possibilities, "for it is the rule with living creatures: what he who is master does, evil or good, the same is done by his subjects; let the wise man take heed of that."[87] The lesson of history, as recorded in these pages, makes clear the double-edged nature of the monarch's effect. But in the same breath in which the chronicler cites this warning, he comments about the royal influence for good: "Thus he was in all his dealings one to whom the teaching of the Buddha was the highest (good), and vying with him all the people also fulfilled the (commands of that) doctrine."[88] About another king he writes: "Everyone in his kingdom cultivated action which leads to Heaven, for as the monarch acts so do also his subjects."[89] Finally, about Dutthagāmanī, whose own struggle with impurity and whose later meritorious actions are both seen as classic, the *Mahāvaṃsa* says: "Thus do the pious themselves perform pure deeds of merit, in order to obtain the most glorious of all blessings; and they, with a pure heart, make also others to perform them in order to win a following of eminent people of many kinds."[90]

In all these instances the basic assumption is made—like king, like subjects. It is possible to find plausible historical factors that influenced this development. Paul Mus has suggested that "the charismatic figure of the Wheel-wielding King (*cakravartin*) grew in size and was credited with increasing soteriological powers, as a compensation for and prospective help against too positive and immediate woes."[91] Walpola Rahula has pointed out its relationship to religio-nationalism, saying that "by about the 10th century, this belief had become so strong that the king of Ceylon had not only to be a Buddhist but also a Bodhisattva."[92] Undoubtedly, as well, there were quasi-magical elements that often trivialized and jeopardized the more profound implications. Without question, in the hands of some the soteriological conception of the king was little more than a clever rationalization for state power. The validity of these and other explanations are pertinent, but they do not exhaust the internal meaning of belief in the bodhisatta-king phenomenon and the relevance of this belief to the social order.

In essence, what one sees unfolding over centuries, influenced both by the Sanskritic notion of kingship and by Mahayana ideas about the bodhisatta, was a merging of two distinct but overlapping notions of sovereignty: one, of the sociopolitical order; the other, of the cosmos at large. Paradoxically, the original choice of vocations put before the infant Siddhartha becomes revealed as a false dichotomy, for as the universal ruler or ideal king is also the Cakkavatti, or bodhisatta, so the Buddha is the supreme monarch, the master of heaven and earth. Whether viewed personally or cosmically, only one who rules oneself is fit to rule others, and one who teaches people Dharma-vijaya, or conquest through righteousness is the ruler of all. Evident here is a kind of parabolic movement, with obvious liturgical ramifications, from king to bodhisatta-king (Buddha) and back to king again, an offering of self to one who taught release from self so that one may serve others with justice, compassion, and tranquility. As Sarkisyanz points out in quoting from the *Kāka Jātaka*, "A king laid his kingdom at the Bodhisattva's feet, but the Bodhisattva restored it to the king . . . beseeching him to shield all living creatures from harm."[93] One is struck by the identical symbolism here with that practiced by Sinhalese monarchs, as they offered their kingdom to the Sangha as vice-regent for the Buddha, or, in one case, to the newly arrived relics as the very presence of Gotama himself.

The explicit connection with the Buddha is, of course, central to the entire conception. Here, too, one perceives a parabola-like movement, as in the *Mahāsudassana Sutta* where the Buddha reveals himself to Ānanda as having been in another life the Great King of Glory. It is important to keep in mind that the only current bodhisatta recognized by Theravada is the Buddha (or Bodhisatta) Metteyya, the Buddha to come. The expectations of his coming have played a major role in the social and political ethos of Theravada communities.[94] The aspirations of kings in both Sri Lanka and Myanmar were to become the Bodhisatta Metteyya in their next life. As noted by Sarkisyanz, "Not only renovation but also fulfillment of Buddhism was expected from Metteyya: universal compassion is to become through him a cosmic reality."[95]

In this conviction is a blending of the three ideas mentioned at the start of this section, namely, a conviction regarding the essential oneness of reality, a vision about the role of the ideal king, and an expectation of the forthcoming City of Righteousness. In the various titles used for the ideal king[96] it was manifest that in him was a symbiosis in which temporal and spiritual domains[97] were harmonized and thus a harmonizing of heaven and earth, humanity and nature, king and people, society as a whole. The image of the Golden Age was projected into the future as a time when the ills of the present age would be cured and its antinomies reconciled. In the meantime, despite the strength of this expectation, there endured the awareness that we are living "between the times," in an age of decline between what once existed and what in time will emerge. The vision of what will become is focused in the concept of a City of Righteousness.

Akin to the notion of an ideal king, the City of Righteousness[98] may be seen by the mind's eye alone. As the presence of the Buddha within the relics, it is incomprehensible, made real only through enlightenment. It is the *sāvaka-saṅgha,* a spiritual community, invisible to all, whose members are known to none. It is a community of attainment where all striving has ceased. It is perceived in time but not limited by it; it occupies space but cannot be confined. It exists everywhere and in each place. It exists now but is eternal. No person is far from it, yet it remains unseen. To some, it seems fulfilled already, but this is blindness to suffering and to ignorance, especially one's own. To others, it has no reality, for they place no hope in release from bondage, including their own. It is a city in which each learns from all and where none is lost. It is a community in which attainment has been reached, yet the horizons are unlimited. Here possession has no meaning, for no one is in need. Here fear is unknown, for love regards each person as him- or herself.

The suttas, the commentaries, the chronicles, and a host of other testimonies bespeak of this city, yet no one who writes has more than glimpsed its possibility. The symbol of the Bodhi Tree, under which enlightenment first shone forth, is a primary image of the distance and of the closeness between wisdom and ignorance, between freedom and enslavement. To make this epiphany possible, the soil must be readied each time. The Buddha's visits to Lanka were to prepare yet another land for its transplant and growth. The vision told by the chronicler in the *Mahāvaṃsa* is of miracles taking place when preparation has occurred: "Hardly had he let it leave his hands but it rose up eighty cubits into the air, and floating thus it sent forth glorious rays of six colours."[99] The chronicler continues: "And while they all gazed, there grew, springing from it, eight shoots; and they stood there, young Bodhi-trees four cubits high."[100]

The glory of its springing forth and yet the sobering fact that people remain ignorant is the essence of the chronicle's tale. Dharma-vijaya has been shown as the way, but conquest continues by means of force. The city where righteousness could be known is at hand, though people settle for accumulations of merit and the promise of heaven. It remains the genius of the Buddhist imagination that each person must begin somewhere; therefore, no place of origin is despised. There will be a time when relics are extinguished (*dhātu-parinibbāna*); in the meantime. these signs of enlightenment merely point the way. The ideal social order is a vision of interdependence, but only when that vision becomes a reality does the process of transformation unfold without constraint.

The grounds for legitimating power in Sri Lankan history is a subject on which considerable source material exists, yet curiously there is little analytical reflection. Specifically, there have been few attempts at perceiving the historic tension between the religious basis for kingship and the tradition of secular statecraft (clearly present within the Polonnaruva period, but also before). While this difficulty remains, it is useful to note that the principal configurations of the *dhamma-danda* tension (perceivable in the *Cūlavaṃsa* particularly) is another approach to the theme of Sinhalese cultural identity and the dilemmas of pluralism.

The more one understands the dynamics of the process, the more one sees its fragile nature, its powers of renewal, its potential for accommodating new ingredients, as well as the constant possibility of its collapsing. And finally, one sees the enduring importance of this process for all its communities. It is the purpose of chapter 2 to explore the process of legitimation with specific reference to the relationship between the monarchy and the Buddhist Sangha within the long Anurādhapura period. Seeing this relationship within an earlier time frame enables one to compare it throughout later Sri Lankan history and, moreover, provides perspective on the contemporary scene.

2

Kingship, the Sangha, and the Process of Legitimation in the Anurādhapura Period, Third Century BCE to Tenth Century CE

The process of legitimizing power and authority in any society is a constantly evolving, complex, and subtle phenomenon. While its configurations vary within all societies, the process reveals numerous interrelated features. This chapter identifies several of these features and examines the process of legitimation within early Sri Lankan society in its responses to opportunities and threats, both internal and external. The specific phenomena within this process are infinitely variable; the features selected here are necessarily tentative. An interpretive essay of this sort highlights several ingredients within ancient Sinhalese history and seeks to test the usefulness of certain concepts in analyzing the legitimizing process per se.

The features examined here include the relationship between the precariousness of social and cosmic order as this connection is sensed by tradition and attempts that are made to fashion forms of existence that are less vulnerable to chaos or anarchy. The second feature is the affirming of both historical and cosmic dimensions of legitimation that provide the structures and values of a particular society within some transcending authority. Also addressed are the tensions that exist between varied claimants to legitimized power within any community and thus the resultant balancing of power, as well as the manner in which legitimation of authority is reinforced in symbolic, ritualistic, and doctrinal modes. Finally, we will examine the validation of power through its ability to bolster a culture's "plausibility structure" in the midst of pluralistic perceptions of reality and in the face of crises threatening personal and communal existence alike. The interdependence of these five features would seem to be clear, yet they hardly exhaust all theoretical possibilities. The ones selected here serve simply as points of departure.[1]

The Precariousness of Order

Historical and comparative studies reveal how all societies struggle to cope with threats of disorder and to create forms of order that lend cohesiveness and durability to social and personal existence. The potential chaos within the perceived orders of every cultural ethos occasions alarm about whether any structure of meaning protects against disintegration and anomie. From social conflict and political crisis to psychic disorder and death the evanescent nature of life and the relativity of all forms of order are constantly experienced. In the face of institutionalized injustice and the seeming irrationality of existence, men and women vacillate between simple assurances on the one hand and terror on the other. History may be viewed as a series of scenarios in which symbols of order and disorder clash for allegiance in human minds and in which societies embrace chaos-averting forces through the legitimizing process. History is in part a search for frameworks of meaning to endure threats of nonbeing and to discover dimensions of order, however fragile and incomplete.

In Sinhalese history, the interplay among the monarchy, the Sangha, and society at large portrays a continuing recognition of the precariousness of order in all senses of the word: cosmic, social, and personal. There is repeated testimony about the contagious nature of disorder, especially when manifested within the Sangha or by kings. The Sinhalese experience of political realism arose from the broader Indian doctrine of *mātsya-nyāya* ("law of the fishes"), reminding rulers and their ministers that power left to its own devices issues in the law of the jungle, in which the strong consume the weak. This perception of political mores was used by astute rulers in ways ranging from crass opportunism to the responsible but realistic exercise of power. Legitimation of authority receives its warrant from the fact that unless the power of others is checked, threats to order keep recurring. In any case, the doctrine of *mātsya-nyāya* was not only part of the Sinhalese heritage from India in a general sense but was specifically part of the early Buddhist recognition within that Indian setting. In the *Agañña Sutta of the Dīgha Nikāya,* there is extensive discussion of the theory of the "Great Chosen One" (*mahāsammata*) to support the centralizing of power in kingly hands as a means of checking those who misappropriate power, in whose hands "order" becomes anarchy.[2]

There is believed to be a connection between this theory and other teachings of the Buddha and models of how power had been exercised by the Emperor Aśoka. The Buddhist doctrine of power and the Aśokan model were used repeatedly to caution later monarchs in Sri Lanka about the norms for legitimate authority. The *sine qua non* of political legitimacy is protection of the populace from anarchy and its consequences.[3] From the *Manusmriti* and other Indian texts to the Chronicles of Ceylon this criterion is a constant. To Sinhalese Buddhists this meant not only protection of the world (*loka*) from disorder but also of the Sāsana, so as to enable promotion of the Dhamma. Early in the *Mahāvaṃsa* the chronicler makes this clear, as King Kālāśoka is first rebuked for being led astray by the Vesālī monks, prior to the Second Council. He then repents by promising to protect and promote the doctrine.[4] Even more significant is the Buddha's last will and testament to Sakka (Sanskrit, Śakra), king of the gods: "In Laṅkā, O lord of gods, will my religion be established, therefore carefully protect him with his followers and Laṅkā."[5] Association is repeatedly made between the welfare of the Buddhasāsana and the well-being of society as a whole. The king who internalizes this kind of legitimacy becomes the Dhammarāja, the protector of humankind from worldly harm and the active agent in basing social order on the order of the cosmos. His kingship becomes one with the lord of gods (Sakka) and with the conqueror himself (Buddha Gotama).

On a larger scale, ontological interdependence among several modes of order is perceived. This assumes mythic proportions in the symbolism of the yakkhas and the *nāgas,* who represent at the very least threats to the human order. As stated in the *Dīpavaṃsa,* "At the time the plane of Laṅkā had big forests and great horrors; different kinds of *Yakkhas,* greatly terrible, cruel, feeding on blood, furious, and demons of various forms having different inclinations."[6] Further, "All the snakes were endowed with miraculous power, all were terribly poisonous, all were faulty, fierce, haughty and dependent. The snakes were quick, greatly powerful, wicked, rough, harsh, irritable, extremely angry, and desirous of destruction."[7] On two of his legendary three trips to Lanka the Buddha encounters these forms of the demonic, reduces disorder to impotency, and ultimately enlists them in service to the Dhamma. Of one piece with this is the authority perceived by King Pasenadi of Kosala, who marvels, in the *Aṅgulimāla Sutta* of the *Majjhima Nikāya* at how the Buddha "tames the untamed, calms the uncalmed," when he subdued the dangerous robber Aṅgulimāla, "without stick or sword."[8] In artistic and doctrinal form these lingering evidences of the demonic, now rendered benign, remind people not only of the Buddha's power in earlier days but of the power of the Dhamma to exorcize latter-day yakkhas and to contain all forms of destruction.[9]

These acts of the Buddha are given perspective by being placed within a continuum extending from the remote past when three previous Buddhas are said to have visited Lanka (freeing it from pestilence, drought, and "a hideous and life-destroying war") to the time when the doctrine was established by the bhikkhu Mahinda, traditionally said to be Aśoka's son.[10] Each of these actions, at least symbolically, removes the consequences of disorder and bases the *promise* of order on the implanting of the Dhamma in the minds and associations of human beings. The establishing of the boundaries (*sīmā*) of the Mahāvihāra to be conterminous with those of the city, by Mahinda at the behest of Devānampiya Tissa, constitutes the conviction that earthly authority gains legitimacy from a Dhamma having cosmic implications.[11] Centuries later, in the reigns of Buddhadāsa (337–65 CE) and his son Upatissa I (365–406 CE), the theme is repeated as both kings display the power of genuine authority in healing the sick and driving plague and famine from the land.[12] While these are the actions of virtuous men, the moral goes deeper than virtue; it points beyond the precariousness of order, beyond the readiness with which people revert to anomic existence, to the fundamental structure of reality that transcends yet makes possible the discovery of selfless freedom.

No less instructive, given the continuing dialectic between order and chaos, is the insistence that the Dhamma's well-being depends on the monarchy's residing in Buddhist hands. From the third-century BCE establishment of Sinhalese Buddhist kingship in the reign of Devānampiya Tissa to its final demise in the early nineteenth century, a persistent refrain attributes legitimacy only to monarchs who support the Sāsana and who perceive the Buddhadhamma as the essence of social order and harmony. As Peter Berger notes, "Just as religious legitimation interprets the order of society in terms of an all-embracing, sacred order of the universe, so it relates the disorder that is the antithesis of all socially constructed nomoi to that yawning abyss of chaos that is the oldest antagonist of all the sacred. To go against the order of society is always to risk plunging into anomy."[13] In this vein, one can appreciate the relief expressed within the chronicles at the wresting of the monarchy from the Damilas by such kings as Dutthagāmanī (161–37 BCE), Vattagāmanī (89–77 BCE), Dhātusena (455–73 CE), and Vijayabāhu I (1055–1110 CE), among others. The passages that "awaken serene joy (*pasāda*) and emotion (*saṃvega*)" in the minds of the faithful stress that the miseries of the world are healed only through the doctrine of the *Saṁbuddha*.[14]

The Ontological Status of Legitimated Authority

The safeguarding of authority rests not only with those who exercise power but also with the institutions, laws, and values of the society that sets criteria for legitimacy. While religious traditions are not unique in being engaged in the legitimating process, religion often invests social institutions with enduring significance, as Berger writes, "bestowing upon them an ultimately valid cosmological status . . . by *locating* them within a sacred and cosmic frame of reference."[15] He continues: "The institutions are thus given a semblance of inevitability, firmness and durability. . . . Their empirical tenuousness is transformed into an overpowering stability as they are understood as but manifestations of the underlying structure of the universe."[16]

If the sacred reality in which society is rooted provides meaning to social and political existence, the ontological reality by which humans endorse their claims to legitimacy remains a double-edged sword haunting those by whom power is abused. The inevitable features of legitimated authority are thus its provisional nature, its susceptibility to using power for its own sake, and its final accountability to that which it purports to serve. Grounding authority in the structure of the universe makes it more, not less, vulnerable to attack. It is essentially the incumbent who is liable, more than the values and traditions that person represents, as these are undergirded with a kind of finality. This fact has immense implications for the process of legitimation.

The history of Sinhalese Buddhism during the Anurādhapura period provides repeated perceptions of authority in ontological terms. Often, it is difficult to distinguish the Sinhalese features of this process from the broader Indian texture (both Buddhist and Hindu) out of which the heritage of Sri Lanka evolved. In other respects, Sinhalese culture is distinctive and original, especially in the manner by which Sinhalese Buddhism has appropriated and modified various elements of Indian models. Three of these are examined here: first, the envisioning of a universe in sacramental terms; second, the enthroning of the Buddha on the sacred lotus seat of Brahmā; and third, the attempted elevation of the monarchy itself to comparable heights. While these fall outside orthodox teaching, they are part of a mythology that orthodoxy rarely discourages and that supports the sacred reality affirmed by that tradition.

Throughout the chronicles there is a poetic envisioning of an organic harmony within the universe that derives from the Buddha's turning the Wheel of the Law. Despite the awareness that most people ignore or violate the teachings of the Dhamma, the ontological structure of existence was believed to remain unfragmented. In *sacramental* terms, evidences are educed from a host of worlds as a way of promoting a vision of reality in which people are drawn by the power of the doctrine and are enabled to participate in a universe of meaning beyond their separateness. Early in the *Mahāvaṃsa* the stage is set for this vision as the chronicler, in reference to Aśoka, writes: "Straightway after his consecration his command spread so far as a *yojana* [upward] into the air and downward into the [depths of the] earth."[17] Geiger's notes suggest that "not only men upon the earth but also the spirits of the air and the earth heard and obeyed Aśoka's command,"[18] the implication being that authority derives from faithfulness to the Dhamma and elicits responses in kind from all corners of the universe. A similar notion emerges from the passage where Mahinda is depicted as preaching to the *devas,* who, like his human congregations, are converted to the doctrine.[19] While these embellishments are partially to stress the Buddha's regnant status over gods as well as humanity, the coherent nature of reality is made vivid.

This notion is expanded in the many descriptions of wonders and miracles said to have occurred in the reigns of Devānampiya Tissa and Dutthagāmanī. From the establishing of the Mahāvihāra to the coming of the Bodhi Tree, from the beginning of the Great Thūpa to the enshrining of the relics, the several events are depicted in the *Mahāvaṃsa* within a framework of cosmic majesty that affirms the ontic unity undergirding the universe: "Celestial instruments of music resounded, a celestial chorus pealed forth, the devatās let fall a rain of heavenly perfumes and so forth."[20] And "All this was completed without hindrance by reason of the wondrous power of the king, the wondrous power of the devatās, and the wondrous power of the holy (theras)."[21] When one has seen the relics, in Mahinda's words, one has seen the Buddha. With their enshrinement in Lanka, the devotional transplanting of the Dhamma is complete. The transmission of the doctrine is not by words alone; what is released is the empowerment to envision dimensions of the sacred beyond the confines of our normal world. "There is, O *bhikkhus,* that which is not-born, not-become, not-made, and not-conditioned. If this not-born, not-become, not-made, and not-conditioned were not, then there would be no apparent release from that which is born, become, made, and conditioned."[22] Whether in the logically clear though often cryptic language of the Buddha or in the allegorical flourishes of the chronicler, a continuity of perspective points to a universe that is sacramentally of one piece, beyond the divisions composing the experienced history of humankind. The implications of this for the legitimation of power and authority are subtle, often unclear, and always indirect. The lesson is for each monarch, for the Sangha itself, and for all persons to discover. In any case, the assertion of the reality from which authority derives is a continuing theme in Buddhist doctrine and mythology.

If genuine authority is ontological by nature and if it embodies the truth of the Dhamma, then the Buddha himself is represented, whether in aniconic or image form, as *sovereign of the universe.* While the chronicles speak from the vantage point of nearly one thousand years of Buddhist history (seven centuries within Sri Lanka alone), they interpret the *meaning* of the relics, the Bodhi Tree, the stūpas, and the images for earlier generations as well as their own. Doubtlessly influenced by Mahayana symbolism and imposing later interpretations on original forms, mid-Anurādhapura mythology was in continuity with a progressively expanding ontological picture of the Buddha's nature. From very early days, the stūpa was regarded not simply as a repository for relics but as a symbol of the cosmos. As Senarat Paranavitana states, "The relics enshrined within the *stūpa,* which at once symbolized the world and the Tathāgata, would convey the idea of the Tathāgata being immanent in the universe. The umbrella, the symbol of sovereignty, suggested to the faithful the idea of the Buddha being lord of the world."[23] It was therefore in relationship to sovereignty of this sort that the authority and power of Sinhalese kings could be and were legitimated.

One intriguing rendering of this theme argues that in the early centuries of Buddhist iconography, first perhaps in Gandhāra but shortly afterward throughout India and in Sri Lanka as well, there emerged the common representation of the Buddha in symbolical form as ascendant to the throne of ultimate power. A. D. T. E. Perera notes: "The Buddha was, according to the canonical texts, a great Being (Mahāpurisa) far above any God or Brahmā (Devātideva, Brahmātibrahma). Thus when the Buddha was taken as the tangible object of worship he had to be represented in supreme qualities that behove of a great Being. The obvious result was the creation, through art, of a supreme Being, who had surpassed earthly limits."[24] This argument proceeds to analyze sculpture and architecture in early Sri Lanka, which finally crystallized in the form of an artistic complex during the latter Anurādhapura period as well as at Polonnaruva that places the Buddha on the sacred seat of Brahmā. While the chronology of this development is unclear, a strong case is made for restructuring the Kailāsa myth whereby "the Buddha (Mahāpurisa) himself was enthroned thus making a suggestion that even the greatest Divine Being of the Hindu pantheon had succumbed before the Buddha by offering him his very lotus seat."[25]

Though space does not permit elaborating on this interpretation, Perera depicts in detail several elements of this sculptural portrayal, providing insight into the meaning not only of the principal figure but of the Nāga guardians (*dvārapāla*), the moonstones (*sandakadapahana*), and the flight of steps leading to the cosmic mountain. In Mahayana imagery, especially that which influenced Buddhist art among the Khmers, the Supreme Buddha takes on the abstract form of Vairocana. In Sri Lanka there is a commingling of iconographic images (with primary stress on the historic Buddha, albeit drastically reinterpreted) with the essential theme being his ontological priority over all beings, spiritual and worldly, divine and human. By understanding this fundamental theme one can appreciate the willingness of Buddhists in Sri Lanka and elsewhere not simply to be tolerant of Hindu gods and local deities but to convert them into service of the Dhamma, a point to be discussed in the final section of this chapter.

A third feature of the ontological underpinnings of legitimated authority proceeds from the above, namely, the association of kingship with the sovereignty of the Buddha. Beyond direct historical ties of Gotama to pious kings such as Bimbisāra and beyond the transmission of Buddhist kingship from Aśoka to Devānampiya Tissa, there was the emerging conviction "that only a Buddhist had the legitimate right to be king of Ceylon" and by the tenth century that the king must be a Bodhisattva as well.[26] While the evolution of this is difficult to trace, there is evidence of a growing elevation of kingship to divine status or, more precisely, a direct ontological association between Buddhist kingship and the Lord Buddha. Canonical warrant for this is, of course, given in the Cakkavatti concept articulated in the *Mahāsudassana Sutta* and the *Lakkana Sutta* of the *Dīgha Nikāya,*[27] wherein the model of a world ruler is one who presides "over the four quarters of the earth, righteous in himself, ruling righteously, triumphant, enforcing law and order at home, possessed of the seven jewels."[28] But this remains abstract until specific kings claim world leadership for themselves, or have ascribed to themselves, direct association with this status.

Though partial ascriptions are made throughout the chronicles of various monarchs, the most deliberate early assertion of ontological parity with the Buddha as lord of the universe is that of Kassapa (473–91 CE), the famed parricide king who built his palace atop Sīgiriya. Paranavitana notes, "As the *Cūlavaṃsa* categorically states, Sīgiri was built as a replica of Ālakamandā paradise on the top of Mount Kailāsa; and Kassapa resided there as the embodiment of Kuvera on earth."[29] While the chronicler's account of the whole Dhātusena-Kassapa-Moggallāna saga hits the salient didactic keys, it is basically restrained on this score. A translation with commentary by Senarat Paranavitana of a purported fifteenth-century Sanskrit history of Sīgiri, on the other hand, unfolds the story of Simhagiri as an Alakā (paradise) on earth and of the attempts of both Dhātusena and Kassapa to be proclaimed *Parvatarāja:* "When it was questioned by Dhātusena what purpose there was in administering the kingdom from a place on the summit of a rock, the Maga Brāhmana replied that *Parvata* was a synonym of *Megha,* i.e., the Cloud, that the Cloud was the source of all prosperity, that if the Cloud did not rain, the whole world would be destroyed and that it would be possible for anyone who had made the world to accept that he himself was the Cloud, [to] bring the whole world under his subjection."[30]

Cynicism prompts the reader to reject the whole account, or at least to view what it portrays as a bald power play, basing legitimation on hoodwinking of the populace. However specious the supposed Brāhmana's reasoning, and however transparent the motives, the account nevertheless suggests the length to which the legitimizing process could proceed and how delicate was the line between genuine and spurious legitimation. As it is said in the *Manusmriti,* the king should "emulate the energetic action of Indra, of the Sun, of the Wind, of Yama, of Varuna, of the Moon, of the Fire, and of the Earth."[31] Likewise, the *Sukranīti* emphatically states that "the king is made out of the permanent elements of Indra, Vāyu, Yama, Sun, Fire, Varuna, Moon, and Kubera, and is the Lord of both the immovable and movable worlds."[32] With mythologies of this sort underwriting political authority and with the even more potent ontological association with the Buddha seated on the sacred throne of Brahmā, the power of the kingship gave the appearance of durability. As Berger explains, "To repeat, the historically crucial part of religion in the process of legitimation is explicable in terms of the unique capacity of religion to 'locate' human phenomena within a cosmic frame of reference. . . . The inherently precarious and transitory constructions of human activity are thus given the semblance of ultimate security and permanence. Put differently, the humanly constructed nomoi are given a cosmic status."[33]

The Extent and Legitimation of Power

In traditional societies threatened by the specter of disorder, authority and power must be buttressed by more than appeals to ontological legitimacy, however acknowledged these may be. With the onset of social instability or with the absorption of heterogeneous subgroups, basic agreements may dissolve and power becomes threatened. Appeals to ontic legitimacy fall on deaf ears, and counterappeals arise. At the very least, order becomes a matter of highest importance, and skill in political statecraft carries its own legitimation.

There is political truism in the assertion that power seeks a vacuum. Maladministration, incompetence, or simply ignorance about the basic problems of a society undermines whatever ideological validation exists. In a hierarchically structured society, leadership often continues in name alone, and authority is maintained only under duress. The fact that this kind of authority is invested with ontological status is ironically more of a liability than an asset, as blame attaches itself to those from whom benefits were expected.

In a monarchy especially the kudos that attends kingship in times of plenty may suddenly collapse when conditions become critical, creating a crisis of confidence that places responsibility on the monarch in power. The jockeying for position that emerges reveals the multiple loci of power comprising any society. Balancing of power occurs as much within a monarchy as in other forms of government. Attempts to secure absolute power are products of despair resulting from the failure to extend legitimate authority throughout the system. Such efforts reveal that effective legitimation has collapsed, that the mandate of authority is recalled, displayed as much by social disintegration as by inauspicious portents.

The task here is to examine the relationship between the concept of kingship and how kings exercised legitimated power in ancient Sri Lanka. While this does not mean ignoring the realms of ideology and rhetoric, since most of the source material is didactic by intention, grains of realism become evident the more one explores the expansion, use, and curtailing of power. The areas to be viewed are as follows: first, how the legitimation of authority is regularized and transmitted; second, how the actual power of kingship is expanded; third, how statecraft is envisioned and utilized; fourth, what bearing traditional expectations of kingship have for each monarch; and fifth, what checks on royal power determine the shape and tenor of legitimacy.

In the entire history of Sri Lanka no event is accorded more importance for the establishment of legitimate political authority than the founding of Buddhist kingship on the Aśokan model during the reign of Devānampiya Tissa (250–10 BCE). This episode constitutes the classical designing of what kingship means and how it is to be regularized. This story is so familiar that one needs only to mention those ingredients that became normative for the institution of the monarchy and how the Indian model of the ideal king, modified considerably by Aśoka, took root in Sri Lanka. If no direct lineage can be traced from the Indian Mauryan dynasty to Sri Lanka, the fact that Aśoka's missionary (the bhikkhu Mahinda) is held responsible for Tissa's conversion to the Dhamma establishes an ideological tie with the earliest of India's great empires. Lanka has, of course, related ambivalently throughout its history to this association with Indian prototypes, utilizing whatever served its own needs and becoming restive when threatened by political realities (especially from South India). In any case, the symbols of office, the modes of consecration, and the forms of administrative practice were largely Indian in origin.[34] It would be naive to imply that these arrived full blown with the advent of Mahinda, unfolding immediately with the *abhiśeka* of Devānampiya Tissa, but over the centuries the regalia, the titles, the ceremonies, and much of the exercising of authority became more Indian in complexion, without losing their primary legitimating feature, that is, the claim of Dhamma.

More significant than the acquiring and confirming of royal power are the means by which this power could be extended through competent handling of the office. In line with the king's basic function of protection, it is clear that military security and political stability were essential conditions for the enhancement of the monarchy. As in the early days of any society, political leadership and military prowess were often merged. In both India and Sri

Lanka the caste basis of this solidified the connection even more. Among the greatest Sinhalese leaders were those whose strategic skills on the battlefield were noteworthy. The reverse is equally true, as many defeats by South Indian armies made clear. Without freedom from foreign attack or civil strife, legitimation was cast in doubt.

The same was true with respect to economic welfare; the necessity of a productive agricultural base and a lucrative foreign trade assumed major importance. The special climatic, terrain, and soil features of Sri Lanka led eventually, because of population increases, to the extensive irrigation system that began to develop under Vasabha (67–111 CE) and continued, with many interruptions, until the final collapse of the Rājarattha civilization in the fourteenth and fifteenth centuries.[35] Safeguarding the economic base was of no less consequence than political protection. In fact, the two were intertwined, as was clear whenever foreign invaders took advantage of domestic unrest and weakness as the occasion to launch an attack.[36] While kings had certain rights over land usage and ownership, and possessed the privilege to levy various kinds of taxation, there was an unwritten law that these rights were in jeopardy unless basic economic and political conditions were met. The lesson for each king was clear: unless legitimation is rooted in effective response to the basic needs of society, its claims to cosmic status were of small comfort. The converse is equally true: with the maintenance of these benefits royal authority is enhanced.

On the other hand, since social conditions are rarely ideal, skills in governance can turn relative losses into relative success. Though power is regularly held in balance by the presence of contending factions, shrewd leadership may defuse factious elements and even convert discord into harmony. While the process is a never-ending dialectic that can easily backfire, there were carefully developed principles in the art of government (*dandanīti*) that stood many a monarch in good stead. As Geiger indicates, the compiler of the first part of the *Cūlavaṃsa* (chapters 37–79) was well-versed in Indian *nīti* literature, especially in the *Arthaśāstra* of Kautilya, and attributed not only detailed knowledge of this to Gajabāhu II (1132–53 CE) but also showed how it was put into practice.[37] While earlier evidence of such statecraft is fragmentary, one may find reference to it in the reigns of Kassapa V (914–23 CE) and Dhātusena (455–73 CE), whose bhikkhu uncle tutored him in these arts.[38]

Though few kings could meet Kautilya's high standards of intrigue and deviousness, there is considerable evidence throughout the chronicles that many Sinhalese monarchs were able practitioners of realpolitik, rewarded by the successful manipulation of power. The standard education of any prince included study of the arts of warfare and of *nīti* in general. Political marriages regularly took place with princesses from South Indian dynasties from the outset of Sinhalese history. Bhikkhus, as well, often engaged themselves in direct political involvement. In reference to Dāthāsiva, whose position at the court of Aggabodhi I (571–604 CE) was similar to that of the *purohita,* Geiger notes this as "the beginning of political influence on the bhikkhus."[39] Long before this, however, in the late third century CE one can see in Samghamitta (during the reigns of Gothābhaya, Jetthatissa, and Mahāsena), a monk whose wiles and manipulation of power took second place to none, at least in the judgment of the Mahāvihāra.[40]

These examples should prove no surprise, for the climate of political practice in India and Sri Lanka made the knowledge of *dandanīti* imperative. Even if Buddhist conscience did not normally approve of duplicity (*dvaidhibhāva*) or if circumstances did not always require spies (*gudhapuruśas*), no leader could afford to be cavalier about the balancing of power (*āśana*), the prospect of anarchy (*mātsyanyāya*), or the regularly practiced system of alliances (*mandala*). While the influence of the Dhamma, as represented by the Sangha, exercised a moderating influence on those who may have been tempted to excesses in statecraft, responsible statecraft and legitimation were perceived to be hand in glove.[41]

In whatever ways a king's legitimacy is established and by whatever means his authority is extended, limits are set to his power by the unpredictable nature of circumstances and by other communities of power within his own society and beyond. The very inflation of status accompanying any ontological grounding of kingship produces a level of expectation and a pinpointing of responsibility that ironically turn the monarchy into a precarious institution. When rainfall is sufficient and the crops flourish and the people prosper, the king may bask in the adulation of his citizens, who attribute all success to his righteousness, all bounty to his protection. When famine strikes, when plague decimates the populace, when a foe puts the king's troops to rout, blame is sought in the person of the monarch. As U. D. Jayasekera notes, "From Vedic times downwards the king has been regarded as the supporter and upholder of the law, the 'dharma.' It was believed that any unhappiness, misery and pestilence among the subjects were attributed to the failure of the king to conform to the duties (*rājadharma*) of the king. It is said that even sugar and salt lose their flavour during the rule of an unjust king."[42] The belief that kingly righteousness is the guarantee of heavenly blessing also attributes repeated afflictions to the absence of righteousness. U. N. Ghoshal observes: "When kings become unrighteous, we are told in a canonical text (*Anguttara-Nikāya,* II, 74–76), the king's officers (*rājayutta*) also become unrighteous. . . . Conversely, when kings become righteous all the reverse consequences follow."[43] A good king is an incalculable blessing, a bad king, a disaster. What legitimation bestows, circumstances may remove, for authority is not inherent in the king. It is provisional, arising from an effective use of power for the benefit of others.

Finally, what were the factors that served to check royal power from becoming tyrannous and contribute to a balancing of power whereby the legitimacy of kingship was actually enhanced?[44] First, on the level of theory, the fact that the king was supposed to rule according to the Dhamma created an *image* of sovereignty that had its effect on incumbents, originally through their early education and later on the throne. Second, there was always the threat of hostile public opinion, which could be capitalized on by adversaries at home and abroad. Third, the lessons of history provide sobering restraints as one reflects on what happens when folly and injustice proceed from the throne. Fourth, in the absence of instant communications and constant surveillance, local communities (the *gāma,* or basic unit of autonomy) and distant provinces (e.g., Rohana) tended to promote a kind of functional independence within the general bounds of fealty. Fifth, the many centers of power within the court, the army, various corporations and guilds, all having their own diversity, were not only vehicles of support but potential threats to the king, depending on his ability to affect balances within and among these groups. Finally, there was the factor of foreign mercenaries, whose numbers grew in importance over the centuries and whose presence was ambiguous in relation to the various allies and foes among South Indian dynasties.

While all of these factors were important in limiting royal power, the most crucial factor was the bhikkhu-Sangha. Because of the Sangha's closeness to the people and because of its role in lending cohesiveness to the realm, a unified monastic community was an invaluable asset to effective kingship. On the other hand, from the reign of Vattagāmanī (89–77 BCE) on, the Sangha was not unified and was often seriously divided, a fact that regularly involved the king or his counselors in disputes and sometimes prompted them to take sides, creating further unrest. Kings were the primary patrons of the Sangha, but they could also become the target of abuse. The following summary by Tilak Hettiarachchy hints at the complexities at work and suggests how royal power was both enhanced by and limited in its relationship to this community.

> Conflicts arose between the king and the Sangha when the king carried his patronage too far and interfered in the affairs of *uposathāgāra.* The Sangha also started taking more interest in politics as they became a landed aristocracy, and the existence of a division within the order aggravated the situation so that the monks tried to put their favourites on the throne in order to secure material benefits. As the orthodox church grew in power

the king was forced to take sides with them, but disputes arose regarding the respective fields of power of these two institutions which led to the ultimate clash in the reign of Mahāsena. When the king realized that his power was no match for that of the orthodox church he made a sudden reversal of policy and instead of attempting to maintain the unity of the Sāsana tried to bring about and maintain as many rival Vihāras as possible, thereby to redress the balance.[45]

The Nurturing of Legitimation

As in the political realm, where power arrangements continuously shift, legitimation of authority is a process needing regularly to be renewed by means of symbolism, mythology, and ritual. Even where no serious threat exists, the process needs to be kept alive among those already accepting it in theory. A central ingredient of this process is for reciprocity to be experienced and confirmed among other key elements in the society. Legitimation is not simply of kingship but of the entire structure of which kingship is the central feature.[46] Authority and power are not granted to the throne for its own sake but to offset the precariousness of order and to foster stability and reasonable prosperity. The very concept of reciprocity suggests that communal existence is a fabric whose integrity depends on the strength of all its parts. While reciprocity takes multiple forms, with different meanings at various levels of society, it is a necessary ingredient in the legitimation process: "Without integration among the elite, integration between the elite and the masses is difficult to achieve; without integration between the elite and the masses, there cannot be an integrated political community."[47] The nurturing of legitimation remains, therefore, essential to any social organism.

Because most available source materials from ancient Sri Lanka come either from the bhikkhu community or from kings in the form of royal inscriptions, one would expect discussions of reciprocity to dwell frequently on the relationship between the Sangha and the monarchy. While this is true, one may read between the lines for evidence of a more pluralistic reciprocity, with various groups within society being as central as the other two. Indeed, as anthropological studies of Sri Lanka, Myanmar, and Thailand reveal, a rich heritage of ideology, symbolism, and ritual exists on the popular level throughout Theravada societies. While present forms of these cannot be projected on earlier centuries without qualification, it is clear that a host of pretheoretical legitimating phenomena has existed from ancient Sinhalese experience. The following discussion identifies three aspects of the nurturing of legitimation, each involving the king, the Sangha, and the wider community in various ways: first, the notion of the Sangha as a merit field (*puññakkhutta*) whose purity was essential to society at large; second, the normative qualities of kingship, centering primarily on its responsibility to protect and further the Dhamma; and third, the role of ritual and ceremony in keeping alive not just the memory of the Buddha but belief in the doctrine's power. These aspects of legitimation go far beyond underwriting royal authority; they attest to and buttress the entire universe of belief that comprises Sinhalese Buddhism.

The stress on the Sangha's purity has been central from the tradition's beginning; the relating of this to an ideology of merit grew gradually over the centuries. Throughout Theravada Buddhism the injunction of the Buddha was that "one of the six duties of a monk toward the laity is to show them 'the way to heaven' (*sagga*) . . . and not 'the way to emancipation' (*mokkhassa maggam*)." This has been taken seriously and helps to explain why, with canonical support, considerable encouragement has been given to pious practices of various sorts.[48] If the path to Nibbāna is too arduous for those not seeking it directly, the Sangha accepts the task of assisting laypeople to build up merit for their next existence and of becoming through the quality of its own life a source of merit to others. The reasons for the Sangha's needed purity are therefore twofold: one, that this may enhance the chances of its own membership for attaining Nibbāna, and two, that the merit accrued by this quest may be transferred to pious followers.

The modern dynamics of this has been discussed by S. J. Tambiah, who shows how the ascetic monk becomes "an appropriate intermediary who can reach up to mystical powers associated with the Buddha and the sacred texts, and who can in turn transfer these powers to the layman in a form that can positively sacralize this life and the next."[49] The practicing of merit is thus accompanied by the receiving of merit, giving concrete form to the reciprocity that needs actualizing in order to have meaning for its participants. As the king is ideally the mediator between the body politic and the cosmic realm, the Sangha's role as mediator can provide sacral meaning to ordinary existence and the human odyssey. For this reason, the quality of a bhikkhu's life must be without reproach. Monks involved in political affairs, engaged in "monastic landlordism," or embroiled in strife among the nikāyas do not give the appearance of being merit fields for others. From the earliest days in India and Sri Lanka the king had an important role in prompting the Sangha to reform itself (*sodhana*) through a regulative act (*dhamma-kamma*) of the Vinaya. This did not place the king above the Sangha in ecclesiastical matters; rather, it reinforced the notion of reciprocity, since the entire society had a stake in the Sangha's purity. Because the Sangha could be an effective check on royal power that had become tyrannous, a unified and healthy monastic community served to create political legitimacy. The ongoing process of purification was thus a central ingredient in the nurturing of legitimation.

The role of the king as protector of the Dhamma was in direct correlation with his role as chief patron of the Sangha, though it went beyond this as well. Aside from various land grants and other endowments that kings made available to monasteries, without which they would not have flourished, royal beneficence was also seen as a model for others, in spirit if not in kind. The importance attached by the compilers of the chronicles to the generosity of kings was not simply out of appreciation for what the Sangha received materially. It was also recognition that monarchs who were well disposed toward the livelihood of the bhikkhus furthered the Dhamma in a number of ways, beyond the maintaining of order and justice within society.

As in other respects, Aśoka was a prime example. The *Dīpavaṃsa* records him as saying, "As much as the monks desire I give them whatever they choose."[50] It is also recorded that the monks had to restrain him in his liberality, though when he pressed the question to Moggaliputta as to whether there were "a kinsman of Buddha's religion like unto me," he received his response: "Even a lavish giver of gifts like to thee is not a kinsman of the religion; giver of wealth is he called, O ruler of man. But he who lets son or daughter enter the religious order is a kinsman of the religion and withal a giver of gifts."[51] It was only fitting that Aśoka's purported son, the bhikkhu Mahinda, should be the one to tell Devānampiya Tissa that not until someone native to Sri Lanka was ordained would the doctrine be planted in that country. Both examples suggest the nature of true giving, and yet the very prodigality of royal patronage was stressed in order to inspire later generations. In response to the lavish gifts of Dutthagāmanī, the chronicler writes: "Merit, that a man has thus heaped up with believing heart, careless of insupportable ills of the body, brings to pass hundreds of results which are a mine of happiness; therefore one must do works of merit with believing heart."[52] Such performance of "pure deeds of merit" prompts others to "give alms lavishly, with a mind freed from the fetters (of lust), mindful of the good of beings."[53]

It was this sort of monarch who was purported to walk among people even as a bodhisatta (e.g., Buddhadāsa in the fourth century) and to be endowed with the ten qualities of kings (*dasa rājadhamma*) and the four heart-winning qualities (*cattāri saṃgahavatthūni*).[54] The models of exemplary kingship are threaded throughout the chronicles, in contrast to others whose lives of evil are due warning. Also, the stories of holy monks and nuns, collected in the *Ariyavaṃsa,* were ordered by Vohārika Tissa (209–31 CE) to be read aloud for the edification of the people.[55] Protection of the Dhamma obviously took a number of forms, involving support of the Sangha, construction of stūpas, and especially living lives founded on the teaching. In the process, not only was the Dhamma enhanced and nurtured; the whole process of legitimation was deepened through this internalization.

The most conspicuous way by which society's roots in the sacred realm were reaffirmed was through ceremony, festivals, and other forms of ritual. While Aśoka's caution about the true nature of ceremony (*dharmamangala*) would rank proper respect for living creatures above the usual ceremonies that people perform, he also placed "the gift of Dharma or the benefit of Dharma" above liberality.[56] The chronicles make clear, however, that orthodoxy saw benefits accruing to the Dhamma by the celebration of its power through ritual. Indeed, among the more obvious emphases throughout the record of the *Mahāvaṃsa,* ending with the reign of Mahāsena (274–301 CE), are its elaborate and unrestrained paeans in response to the rituals of stūpa building, relic worship, reverencing of the Bodhi Tree, and other forms of paying homage to the Buddha.

Unquestionably, the focus is on the Buddha and the Dhamma, but it is on their cosmic significance, not simply their historic features. Access to this realm comes preeminently through attitudes of reverence stimulated by symbolism, mythology, and ritual. While many have suggested that these occasions were primarily for the populace, this argument is not convincing. The bhikkhu community was as much involved in glorifying the Buddha's relics and in celebrating the Wheel of the Law as any others. If the proper aspiration of each monk was the attainment of Nibbāna, paying homage to the Buddha formed an intrinsic avenue of approach, even if the path finally required the extinction of all dependence.

It is true that the performance of ritual clearly had its less elevated dimensions. Kings were often engaged in constructing stūpas and image houses as much for their own advantage as for the benefit these brought to the Dhamma. Political opportunism often played its part as forms of bread and circuses for the populace and amassing of credit with the Sangha. A touch of cynicism is called for in trying to assess motivations, though there was undoubtedly sincerity in the intentions of many monarchs. At any rate, the value of renewing legitimation liturgically was not lost to the ingenuous and the scheming alike. Because people forget or disregard the ontic dimensions of their social existence, they need reminding. Berger notes: "Religious ritual has been a crucial instrument of this process of 'reminding.' Again and again it 'makes present' to those who participate in it the fundamental reality-definitions and their appropriate legitimations . . . in the context of a history (fictitious or not) that transcends them all."[57]

The single most important Sinhalese Buddhist festival was that of the

Tooth Relic, brought to Sri Lanka in the reign of Sirimeghavanna (301–28 CE), which became an annual event continued down to the present and now accompanied by the Kandy Perahara. While associated with the Abhayagiri-vihāra and not even mentioned by the Pāli commentaries of the fifth century, the Tooth and the Alms Bowl (*pātra-dhātu*) of the Buddha came to be considered "essential for a prince who wished to be the recognized king of Ceylon."[58] Indeed, in an act of devotional symbolism, Sirimeghavanna was said to have offered the whole kingdom to the Tooth Relic, whose annual festival scored the reliance of genuine sovereignty on the sovereign rule of the Buddha in cosmic terms. Reinforced by the reverencing of the Hair Relic (*kesadhātu*), begun in the reign of Silākāla (518–31 CE), "there were also public festivals in connection with the older objects of religious veneration, the Bodhi Tree and the *stūpas*, in which the king and the people took part. A festival regularly celebrated in honour of the Bodhi Tree was known as *sinānāpūjā*, the ceremony of bathing the holy tree, still conducted in the height of the drought as a means of causing rain to fall."[59] While it is not appropriate here to explore the vast subject of *pirit* (Pāli, *paritta*), it must at least be said that the importance of the Protection Suttas and their use in dealing with public and private calamity are central to the problem of evil that ensues when forms of anarchy threaten the cosmic order. While close to magic on one level, they may partake of spiritually more profound quests on another.[60]

In conclusion, it should be stressed that all forms of ceremony and ritualistic action on the public level in ancient Sri Lanka were party to the nurturing of legitimation, provided one interprets this as legitimation of society's definition of reality and not simply of royal authority and power. In this vein, one may see the deeper significance of stūpa building, that has always been regarded in Theravada countries as the apogee of merit making, as a form of ritual itself, and as the prime symbol of the Buddha's authority. The following comments by Edward Conze make this clear:

> It was because Buddhism assured this harmony with the cosmos on which all social welfare depends that the laity was so eager to support the Order, house its members, and erect fine monuments in honor of their teachings. The world would not have put up for long with a community of monks which would merely turn their backs on those who fed them if they had not given something priceless to the world it could not get in any other way. The visible manifestations of this concern for cosmic harmony are the magnificent stupas which adorn all parts of the Buddhist world and are the tangible focus of the religion. It was the business of the laity to build those stupas, though only the relics of the Lord Buddha could give them

> life. The stupas are as fundamental to Buddhism as the four holy truths, and it has been shown beyond doubt that they have a cosmic significance, that they are representative of the universe. . . . This "cosmic architecture represents the world as a theatre for the working-out of the Dharma and for the awakening of all beings by its piercing rays." Each stupa is an 'imitation' of the life, or rather lives, of the Tathagata. . . . They allowed a whole society to unify in one common celebration, and thus had not only great moral, but also political consequences.[61]

The Collapse of Legitimation

It has been the thesis of this chapter that each human community requires for its social and psychic existence a significant consensus about what Peter Berger calls its "plausibility structure." This entails the defining of reality employed by a community to provide meaning to its corporate life and to cope with the forces of disorder within and among people. The two central ordering principles in traditional communities are the political and the religious, both of which seek to relate the affairs of society in different but complementary ways to a perceived transcendent sacred reality. In this manner, authority and power are identified and in various ways gain legitimacy—of the plausibility structure itself rather than of those in positions of leadership at any point in time. By definition, the structure is a seamless web and cannot easily endure sustained challenges to its authenticity without being radically affected. Finally, the process of legitimation is a continuous one, needing reaffirmation regularly if its meaning is not only to persist but to become more inclusive. The notion of inclusivity has major implications for the contemporary situation in Sri Lanka.

A question that became acute in the latter half of the twentieth century, as traditional forms of societies succumbed to new means of ordering reality, is what happens to human communities in the face of immense pluralism when their plausibility structures are shattered or seriously threatened? The fact that we are presently more aware of this issue does not mean the phenomenon is new. In the West, for instance, we have been dealing with this fact in a host of forms ever since the breakup of the Holy Roman Empire in the late Middle Ages. This also does not suggest that new structures of meaning cannot emerge, for they obviously have. But these structures possess less scope today and rarely inspire the same confidence as those existing for centuries without radical challenge. On the other hand, history records successive efforts at weaving new patterns from the ruins of the old, using many former threads but adding new ones as well. The process is not a simple evolution from an originally affirmed plausibility structure. More likely, the process often involves consensus, challenge, collapse, and attempts at new forms of consensus, ad infinitum. If consensus appears to be enduring, based indeed on the perceived structure of reality, its collapse may appear to preclude all possibility, at least until new visions become convincing.

While the final section of this chapter is no place to introduce new themes, it may be appropriate here to suggest nuances of the original theme that could profit from further research and reflection. The history of the Anurādhapura period affords considerable evidence that the culture dominated by the ethos of Sinhalese Buddhism was remarkably diverse. This was somewhat the case from the beginning, though it became more so through centuries of increased exposure to the political arenas of South India, the world trading community with which Sri Lanka was involved, and the changing patterns within Buddhism (in Theravada and Mahayana circles alike). The traditional documents for studying the Sri Lanka scene are well known. While presenting an extraordinarily full picture, they are now being enriched by comparative historical studies of other Theravada cultures especially, as well as by further anthropological case studies of the sort done by Hans-Dieter Evers on the interplay between the *vihāra, dēvāle* and palace systems in the Kandyan period.[62] This suggestion is made on the assumption that sufficient evidence is obtainable for a fuller historical picture than we presently have of the diversity within the Sangha, the increasing influence of Purānic Hinduism, and the impact of various forms of popular religion.

The value of understanding this broader picture is obvious from a number of standpoints, but it is essential if one is to grasp the factors leading to a radical challenge of the orthodox plausibility structure, beginning in the late Anurādhapura period. The main configurations of Mahayana history in Sri Lanka, from the reign of Vohārika Tissa (209–31 CE) to the introduction of Vajrayana and Tantrayana in the ninth and tenth centuries, are familiar, but detailed studies of *nikāya* history (involving the problems of schism, sectarianism, and Sangha unity) have only recently been broached. Likewise, knowledge about the general patterns of Brahmanic culture, especially in the North, is available, but further studies that seek to appraise in depth the influence of Indian popular religion, Sanskritized Tamil Brahmanism, and the highly important Bhāgavata cult on forms of Sinhalese Buddhist life and practice remain to be attempted (as of this writing). Finally, while anthropological work of increasing sophistication has been done on the national cults of Sri Lanka and on various indigenous forms of popular religion, it is crucial that these be studied on a comparative basis and that we learn further about their role historically in affecting more orthodox forms of mythology, symbolism, ritual, and piety.

Traditional forms of legitimation may retain their credibility long past their zenith, but unless they absorb creatively new elements into the plausibility structure, they cease to be vibrant. Until we know more about the history of relationships between the major *vihāras* and the *nikāyas,* not to mention their associations with political figures in Rājarattha and the provinces, one can only speculate about the tensions that were present in the constant struggle over legitimacy. Glimpses of the picture are available. We know the side that several kings took in disputes between monastic communities. Evidence affords some insight into the role of bhikkhu influence on affairs of state. But only a skeletal perspective is thus far available. The same holds for how diverse branches of the Sangha responded to the mounting Indian influence in the last two or three centuries before what the chronicles call the "pillage of Laṅkā" (by Māgha in 1215).

A synoptic account exists, but we learn little about the dynamics of a culture wrestling desperately to retain its definition of reality in the face of competing alternative views. Were there, for instance, important attempts to fashion new syntheses that were nipped in the bud but were never even reported? Does the Sangha's livelihood depend, in fact, on patronage from the political arm? What creative resources emerge in such a community when it becomes clear that this dependence is no longer possible? Obviously, there were many stages in the history of Sinhalese Buddhism, long before the colonial and modern periods, when royal patronage and political stability were either precarious or nonexistent. How did the bhikkhu community deal with these crises? One may suspect that during these times the plausibility structure was at most in abeyance, not extinct, but thus far we have insufficient insight into what this actually meant for the life of monks. Moreover, the picture of lay Buddhism during the vast scope of ancient times is inadequately known. While this is often true in the records of early societies, it is particularly the case here. Again, comparative historical and case studies from other Theravada societies would enable speculation to be better informed.

To conclude, the process of legitimation involves the linking of normal social existence to a perceived sacred reality, indeed involves the perception of how this reality may help to transfigure, even regenerate such existence. The more one understands the dynamics of the process in detail, the more one sees its fragile nature, its powers of renewal, its potential for accommodating new ingredients, the constant possibility of its collapsing, and the enduring importance of it for all communities. All of this is germane to understanding the nature and process of how power and authority are legitimated, as well as their inherent vulnerability.

The following chapter is primarily theoretical in nature. Specifically, it addresses the process of assimilation in ways that indicate how Sinhala Buddhists became skilled, yet sometimes threatened, in their relationships to other religious traditions. Its intent is to describe different forms or styles of assimilation within early medieval Sri Lanka. By such an approach one discovers how Sinhala Buddhists have crafted varieties of response to changing situations as these have arisen within the Sāsana or have impinged on it from the outside.

3

Varieties of Religious Assimilation in Early Medieval Sri Lanka

Over the centuries and particularly during the early medieval period there is abounding evidence of a doctrinal, iconographic, and cultic sort that Sinhalese Buddhism accommodated itself to varied religious influences, including those of the Mahayana tradition. On the other hand, if one takes the Chronicles of Ceylon literally, one has a picture of so-called orthodox, Mahāvihāra Buddhism staving off both Mahayana and Brahmanic influences, not to mention folk religious beliefs and practices. This *image* of orthodoxy, as presented in the *Mahāvaṃsa,* has been challenged by a number of modern scholars. What the chronicles do provide is a clear portrayal of the Mahāvihāra position—its ideology, its anxieties, its connection with political power, as well as its vision of what the Dhamma means. As D. K. Dohanian notes, "The prestige of the Mahāvihāra monks depended completely upon their maintaining a strong and obvious historical connection with the earliest days of Buddhism in Ceylon."[1] One needs to recognize the bias of this community. The very vehemence of its conservative stands suggests alternate positions within the Sangha. As R. A. L. H. Gunawardana has written, "Though the Mahāvaṃsa seeks to present a picture of a unified kingdom in the island which had existed long before the time of Dutthagāmanī [r. 161–37 BCE], it is possible to recognize certain elements lying scattered in the body of the chronicle as remnants of a discordant tradition which points to a totally different situation."[2]

This discordant tradition is frequently attributed to the Abhayagirivihāra monks, who tended to be more receptive to new ideas and practices stemming from India, including Mahayana as well as Tantrayana, or Mantrayana, forms of Buddhism. While the early clashes between these two markedly different sects within the Sinhalese Sangha entailed matters of monastic discipline (Vinaya), by the fifth century it becomes clear that the Abhayagiri monks were being strongly influenced, for example, by Mahayana teachings about the nature of the Buddha. Suffice it to say that one needs to be aware of this diverse picture as one seeks to understand the various approaches of the Mahāvihāra monks to the whole issue of religious assimilation.

The image presented by the chronicler and maintained by the Mahāvihāra monks is, instead, a depiction of Urbuddhismus, of "original" Buddhism, and its implications for the Sāsana in Sri Lanka. Since this perceived image is intertwined with that of Sinhalese nationalism and the society's search for ethnic identity, it raises a research problem of considerable importance. How is one to understand what actually happened during early medieval times from the late Anurādhapura period through the Polonnaruva era (i.e., early ninth to late thirteenth centuries), not to mention what Sinhalese Buddhism evolved into as a consequence of these influences? Did the Buddha Sāsana resist changes of an important sort? If not, how was it modified by newly emerging practices and beliefs as these arose from within Sri Lanka or came from abroad? Was it able to sustain significant continuity with its own past, at least its perceived past, and with that of early Buddhism in India?

While conclusive evidence going back several centuries is difficult to secure, there is no lack of testimony, however piecemeal at times, throughout the history of Sri Lanka. One finds this documented in the chronicles and the commentaries, the inscriptions, the ancient festivals and rites (many of which continue into the present), and in sculptural and architectural remains from both the Anurādhapura and Polonnaruva periods. Aside from these forms of evidence, modern ethnographic and anthropological studies lead one to speculate that many of the forms existing within Sinhalese Buddhism today were also existent in ancient times.

This chapter is primarily theoretical in nature. Several methods and types of material are used as a way of suggesting that Buddhism throughout its history in Sri Lanka was more diverse than has often been assumed and of indicating that Sinhalese Buddhists became skilled in adjusting to other religious traditions. An attempt is made to develop a theoretical spectrum of stances taken by the Sāsana toward these other beliefs and practices. Such a portrayal would include rejection of influences from other religious positions at one end of the spectrum to nearly wholesale acceptance of other positions at the opposite end. In between, one can detect a variety of intermediate positions in which elements of these influences were assimilated and transformed in various ways over the centuries. This chapter is part of a more extensive study by various scholars of religious assimilation within several traditions of Theravada Buddhism from its emergence and development in India and Sri Lanka to its spread throughout large areas in Southeast Asia. The intent here is to advance the concept of a spectrum, to provide enough examples within the context of early medieval Sri Lanka, and to suggest a number of areas that could benefit from further exploration.

It was during the Polonnaruva period (ca. 993–1293 CE) that Sri Lanka began to relate to and influence various Buddhist communities in Southeast

Asia. It may seem ironic that the form of Theravada that emerged after periods of intense exposure to Mahayana and Mantrayana Buddhist elements was precisely the form that became the standard of orthodoxy in these other countries. While this fact attests to the resourceful manner in which this tradition incorporated varied religious features, it also weakens any claim to unalloyed continuity with the world of early "canonical" Buddhism in India. The actual process of assimilating certain new forms while rejecting others reveals the tensions that arise in encounters between any tradition and plural elements both inside and outside itself. As we shall see in chapter 4, this process is analogous to a similar one within the political order of the Polonnaruva era in which centripetal and centrifugal forces were constantly being rebalanced.

Part of analyzing "orthodox" Buddhism and its relationship with other religious beliefs and practices is the need to clarify one's terminology. Because the term *syncretism* is commonly misunderstood, it is preferable to identify the process as one in which a religious tradition (in this case, Sinhalese Buddhism) assimilates, subordinates, transforms, and is itself modified by elements of belief and practice from other religious traditions or communities. Any process of this kind is subtle, complex, frequently reciprocal, and dynamic, and it is clearly found in areas such as ritual, symbol, cosmology, and institutional structure. The various Chronicles of Ceylon provide limitless raw material for study, but it is in cultic practices and archeological complexes that one can understand even more deeply the intricate process of assimilation and synthesis that has occurred throughout history.

Fundamentally, religious assimilation is the process of incorporating, subordinating, and transforming diverse elements into an ongoing tradition of belief and practice. This process is a continuous one within which what is assimilated changes, as does the matrix into which it is incorporated. It is thus dynamic, dialectical, and reciprocal. These new elements frequently emerge from within a tradition; they do not simply impinge upon it from the outside. Reform movements from within a religious community are the most common case in point, even though they are obviously influenced by outside forces as well. One sees, therefore, in the process of religious assimilation continuing efforts to balance centripetal and centrifugal tendencies. The crux of the dilemma, from the standpoint of the dominant tradition, is knowing how to be responsive to changing circumstances without losing a sense of its own self-identity. In actual fact, the most surprising and interesting outcome is when there is an increasing and perhaps deeper sense of what this self-identity comes to mean.

Edward Shils has ably expressed this notion of consensus and the tensions that arise within it:

> The centre, or the central zone, is a phenomenon of the realm of values and beliefs. It is the centre of the order of symbols, of values and beliefs, which govern the society. It is the centre because it is the ultimate and irreducible; and it is felt to be such by many who cannot give explicit articulation to its irreducibility. The central zone partakes of the nature of the sacred. In this sense, every society has an "official" religion, even when that society or its exponents and interpreters conceive of it, more or less correctly, as a secular, pluralistic, and tolerant society.[3]

One issue, of course, is what happens when there are many subordinate centers, whatever their association might be with the principal center. Another issue is the relationship of "civil religion" to a historic religious tradition such as Theravada Buddhism (in this case, Sinhalese Buddhism). The other side of Shils's coin is that tensions within a consensus are as necessary to examine as the consensus itself: "The central value system which legitimates the central institutional system is widely shared, but the consensus is never perfect. . . . Active rejection of the central value system is, of course, not the sole alternative to its affirmation. Much more widespread, in the course of history and in any particular society, is an intermittent, partial and attenuated affirmation in the central value system."[4]

In discussing the center-periphery relationship, S. N. Eisenstadt states that we may "distinguish between a generally positive as against a negative attitude to change." He refines this by sketching "various concrete types of response to change," especially the following:

> (a) a totally passive, negative attitude often resulting in the disappearance or weakening of such resisting groups; (b) an active resistance to change through an organized "traditionalistic" response aiming to impose some, at least, of the older values on the new setting; (c) different types of adaptability to change; (d) the appearance of what may be called transformative capacity. This last position is the capacity not only to adapt to new conditions but also to forge new general institutional frameworks and new centers. Transformative capacity may vary according to the extent of coercion which it involves.[5]

While Eisenstadt's typology is useful in examining many of the dynamics within Sinhalese Buddhism historically, it does not sufficiently allow for certain elements that are unique to Buddhism. We proceed now to describe what is essentially a complex spectrum of positions within Sinhalese Buddhism. A spectrum of this sort reveals this tradition's efforts both to remain in continuity with what it perceived to be canonical Buddhism and to respond to changes within itself and to pressures from different sources over the centuries. By definition, a spectrum is a model, a portrayal of distinctive positions along a continuum. It is not definitive, only suggestive. In the process of outlining these positions, it is necessary to include caveats to this particular model as well.

Various Modes of Assimilation within Sinhalese Buddhism

The purpose of this section is to identify modes or nodal points along a continuum as a means of illustrating the infinitely varied yet characteristically patterned ways in which Sinhalese Buddhists have reacted to changes of various sorts, both as these have arisen within the Sāsana and as they have impinged upon it from the outside. To begin, what is meant by *Sinhalese Buddhism?* Only a longer study could do justice to the tremendous variety implied in answers to this question over more than two millennia. Suffice it to say that, here, we are talking primarily about the Mahāvihāra community as this can be discerned within the chronicles.

The six positions outlined below are by no means mutually exclusive. They overlap at various points in time. Their relationship may shift rapidly or evolve gradually, depending on the circumstances. But whatever qualifications can be made, the principal point is that these are distinguishable positions and that considerable evidence for each exists in the history of Sri Lanka. This section discusses all six positions and provides evidence from a variety of sources. The brief concluding section identifies future studies that might advance the discussion further.[6]

While examples can be drawn from many periods of Sri Lankan history, the largest share is drawn from the early medieval period, the late Anurādhapura through the Polonnaruva period (ca. 800–1300 CE), in part because these issues were exceptionally alive during that time. Indeed, one wonders whether there was a move during the Polonnaruva era toward renewed orthodoxy as well as, paradoxically, an increasing modus vivendi with various noncanonical beliefs and practices that flourished at the same time. These included forms of Mahayana and Mantrayana Buddhism that were especially strong in the early centuries of this period, the vital bhakti movements as these spread from South Indian Śaivism and Vaishnavism, and continuing elements of folk religious belief and practice. Was the result a new orthodoxy? Also, was Polonnaruva as a ceremonial complex more conducive to these features than Anurādhapura had been in earlier centuries? Or was this process of "synthesis" not new at all but simply a case of varied religious expressions being allowed by, but kept distinct from, "canonical" Buddhism?[7]

RESISTANCE TO ASSIMILATION: A STANCE OF OPPOSITION

The first two positions may seem to be opposites but often emerge as reactions to each other. They are at antipodal ends of any spectrum and would not seem to characterize historical Sinhalese Buddhism in its most typical forms. On the other hand, they are not unrepresentative of Buddhism, for at certain times they have characterized the dominant mode of the tradition. Of these two, the first typically opposes what it sees as violations of the normative beliefs and practices of Buddhism. If one designated the dominant tradition by the symbol *x* and challenges to it by the symbol *y*, radical opposition would appear as *x* against *y*. While degrees of resistance against extracanonical styles of life and ways of perceiving reality exist in all religious traditions, the basic posture here is rejection of heterodoxy in any form.

But the other side of protest is affirmation of traditional norms. In one sense, it is separatist in orientation. It perceives alterations in doctrine and regimen to be contaminations that would undermine the essence of the Dhamma. Though "false bhikkhus" are often singled out in the chronicles, a stock phrase is usually reserved for kings who accept heretical views; namely, they are "as the grasshopper [that] leaps into the fire taking it for gold." A specific case in point is the monarch Silākāla (524–37 CE), who welcomed the arrival in Sri Lanka of a famous text entitled the *Dhammadhātu* that contained the heretical teachings of the Vaitulyavādins (the Vetulla School, a Mahayana sect). This group was first mentioned in the reign of Vohārika Tissa (209–31 CE) and was affiliated with the Abhayagirivihāra in Anurādhapura. For his inadvertence, the king was portrayed as being "incapable of distinguishing truth from falsehood as the moth which flies to the lamp it takes for gold, when he saw it, believing it to be the true doctrine of the Buddha [who] received it with ceremony."[8]

The various chronicles are replete with comparable evidence. While the *Mahāvaṃsa* and the *Cūlavaṃsa* are especially important documents, a late fourteenth-century Sinhalese work entitled the *Nikāya Sangrahāwa* is of special value in cataloging the various schisms that occurred within the Sangha over the centuries and the reasons for these schisms.[9] When one juxtaposes this work with an early thirteenth-century noncanonical Pāli work, the *Saddhamma-Samgaha*, which stresses the importance of compiling, writing down, and expositing the Pāli canon and its commentarial literature, the strenuous emphasis on orthodox teaching may be felt.[10] Intrinsic to this position is the repeated attention given to reform of the Sangha. Normally, what is at stake is purification of the lifestyle of the bhikkhus (to make behavior conform to the Vinaya or its accepted modifications according to time and place) and the unifying of dissenting elements within the monastic community. For the most part, during the Anurādhapura period the emphasis was on purification, though many instances of doctrinal strain also exist among and within the four main sects: Mahāvihāra, Abhayagiri, Jetavāna, and Vaitulyavāda.

According to W. F. Gunawardhana, in his introduction to the *Nikāya Sangrahāwa,* it was not until Sena II (853–87 CE) that the Mahāvihāra began to regain its dominance. Sena "now made the other three formulate their ritual, and enjoined their strict conformity to religion. This may be considered as the deathblow to the survival of the three new Nikāyas. It is true that while they received a constitution, it was a constitution that deprived them of their expansibility and the power to adapt themselves to the changeful fortunes of their struggle. From this time forth, therefore, they begin to decay, and they linger on till the time of Parākramabāhu the Great, when that mighty monarch bids them cease and they are heard of no more."[11] Following the example and admonitions of Aśoka, Sinhalese monarchs involved themselves in monastic disputes from the beginning, as well as in actual Sāsana reforms, after the early sixth century CE. It was during the Polonnaruva period, however, that the most noteworthy involvements took place; it was within the reigns of both Parākramabāhu I (the aforementioned "Great") and Parākramabāhu II that *sāsana katikāvatas* (codes of regulation) were promulgated—in 1165 and 1266–67, respectively. Aside from the standard stress on purification and on unity within the Sangha, which Parākramabāhu I enforced in an unprecedented manner, one sees in these codes important developments toward organizational centralization within the monastic community, a trend stimulated by the confused nature of social and political affairs in the twelfth and thirteenth centuries.[12]

It is clear that the stimulus for reforms within the Order frequently came from forest-dwelling sects (*āraññika*). In *Robe and Plough,* R. A. L. H. Gunawardana makes this point convincingly. Indeed, one can say that the traditional distinction between the forest-dwelling monks (*āraññavāsī*) and the town- or village-dwelling monks (*gāmavāsī*) separates those who are less accommodating (with respect to strictness of regimen) from those who are more so. This is parallel to what one finds in the modern period, where groups among the laity arise in protest against monastic slackness and impurity of doctrine.

Among many examples of the stimulus for reform one may point to the Sri Lanka Vinaya Vardena Society.[13] In such cases one is dealing with a reform movement that seeks to reaffirm purity of discipline and to reestablish doctrinal continuity with early Buddhism, both in its Indian forms as perceived in the *Tipitaka* and in its Sinhalese forms as indicated through the chronicles. Inevitably, this stance inclines toward a rejection of much that has actually evolved in historical Buddhism, in Theravada as well as Mahayana. While contact with the world cannot be avoided, it seeks more extreme forms of separation than most Buddhists are willing to take. Paradoxically, while frequently perceived as closer to normative Buddhism and thus held in high esteem, this stance is not typical of how most Buddhists, whether monks or laity, relate to the world.

PRONENESS TO ASSIMILATION: A POSITION OF ACCOMMODATION

The second position would seem to be a polar opposite to the one just discussed. In this instance, *x* capitulates to *y*. The grasshopper leaps into the fire, undoubtedly with the best of intentions. In the process, the basic identity of Buddhism is endangered either by accommodation to other forms of culture or by being co-opted for purposes inconsistent with its principal mission. The manners in which either of these can happen are, of course, infinite. Whether the *x* factor is extinguished in some violent fashion or is gradually subsumed under *y* may make little difference in the long run. In either case, the tradition's very identity is threatened. An example of the former would be what happened to Buddhism in ancient India with the Muslim advance into Bihar and Bengal. Coupled with its own internal problems at this point, political misfortune effectively put an end to institutional Buddhism (with some exceptions in East Bengal and the South) until its partial revival during the past century and a half. For different reasons and in different ways one sees a severe weakening of Buddhism in Sri Lanka during the long colonial period, especially under the British, until its various forms of revival beginning in the mid- and late nineteenth century. A recent example and one that is more dramatic would be the fate of Buddhism in Tibet since the 1950s, even though it has in many ways thrived in exile. The several persecutions of Buddhism in China, especially in the fifth, sixth, and ninth centuries, took their toll, though the tradition survived in less vigorous forms. Again, in Sri Lanka, one can track the fortunes of the Sāsana resulting from various Tamil invasions in the early Anurādhapura period, and later with the Cholas in the eleventh century and with Māgha in the thirteenth.

These sorts of adversity are, of course, more dramatic than when the tradition is seduced into serving ends that are non-Buddhist in nature. Naturally, there is a distinction between extensive assimilation of non-Buddhist beliefs and practices and a virtual loss of Buddhist identity. There is clearly a continuum between these two positions. An important kind of example is where appropriation of religious symbols, institutions, and personnel by social, political, or economic forces provides sanctity to what are basically non-Buddhist ends. We are referring here to what is commonly called "civil religion," or the use of sacralizing powers for essentially worldly purposes. This is not to imply that Buddhism lacks interest in justice or in the responsible use of power. The evidence throughout Buddhist history in various countries is otherwise. The point here is where the Sāsana becomes virtually captive—even though for good, if naive reasons—to forces and powers that undermine its functional independence.

It would be simple to supply evidence from the modern period (in Sri Lanka, Southeast Asia, and elsewhere) where developments in so-called posttraditional societies threaten the identity of traditional religions and force them to pose fundamental questions. The primary example here, however, is from the Polonnaruva period. Though use of the Sangha by kings and other claimants to power for political purposes is common throughout Theravada history, one may observe in the reign of Parākramabāhu I (1153–86 CE) and in that of Parākramabāhu II (1236–70 CE) explicit but different forms of civil religion being employed.

In the latter case, the sources suggest that the Sangha was a willing participant. Indeed, one could see this as a classic case of symbiosis between monarch and Order. Each retained a basic independence, yet the relationship between the two added to the strength of both. One gets the impression of a pious king who anticipates the needs of laity and bhikkhus alike. As one reads more closely, one perceives an exceptionally shrewd leader whose political astuteness seems matched by his religious sincerity. The result for both the Sāsana and the social order appears as beneficial as can be expected considering the threatening nature of the times. In this case, one has an example of Buddhism's not being consumed or misused by civil religion.

The other example is less clear. The more one tries to grasp the attitude of the chronicler toward Parākramabāhu I, the deeper the sense of ambiguity. Unquestionably, the 240-page account of this figure is told in the language of *kāvya*. The words are classic encomium. His exploits are praised; his power, skill, and courage are held in awe. All the obvious signs and portents appear to be auspicious. He is a paradigm of paradigms. If only his *kamma* had fated him to be born in Jambudīpa (India), he would have rivaled Aśoka. None but the Buddha outshines him, and the two are clearly associated throughout the tale. On the other hand, we have depictions of a person whose ends frequently are made to justify his means and whose powers of artifice have no equal. He dispatches his foes with an obvious touch of cynicism. He rewards his followers "to each according to his merit"—a common phrase harking back to the *Cūlavaṃsa*—[14] as though he were the dispenser of kammic destiny. Like the Buddha, he is the allayer of fear, striking the *abhaya* pose in one guise or another, yet, unlike the Buddha, he uses fear to make cowards of his foes.

The ironic tone is too transparent to miss. Even his resolute purification of the Sangha, especially his determination to rid it of all division, makes cynics of careful readers. One suspects that his motives were fundamentally political and that his purpose in promoting organizational unity was to reduce the chances of factionalism. From the standpoint of political realism, this makes good sense. Again, Aśoka provides a model. From the standpoint of the Sangha's independence, however, it did not bode well for long. The chronicler appears to be raising a flag of warning about an imbalance of power that was taking shape during this reign. The pitfalls as well as the advantages of civil religion are obvious from a reading of Sinhalese, Burmese, and Thai history, whether ancient or modern. The issue at stake here is the danger of diminished freedom that results from too close identification with the political order, no matter what the passing benefits may be.

FROM ASSIMILATION TO SYNTHESIS: A PROCESS OF INCORPORATION

The third position is where *x* assimilates *y*, the fusion creating a new entity, *xy*. This form of religious assimilation is often labeled as *syncretism*, though that term could be used for other forms as well. Or, it might better be termed *synthesis*, which technically means a mixing together of different elements to form a new and different whole, creating something that did not exist in the same fashion before. If the word is used loosely, any number of examples can be found, since the process of fusion and synthesis occurs regularly and is part of what one means by religious assimilation. But when used strictly, it becomes a distinct mode by itself, requiring examples that are more selective. Two sorts of illustration serve. The first is broad in scope and suggests what was happening throughout the country over centuries; the other is more precise, namely, the process as it developed within an important temple in the fourteenth century. Each of these reflects the impact that popular Hinduism (particularly Purānic Śaivism) was having on the religious practice and worldview of Sinhalese Buddhists. While Brahmanic influence in Sri Lanka is as old as that of Buddhism and while India's influences on Sri Lanka (intellectually, artistically, religiously, sociopolitically) continued through the centuries, a different sort of movement gained momentum around the ninth century, lasting for at least six hundred years. It was out of this movement, Mahayana Buddhist as well as Hindu in nature, that what we are calling a "synthesis" emerged.[15] Vincent Panditha writes of the Hindu influence: "With the increasing instances of Indian rule over Ceylon, Hinduism too began to influence Buddhist practices. Sinhalese kings like Mahinda II (787–807 CE) and Sena II (866–901 CE) put up temples for Hindu gods. During the Polonnaruva period influences of Shaivism and Vaishnavism were felt strongly. Shaiva and Vaishnava shrines were erected at Polonnaruva, and they possessed bronze images of Shaivite and Vaishnavite gods. . . . In a comparative study of the moonstones of the Anuradhapura and Polonnaruva periods, one sees a marked difference in design guided by Hindu ideals."[16] N. Mudiyanse also notes Hindu and Mahayana influences: "From the 12th century onwards we find the influence of Hinduism on the faith of the masses of Ceylon and Hindu deities such as Vishnu have since been absorbed into the popular religion of the Sinhalese people. Of the doctrines that the rivals of the orthodox monks had preached, some, like the theory of perfections (*pāramitā*), the belief in Bodhisattvas, and the emphasis on devotion (*bhakti*) had been accepted by the Mahāvihāra and incorporated into the Theravada. It should be noted that these doctrines are mostly Mahayanist in character."[17]

As general depictions, those two quotations are reasonably representative of what was happening from about 800 to 1500 CE. As of this writing, a detailed history of religious assimilation during those centuries has not yet been written. The reasons for the increasing influence of Hinduism are several. Among them one would include the impact of growing numbers of Indians (mainly Tamil Hindus) who came to Sri Lanka as mercenaries, merchants, and immigrants during this period. Other factors would be the spread of Mahayana, especially during the Gupta age (*c.* 320–550 CE), giving a strong impetus to the study of Sanskrit, the important revival of Hinduism occurring in South India in the seventh century and the great literary activity that took place under Parākramabāhu I in the twelfth century, stimulating studies in Pāli, Sanskrit, and Sinhalese in subjects both religious and secular.[18]

It was not primarily in the area of scholarly activity, however, that the synthesis or fusion with which we are concerned occurred. It was rather in the growth of devotional expression (*bhakti*), and not simply on the popular or folk level. While obviously manifested there, it became characteristic of the society more generally, engaged in by king, monk, priest, and layperson alike. The origins of this devotional expression in Sri Lanka are obscure. From the reverencing of the Buddha and his relics described in the *Dīpavaṃsa* (fourth century CE) and the *Mahāvaṃsa* (fifth century CE), it is clear that a cult of the Buddha existed then. The cult may have had its liturgical beginnings with the formal establishment of Buddhism in the reign of Devānampiya Tissa (250–10 BCE). The arrival of the relics, the receiving of the great Bodhi Tree, the construction of the Mahāthūpa, and the enshrining of the relics during Buddhism's first hundred years had already been heralded with effusive devotion.

As indicated earlier, understanding the evolution of belief and practice over the centuries in Sinhalese Buddhism requires one to recognize the ongoing struggle between the more conservative position of the Mahāvihāra monks and the greater receptivity of the Abhayagirivihāra to evolving forms of Buddhism that were arising in India. Dirian K. Dohanian elaborates on the Mahayana influence in this struggle: "The Mahayana features which find a place in the mixed Buddhism of the Abhayagiri fraternity are the most general, striking and obvious ones: worship of the Bodhisattvas and the Buddha who are preternatural and innumerable; belief in Buddhahood as the ultimate destiny of all sentient beings who win their way to universal salvation by faith and through grace; belief in the transfer of merit, earned through the performance of pious deeds, to others in order to awaken the Bodhi in their hearts; and reliance upon the magical efficacy of word-charms, diagrams and other contrivances."[19] These features were foreign to canonical Buddhism as interpreted by the Mahāvihāra community, but it is also true that the Buddhism that evolved in Sri Lanka from the fifth century CE on gradually incorporated more and more from the Mahayana tradition and even from forms of the Hindu *bhakti* tradition.

We know that in the fifth century CE, when the Chinese pilgrim Fa Hsien visited Sri Lanka, there was an active cult of the Tooth Relic, with large-scale festivals being promoted by the Abhayagirivihāra (which thrived during these years). We also know that the Tooth Relic was brought to Sri Lanka in the first year of Sirimeghavanna's reign (301–28 CE) and that the history of this relic was written in Elu (the ancient language of the Sinhalese), supposedly in the year 301. In line with our thesis about the strong emergence of devotional expression during the late Anurādhapura period and its flourishing for centuries thereafter, it is not coincidental that a Pāli translation of this history, entitled the *Dāthāvaṃsa*,[20] appeared about the year 1200 and that the cult of the Tooth Relic was of exceeding importance throughout the medieval period of Sinhalese society for both political and religious reasons. Nor was it coincidental that the *Thūpavaṃsa* was written during the reign of Parākramabāhu II (1236–70 CE). As an account of the construction of the Mahāthūpa in Anurādhapura during the reign of the hero-king Dutthagāmanī (161–37 BCE), it associates the mid-thirteenth century (an era witnessing the decline of Sinhalese greatness) with an earlier age of emerging Sinhalese national and religious identity. As such, the *Thūpavaṃsa* was not simply a remembrance of former greatness but a recalling of a people to their spiritual destiny.[21]

The essence, therefore, of the "synthesis" that was strongly characteristic of this period was its fashioning of a form of *bhakti* or pious devotion that had elements from more than one religious tradition. In a note to his translation of the *Cūlavaṃsa*, Wilhelm Geiger mentions the use of the term *bhakti* (Pāli, *bhatti*) in the twelfth and thirteenth centuries, ascribing its influence to

Hinduism but showing how it was applied to forms of reverencing the Tooth Relic, the Bowl Relic, and the sacred footprint (*śrī pāda*).[22] A further example of synthesis was the promoting of pilgrimages to Sumanakūta (Adam's Peak) by various kings within the Polonnaruva era (including Vijayabāhu I, Parākramabāhu II, and Vijayabāhu IV) so that Buddhists could honor the sacred footprint and also pay respect to Sumana (Saman), the god of this mountain and one of Sri Lanka's traditional protectors. As Senarat Paranavitana says,

> The acceptance of Buddhism by a people is not necessarily followed by the disappearance of the gods whom they were wont to worship. The conversion of a people to Buddhism generally results in the conversion of the gods of that people also to the same faith. The Buddha is the teacher, not only of men, but also of gods. The gods thus continue to exist, but not the same as before. . . . But the cults of these gods, as well as the worship of the Footprint on Adam's Peak, though not encouraged by the orthodox religious leaders in Anurādhapura, were probably prevailing in places away from the main centres of Theravada Buddhism; it is, in fact, after a prince belonging to a branch of the royal family that had been in Rohana for several centuries, established himself at Anurādhapura in the eleventh century, after repelling the Chola invaders, that we have a record, for the first time, of a royal benefaction to Adam's Peak. Similarly, it was after the centre of political gravity shifted away from the ancient capitals in the thirteenth century, that there is mention in the chronicles of a king of Ceylon concerning himself with the worship of Saman.[23]

A second example of such synthesis will be mentioned only in passing. It appears as an interesting development in the mid-fourteenth century, apparently occurring for the first time with the construction of the Lankatilaka Temple (the state temple of the Gampola period), of locating Hindu dēvāles, or shrines, *inside* Buddhist monasteries. While it was becoming increasingly common for dēvāles to be attached to vihāras, the instance of Lankatilaka is considered to be the first of its kind. Since this has been described at length by Hans-Dieter Evers, it is cited here simply as a particularly graphic case of synthesis.[24] In saying this, we do not imply that either Buddhism or Hinduism loses its identity by this sort of functional and symbolic fusing. This third position along the spectrum is unlike the second, where the danger of lost identity is very real, although, as Evers indicates, both monk and priest here are at the behest of the palace system, with all the implications of civil religion again. The most interesting feature of this relationship between vihāra and dēvāle is that, while the former nominally retained supremacy, the more insecure the times became, the more people resorted to what the priest had to offer, namely, protection against a threatening world. The shifting relationship within this fusion was based naturally on circumstance and need, but its unique feature lay in its encouragement of a roughly equal and mutually advantageous coexistence.

ASSIMILATION WITHIN LIMITS: A PYRAMIDAL STRUCTURE

The fourth position is one in which a hierarchical arrangement exists among the related elements. Symbolically, it is *x* over *y*. This pyramidal relationship has been described by many anthropologists of Sri Lanka, especially by Gananath Obeyesekere, Michael Ames, and Nur Yalman. Similar observations have been made by scholars dealing with Myanmar and Thailand. While one cannot automatically project these perceived structures back into time, sufficient material of a mythological, ritualistic, and artistic nature remains from earlier periods to indicate how these relationships have evolved and how plausible the hierarchical theory is, as far as it goes. In a sense, the concept of "hierarchy" is endemic to Buddhism. By definition, the Brahmanic deities and later the Hindu gods (as well as the entire Mahayana pantheon) are subordinate to the Buddha, who has extinguished his *kamma,* as comparable Buddhas had earlier. All others remain on the wheel of suffering, however high or low their status.

The question of differential status and authority, nevertheless, is intrinsic to a pyramidal structure. Equality is an illusion: differences between beings derive from merit earned or lost in former existences. Built into the fundamental distinction between the Buddha and all others is a division of labor separating those persons, institutions, rites, and supernatural beings that are oriented toward Nibbāna (the extinction of kammic existence) from those whose aim is further pleasure or less pain. In a hierarchical schema, there are gradations of merit accrual, but there remains a difference in kind between the most meritorious and the Buddha. The very concept of a hierarchy suggests an infinite distance between enlightenment (freedom from attachment) and nonenlightenment. In order to accommodate that fact, religious traditions create universes of differentiated beings whose assistance humankind seeks or whose malevolent intent one avoids.

This pantheon, with its various levels and numerous ways of being approached or protected against, has been capably portrayed by Gananath Obeyesekere.[25] Under the Buddha in importance there is first Śakra (Sakka), king of the gods, to whom the Buddha entrusted the welfare both of the Sāsana and of Lanka. The latter's care was delegated to Uppalavanna (Upulvan) or Varuna (later seen as Vishnu). The other pan-Sinhalese deities, essentially *lokapālas* or guardian figures of the Sinhalese world, are Saman (Sumana), Skanda (Murga), Vibhīsana, Pattinī, and Nātha (Avalokiteśvara). These figures are, according to Obeyesekere, "gods in a conventional sense, for they grant favors, intercede on behalf of humans, help them in worldly affairs, and cause weal or woe in the human world."[26] Beneath them, in feudal-like fashion, are area or district deities, who in the modern period have faded in importance as people move more easily from one locale to another. On lower levels, at the pyramid's base, are first "a host of very powerful demons who are completely malevolent and 'irrationally punitive.' . . . Below them are spirits of dead relatives (*pretas*), goblins, and ghosts, who are all spiteful, causing fear in men's hearts."[27]

The Sinhalese pantheon, with its ritualistic features, has often been described. Only a few additional comments are called for here. First, when observers have noted a complementary division of labor, for example, between Buddhism and the healing rituals, whereby in practice they are closely intermingled but in theory are distinct, it is my impression that this is more true now than in the premodern era. The effects of modernism and the quite natural desire of bhikkhus (most laity also) to distinguish normative Buddhism from what might be seen as magic are products of a "scientific age." Such an association would have been less problematic in previous centuries, but this is an issue that needs further exploration.

A second topic for further exploration is "the process by which a 'foreign' god or demon is incorporated into the pantheon."[28] If one uses the model of superiority-inferiority, then the newly incorporated member accepts the suzerainty inherent within the pantheon. The most interesting feature, however, is the process that occurs (sometimes gradually, sometimes quickly) between various deities and bodhisattas, a process in which shifting relationships may be observed and in which the notion of a fixed hierarchy is less appropriate. At any rate, the process is exceedingly complex and suggests the need for more fluid models, arising out of historical and comparative research that focuses primarily on the process by which religious assimilation takes place.[29]

POLARITY AND TENSION: A DIALECTICAL MODE

The fifth position poses the central dilemma within Buddhism as a historical tradition, and within Theravada especially: the task of helping monk and laity alike to live within a world of suffering without compromising the basic principles of the Dhamma. This dilemma creates an inevitable tension between *x* (the dominant tradition with its normative beliefs and codes of action) and *y* (social values and behavior that are in conflict with that tradition). Conflict of this kind may arise within the Sangha, not simply within society. Arrogance and corruption may exist in any context. This dilemma makes the relationship one of continuing paradox, for it acknowledges both sides of the tension with equal force. It recognizes that Buddhists live in a world of compromise and that they do so in a less than perfect fashion. It neither rejects this world, nor can it live easily within it. While it clearly values forms of religious assimilation, it coexists uncomfortably with them and perceives their threat to the Dhamma more deeply than do positions three (*x* assimilates *y*) or four (*x* over *y*). This dilemma may be more sharply felt by bhikkhus who have left village or city life, choosing instead to live either in a hermitage or in a community of forest-dwelling monks. But it is in fact a tension that is widely experienced within Buddhist societies from Sri Lanka to Southeast Asia. This dilemma is unquestionably severe in the modern world, recognized as much by laity as by bhikkhus, but it is clearly not a modern phenomenon alone. The historical documents give repeated evidence; rituals, mythology, and symbols attest to it in all ages. The tension is indeed intrinsic to the Buddhist worldview and may be found in its earliest Indian forms.

On the other hand, it is also true that the more disturbed the times and the more threatened the Sangha, the greater the dilemma becomes. It is precisely at times such as these that men and women are attracted to noncanonical means of release. Individuals and communities under serious stress resort to protective devices in relatively stable times, but the more the forces of *adhamma* appear, the greater the inclination. It is the thesis of this chapter that early medieval Sinhalese society increasingly experienced this sensation and that this was a major reason, though not the sole one, why religious assimilation quickened during this period. If this thesis has sufficient validity, one would expect a heightened sense of dilemma at the same time. By paying attention to the increased liturgical and ritualistic emphasis that evolved in the Polonnaruva era and by noting the interesting historical studies done by Obeyesekere and others on the relationship between myth and history (see note 28), one detects an interesting correlation and tension between cultural anxiety and religious syncretism.

In an analysis of changing status relationships among gods in modern Sri Lanka, Obeyesekere states that "wherever uncertainty prevails, astrology flourishes."[30] While he limits that observation to South and Southeast Asia in recent times, its implications pertain to any period of history, especially if one sees astrology as but one means of seeking to resolve the tension. In an earlier essay, entitled "Theodicy, Sin and Salvation in a Sociology of Buddhism," he examines the dilemma existing between orthodox, classical Buddhism and "practical secular Buddhism." In that essay he cites two prominent ways in which this dilemma has been resolved—by the bodhisattva (savior) cult in Mahayana, and by the concepts of counterkarma, transfer of merit, and the importance of one's last thoughts before dying in Theravada.[31] He mentions also how normal monastic life can be an obstacle to enlightenment (hence the decision of some to become forest monks) and how laity regard the purity of the Sangha as a social necessity (i.e., as a vehicle of transferring merit—hence its need for regular reform). In his article "Magical-Animism and Buddhism: A Structural Analysis of the Sinhalese Religious System," Michael Ames states the problem concisely: "The fundamental paradox facing the Sinhalese is that they have such a high and noble ideal they can never fully realize it in this life. Not only are they bound to endless rebirth, they also require rebirth. They must somehow learn to escape from it."[32]

Sinhalese Buddhists, however, have nevertheless developed ways of embracing the dilemma as well as trying to resolve it. In a discussion of the *pataha* ritual (see note 28, item 2) Obeyesekere shows how this ritual becomes a means of inverting or challenging misuses of the theory of divine kingship: "What is at issue is not so much the theory of divine kingship per se but the form it took in an era of troubles. . . . [This] neither implies a rejection of notions of divine kingship nor the authority of the king. Similar rituals of humiliation are directed against gods and demons: yet they are respected, venerated or feared."[33] The ritual acts, as it were, to redress an imbalance. Functionally, it is similar to the ongoing tension between the monarchy and the Sangha, between the two wheels of the Dhamma. One may see this balancing occur within a ritualistic context more than in any other. The elemental function of liturgy is precisely not to collapse the tension between levels or dimensions of reality but to register their actual separation and to reenact their essential oneness. Some have referred to this separation as this-worldly and other-worldly in nature, but such a distinction seems more confusing than edifying.

The dilemma of separation between reality as commonly experienced and reality as seen upon awakening is a continuing Buddhist dilemma. The difficulty of sustaining this tension, even of recognizing its deeper implications, is clear. While Sinhalese Buddhists have no less difficulty with this sort of tension than persons in other religious communities, they have certainly experienced the dilemma profoundly and have sought to live within it as a way of discovering how to transcend it. Frank Reynolds makes a case for how the Mahāvihāra community in Sri Lanka has reacted over centuries to the stimulus of Mahayana and Mantrayana forms of Buddhism on the one hand and varieties of Hinduism on the other. It was not by a "grudging acceptance of the newer views and practices" but by a "persistence and resilience" that enabled Sinhalese Buddhism to sustain a balance between significant continuity with its historical tradition and significant change in the face of major social and ideological challenges. The result was a perceptively altered form of Buddhism that became the model for the forms the Sāsana took in Myanmar, Thailand, and Cambodia.[34]

FROM FORM TO FORMLESSNESS: A TRANSFORMATIVE APPROACH

The sixth and final position on the spectrum is peculiarly important in that it may be closer to the essence of what the Dhamma means to reflective and sensitive Buddhists. Yet it may also be the furthest from how Buddhism is typically conceived as well as practiced. It might be portrayed as an ongoing process in which x (the normative dimensions of the dominant tradition) relates to y (again, those elements of mundane existence that arise inside and outside the Sangha) in a manner transformative of both x and y. The first neither rejects nor succumbs to the second. The two are not simply combined into a "higher" or "lower" synthesis; nor does the notion of hierarchy fit the relationship. While the position of "tension"—also called "dialectic" or "paradox"—approximates it more closely, it falls short for the obvious reason that the notion of transformation includes but goes beyond tension, makes room for but is not defined by paradox, and engages in but does not settle for dialectic.

To some, the position in question is a goal or an ideal. To others, it is the fundamental nature of reality, whether realized by men and women in history or not. In a real sense, it appears as an impossible ideal, but it is also one that tradition believes was realized in the Buddha, and in all awakened persons. However conservatively tradition acknowledges its realization, the ideal is perceived as a genuine if rarely achieved possibility. In Buddhism, as in other traditions, concrete historical models (however idealized) and abstract ideals exist side by side. While the former appear more accessible, they are in fact as far removed from ordinary experience as the latter.

At this point, the distinctions between Theravada and Mahayana portrayals of enlightened beings overlap and begin to blur. An ideal is inevitably an abstraction until it is realized. The sixth position, therefore, is not descriptive of historical reality as typically experienced by those on the path but only as indicative of its possible realization. This possibility serves as a transforming influence, since other positions along the path, however efficacious they may appear, are perceived as incommensurate with the ultimate Dhamma. It is being suggested here that whatever emerged within early medieval Sinhalese Buddhism, it was a blending of positions, not into a stable synthesis but into an interrelationship among diverse ingredients. These ingredients had a transforming effect on each other. For perhaps the first time in Sinhalese history, the role of Mahayana changed from being essentially external to mainstream Buddhism in Sri Lanka to one that subtly exercised a transforming, impact, however briefly. The effects of the impact, however, were more enduring. As Dirian Dohanian put it,

> Parākramabāhu I, in the historical mythology of Lankā, is regarded as the Sinhalese ecumenicist *par excellence* whose greatest kingly act was the reconciliation of Ceylon's Buddhist sectaries and the restoration of ecclesiastical supremacy of the followers of the Theravāda. Still, the Mahāyānist character of the Wata-dā-ge at Polonnaruva, and of its model, does not reflect a cultural abnormality. The role of the Mahayana in the cultural development of Ceylon has been grossly underrated, both in the traditional histories and in modern commentary. (It may be said also that the special character of ecclesiastical reform in ancient Ceylon has not been understood.) The archeological remains alone suggest a widespread Mahāyāna cult flourishing from the seventh century until the devastation of Anurādhapura in the tenth. And there is considerable evidence for the survival of Mahāyāna institutions well into the fifteenth century.[35]

While this transformative capacity may be present anywhere along the spectrum that is being sketched, it is perhaps more clearly portrayed through artistic means than elsewhere in Sinhalese Buddhism. An interesting article by Senarat Paranavitana, "The Significance of Sinhalese 'Moonstones,'" suggests how a specific Buddhist symbolic complex assimilates and transforms, in this case, Brahmanic and folk elements for its own purposes and how this symbolic gestalt or synthesis is then used in ritualistic fashion.[36] Moonstones first appeared around the fourth century CE in Anurādhapura (with Indian counterparts earlier) and continued through the Polonnaruva period. These symbols, representing the plane of suffering (*bhava-cakra* or *saṃsāra*), were stepping stones, as it were, to the image shrine or mount upon which the Buddha sits (*pabbata*). The pilgrimage symbolically is from the world of psychic suffering (*samkhāra-loka*) to the Abode of Pure Beings (*brahmā-loka*), where *tanhā* has been extinguished.

Discussing the iconographic and floral detail, Paranavitana relates this to Brahmanic and Buddhist mythology, elaborating on its spiritual implications and pointing to evidence of religious assimilation. His discussion deals with the basic process of symbolization. He sees this process as an attempt to make intelligible, through the use of symbols or ritual or cosmology, that which is essentially unknowable—to interpret the unknown by analogy with what is known, however relatively. Thus, by recognizing the pluralistic nature of all symbolic interpretation and by experiencing the inadequacy of symbolization itself, one is led liturgically and psychically to the nonsymbolic, beyond potentially infinite symbolization.[37] The transformation that can occur is within the imagination of the participant. Concrete reality is viewed symbolically. By stages, the imagination opens doors to the nonsymbolic, finally integrating this with the perception of concrete reality. In the words of Paul Mus:

> Here we see why the ancient Buddhist kings undertook "cosmic" architecture. . . . It is simply for the Buddhists a theatre in which the Law is unfolded and all things awake in all their radiance. In a word, it is not descriptive architecture but normative, a catharsis. It isolates itself from the world that is nothing but confusion and it points to the way out. The order of its parts and the imagery that meets the pilgrim coming there emphasizes what leads from evil to good. This indicative value, which one must listen to as one does an injunction, makes of the stūpas . . . by the force of their example, a "replication" of the life, or rather the lives, of the Tathāgata.[38]

Ritualistic reenactment is central to the transformative process, but transformation cannot be captured by particular forms. The formlessness to which this process leads inevitably partakes of forms, but these are freed to become vehicles of the Dhamma.

The sixth position is, therefore, not a point along a line within a spectrum, but the qualitative fulfillment of any point. It is both *no* point and *every* point. While it would be false to claim this characterized actual Buddhism in early medieval Sri Lanka, one can say that in the midst of social and political confusion new insights emerged, largely through the process of religious assimilation of a varied sort, and that these enriched an entire culture. That these insights were not enduring in the common life of monks or laity does not negate their emergence. One may still detect them, in somewhat hidden form, within archeological remains and in fragments of a mythic and ritualistic nature. As largely inert forms, they remain paradigms of the formless. As such, they retain the potential of taking on new forms, keeping alive the Dhamma's relationship to changing existence in one mode or another.

Conclusion

The depiction of a spectrum of positions is simply one way of looking at evidence. It is not descriptive of reality but is another means of examining material of a varied sort. The examples used cannot do full justice to any one context. The variety itself precludes this. Furthermore, new moments of time bring new images into focus and create new realities. Again, as H. A. L. Fisher argues, the "one safe rule for the historian: [is] that he [or she] should recognize in the development of human destinies the play of the contingent and the unforeseen."[39] This applies as much to religious assimilation in early medieval Sri Lanka as to any subject. Endless caveats could be made, beyond those already suggested, about the difficulty of defining canonical Buddhism or of depicting Sinhalese Buddhism. A more appropriate way of ending this discussion is to recommend areas for future research that, as of this writing, would illuminate both the wider topic of religious assimilation and the more specific historical period of Polonnaruva Sri Lanka.

One area entails the study of South India and Sri Lanka as an interrelated microcosm (during this period of history) within a larger developing orbit, including India as well as larger parts of Southeast Asia. A study of this magnitude would call for a series of projects, utilizing specialists in many fields. To begin, it would require a more integrated study of Sri Lanka and South Indian history and culture from the ninth through the thirteenth or fourteenth century. Too often, these areas are studied in relative isolation from each other, touching at obvious points but only so far as the competence of a particular scholar allows. This calls, therefore, for a series of projects, involving many scholars in long-term and extensive research.

A second area of importance would be a comparative study of Buddhism's relationship to Hindu culture, specifically to forms of Hinduism within Theravada contexts of Sri Lanka and Southeast Asia. This would entail examining Mahayana and Mantrayana forms of Buddhism. Indigenous folk religion would likewise be germane to such a project. While many individual studies have been done, as of this writing, nothing of a comparative nature has as yet analyzed the different modes of religious assimilation occurring in various cultures at several points in time.

A third area would be a comparative analysis of the organization of the Sangha and of various factions within it during this period in both Sri Lanka and Southeast Asia. Part of this would be the relationship of these groups to the political sector (examining the nature of civil religion itself) and to broader aspects of the socioeconomic order. It would also include a comparative study of stratification within the Sangha and the process whereby elites emerge within the Order.

A fourth area for study that would be useful is relating the symbolic and cosmological implications of religious architecture, sculpture, and painting to ritual, festivals, pilgrimage, and other forms of religious devotion. Attention to the sociopolitical aspects of this area should be included as well. A comparative study on religious assimilation or synthesis would analyze the process by which different ingredients become related to each other. A basic feature would be examining how these assimilated beliefs and practices are appropriated in different ways by laity and by members of the Order. Intrinsic to this process are the distinctions between doctrine and praxis in terms of religious assimilation.

While other areas are worthy of study, the four highlighted here would be of special interest. Further clarity about them could shed light on how we understand religious assimilation more broadly.

Chapter 4 examines the principal forces at work in the Polonnaruva period, by means of three approaches. To begin, the political and socioeconomic developments of this three-hundred-year period are examined, as well as the implications these had for Polonnaruva and other regions of the country. This approach focuses on how developing forms of pluralism were in ongoing tension with a centripetal process, generated from the capital, that sought to maintain equilibrium and to resist threats, from whatever region, to the prevailing social and cosmic order. The continuing pursuit of equilibrium is an attempt to maintain Sinhala cultural identity in the midst of accelerating pluralism. The genius of a ceremonial complex lies in its ability to fashion and maintain a viable equilibrium between and within the diverse components that compose any social order.

On the other hand, this very pursuit reveals conflicts, stalemates, and disintegration, despite the possibility of renewal at various points in Sri Lankan history. The failure to maintain this equilibrium beyond a relatively short period of time, however brilliant the efforts, spelled the death knell of the classic, nationwide form of a ceremonial center in Sri Lanka. Without a center of this kind and without a revived process of inclusivity, the seeds were sown for what one finds in subsequent periods of Sri Lankan history. At the same time, a sober realization of the relationship between newly imagined forms of inclusivity, for instance, in contemporary Sri Lanka, has enormous implications for the possibility of a previously unimagined sense of identity.

4

The Pursuit of Equilibrium

POLONNARUVA AS A CEREMONIAL CENTER, 993-1293

The focus of this chapter is on the premodern capital city of Polonnaruva and how it relates to other centers of power and influence within Sri Lankan society over a three-century period. At stake then was the continuing problem found within any complex society, namely, the relationship between unity and diversity, between a so-called center and its periphery. While manifest today in countries such as the former Soviet republics, India, Canada, and the Peoples Republic of China, this problem was no less pervasive in premodern societies. The example of T'ang China (618–906 CE) was a striking one, although Chinese history in general reveals a conspicuous and ongoing tension between the centralization of authority and the forces of regional autonomy. While one could also write Sri Lankan history focusing on a similar theme, this chapter examines how centralization and provincial autonomy were in a conflictive relationship especially during the time when Polonnaruva was the capital (993–1293 CE).

Among seminal interpretations of premodern cities is Paul Wheatley's discussion of ceremonial centers and complexes in *The Pivot of the Four Quarters*. There he analyzes the origin and character of ancient Chinese cities by examining the genesis, morphology, significance, and transformation of ceremonial centers and by setting these in comparative perspective in various cultures and historical periods. Basic to his discussion is how the *centripetalizing* function of such complexes relates to what occurs over time as a society becomes more pluralistic. In his words, "All social action was indeed reinforced by religious authority, a situation which nurtured the seeds of its own dissolution, for as society became yet further differentiated, so the problem of legitimizing the increased autonomy of each institutional sphere of society became more complex."[1]

In other words, as pluralistic forces grow within a society, they challenge earlier forms of normative belief and structure. Divergent views typify social interaction; they are not atypical. If new patterns of unity are to emerge, a culture must be hospitable to its own social and religious diversity and contradictions, becoming in the process more inclusive. Without accommodation to such differentiation, a society's centripetal and centrifugal forces remain antagonistic to each other. The issue is how a society incorporates unprecedented diversity, especially when a return to traditional patterns of social order is impossible. The problematic of Polonnaruva was precisely the degree to which its social equilibrium could tolerate diversity with all its attendant conflicts. While there is no enduring equilibrium without conflict, chronic disequilibrium undermines the potential for a tolerable social order.

Again, to employ Wheatley's thesis about the ceremonial center and its centripetalizing function suggests one way of understanding the dynamics of Polonnaruva as the capital of Sri Lanka from the mid-ninth century until its final abandonment in 1293. While occupied by foreign troops during several decades of this period, it reached its apex of power and influence in the reign of Parākramabāhu I (1153–86 CE) and retained its function symbolically until the end. As such, it represented one of the great ages in Sinhalese history and, because of its immense complexities and increasing forms of pluralism, remains an enigmatic yet compelling period for study.

The full scope of this chapter covers a major period in the history of Sri Lanka, beginning with the initial transfer of the capital from Anurādhapura to Polonnaruva during the last days in the reign of Sena I (833–53 CE) through the reign of Parākramabāhu II (1236–70 CE). The period as a whole may be called the Polonnaruva era even though there were many decades (especially during the eleventh and thirteenth centuries) in which the capital was occupied by foreign troops and the region known as Rājarattha was controlled by South Indian dynasties. One assumption of this chapter is that while the relationship between the capital and the other Sinhalese kingdoms (or provinces) of Dakkhinadesa and Rohana was central to the dynamics of this period, it was only part of a larger spectrum of tensions. Out of these tensions arose conflicting factions that appeared within the court, the wider Sinhalese nobility, the Sangha, and an expanding mercantile and agricultural community. This situation will be examined from three different perspectives, to be introduced shortly, each of which points to the various forces that contributed ultimately to the breakup of traditional Sinhalese culture and polity.

The long Anurādhapura period from the third century BCE to the tenth century CE unquestionably had its own share of what could be called *problematic multicentricity.* The developments leading to the decline of Anurādhapura, the conquest and occupation by the Cholas in 993, and the establishment of a new capital at Polonnaruva (Pulatthinagara) initiated a phase of Sinhalese history that spanned more than three centuries. While still under the shadow of Anurādhapura, the nation's capital for more than a millennium, Polonnaruva became in all respects the political and ceremonial center and was in significant continuity with the past even when occupied by enemy forces. Yet, because of the infusion of new elements, it set in motion a stage of history involving marked discontinuities with former structures of society. In the process, the Sinhalese social and ideological order was significantly altered.[2] Moreover, these developments contributed to what irreversibly changed the nature and influence of premodern capital cities in Sri Lanka. After the collapse of the Polonnaruva era there was never again a center of Sinhalese culture and religion that could match the glory that had been Polonnaruva's, let alone its prototype, Anurādhapura.

Throughout this transformation from what may be called an *orthogenetic* society to one that became increasingly *heterogenetic,* the nature of Sinhalese identity was always an issue. In fact, throughout this transformation the nature of Sinhalese identity itself was at stake. The encounters with changing religious, intellectual, political, and economic forces from within and abroad were both intense and relatively rapid. Responses ranged from those evincing confusion and indecisiveness to those that were bold and powerful. The interpretation of these forces and of responses to them is far from simple.

Even the dating of the period can be argued.[3] As early as the late seventh century kings made Polonnaruva their periodic base, though Anurādhapura remained the capital either in fact or symbolically until its final collapse with the Chola occupation. At the end of the period one may date Polonnaruva's demise with the emergence of successful resistance out of Māyārattha (Dakkhinadesa) to another invader, the Kālinga ruler Māgha (1215–36 CE), and the beginning of the era in which Dambadeniya, Yāpahuva, and Kurunāgala served as seats of royal authority (1232–1341 CE). Even after Polonnaruva ceased to be where the court was located, it is clear that it retained its symbolic hold on the Sinhalese imagination through Parākramabāhu III's long reign (1287–1341 CE), at which point it succumbed to a host of forces. The base of operations then shifted, along with the critical mass of Sinhalese population, to the southwest.

As noted, the intent of this chapter is to understand the principal forces at work in the Polonnaruva period by means of three approaches, each of which forms a separate section. The first inquires into the primary political and socioeconomic developments of this three-hundred-year period and the implications these had for Polonnaruva as well as other regions of the country. This approach focuses on the way in which rapidly developing forms of pluralism were in ongoing tension with a centripetal process, generated from the capital, that sought to maintain equilibrium and resist threats to the prevailing social and cosmic order. In order to understand the role of a ceremonial center in this process one needs to examine the ingredients in this emerging pluralism in some detail.

The second approach is to assess the process of legitimizing authority within this era. For instance, what alternative concepts of kingship arose from this changed political and economic context? And were these in basic continuity with notions about legitimacy that had characterized the Anurādhapura period? In the course of such an assessment one comes to suspect that there is a positive correlation between the existence of increased threats of disorder and the pursuit of strengthened efforts to undergird traditional sources of power. Again, the role of a ceremonial complex is central to this process, especially in times of actual or threatened disequilibrium.

Third, it is important to observe how the Buddhist Sāsana in Sri Lanka, as part of the society's overall response to cultural and social pluralism, dealt with new forms of religious expression and, in the process, to examine developments in ritual, symbolism, and cosmology, which are typically central to the whole phenomenon of a ceremonial complex. To what degree were these developments continuous with traditional formulations of reality, as expressed in the *Dhammadīpa* mode articulated within the *Mahāvaṃsa?* And to what degree were they new departures? In developments of this sort one sees in what ways the sacred may be enacted within society and how these enactments both affect the sociopolitical order *and* are affected by it.

The continuing *pursuit of equilibrium* therefore emerges as a theme that may be perceived throughout this period. It was essentially an attempt to maintain Sinhalese cultural identity in the midst of accelerating pluralism. The very pursuit reveals conflicts, stalemates, disintegration, and the possibility of renewal at various points in Sri Lankan history. The failure to maintain this equilibrium beyond a relatively short period of time, however brilliant the efforts, spelled the death knell of the classic, nationwide form of a ceremonial center in Sri Lanka. The genius of a ceremonial complex lies in its ability to fashion and maintain a viable equilibrium among the diverse components that compose the social order. Its vulnerability lies in generating new forces that it may not be able to control. By its very nature, equilibrium is precarious and unpredictable. The case of Polonnaruva is one among many interesting examples of such interwoven and tension-generating relationships.[4]

A Centripetal Process and Its Impact on Pluralism

Pursuing Paul Wheatley's thesis about the capital as a ceremonial complex or center, one asks in what sense Polonnaruva was a ceremonial as well as a political-military complex. One also enquires into the factors responsible for its collapse and begins to inspect its role and eventual fate in relation to developments of a complex sort. An inquiry of this nature requires consideration of Sri Lanka's relationship to the South Indian political arena and to new political and economic developments not only there but in the subcontinent as a whole and in areas within Southeast Asia more broadly. It also entails examining the relationship between Rājarattha (the region in north-central Sri Lanka of which Polonnaruva served as capital) and Dakkhinadesa and Rohana, especially the latter

This situation is composed of continuing dynastic alliances and warfare, complicated by steady infusions of refugees, adventurers, mercenaries, and mercantile communities from South India. During this period the position of kingship became increasingly precarious, and monarchs resorted frequently to foreign assistance and marital alliances, only to incur greater burdens, which in turn weakened their power base, fragmented the dynastic lineage, and created lasting divisions within the Sinhalese nobility through ties with Pāndyan and Kālingan nobility in South India.

Part of the overall picture is the relationship between elements within the Sangha and among various political power bases in Rājarattha, Dakkhinadesa, Rohana, and even South India. The political divisions these relationships engendered reached such proportions during the reign of Parākramabāhu I (1153–86 CE) that it led to a purging of the Order, with implications that were unprecedented in Sinhalese history and were motivated not simply by the desire to rid the Order of corruption but to disengage it from political involvement. It is germane to ask what effect this had on the traditionally "symbiotic" though never conflict-free relationship between the Sangha and the monarchy (as portrayed in the chronicles of Sri Lanka). As of this writing, there is need for further research on this topic within various historical periods, including the centuries after the demise of Polonnaruva as its capital.

Also of importance was the emergence of a powerful class of mercantile groups and an agricultural gentry whose fortunes rose and fell with the political and military situations, contributing eventually to new and smaller-based forms of regionalism in the first half of the twelfth century and especially after the reign of Parākramabāhu I. The latter's policy of imperial centralization crushed all forms of resistance, particularly in Rohana, ending the so-called Trisimhala-rājaya, the three kingdoms or provinces of Sri Lanka.[5] While this policy was effective under the leadership of Parākramabāhu I, it triggered a radically centrifugal process following his death. Consequently, there emerged not only the *vanni* (forest chieftains), who established power bases in areas inaccessible to the Chola conquerors, but also remnants of the court who secured for themselves rock fortresses that were precursors to the post-Polonnaruva capitals of Dambadeni, Gampola, Kōtte, and Kandy.

Each of these developments influenced the way in which Polonnaruva served as a ceremonial center over this three-hundred-year period of time. At the height of its power under Parākramabāhu I, it ruled supreme only by decimating provincial autonomy, thereby altering the traditional bases of relationship among numerous centers of power on the island. While an effective center of power for a short span, its success did not continue into the thirteenth century. Part of the task here is to assess the meaning of the centripetalizing process in this new but short-lived ceremonial complex, to view this complex in relationship to both traditional and new elements within the society and from abroad, and to question whether the impact of pluralistic forces contributed to heterogenetic forms of transformation at the price of weakening significant continuity with tradition itself, thereby calling into question the very meaning of Sinhalese identity.

As one analyzes the complex factors leading to the decline of the ancient capital of Anurādhapura, the establishment of a new one, and the gestation of forces that altered Sinhalese society and culture markedly, one looks for many clues. A statement by B. J. Perera is a helpful starting place to assess the impact of pluralistic influences on Sinhalese cultural identity:

> The civil war of the 7th century which lasted nearly three fourths of a century had far-reaching repercussions on the political history of the island. Trends that had their origin in this period of civil strife lasted throughout the late Anuradhapura and Polonnaruwa periods and only ceased to exist after the abandonment of the Raja rata. This civil war, it is true, was a dynastic struggle fought by the rival claimants to the throne with mainly mercenary troops in a limited area around the capital, but the indirect results of this period of prolonged struggle on the political conditions of the country were disastrous.[6]

Identifying the key trends from the seventh to the tenth centuries helps one to focus on later developments: (1) dynastic struggles that contributed to regional factionalism, with Rājarattha, Rohana, and Dakkhinadesa frequently pitted against each other; (2) Tamil mercenaries implicated in these struggles who were neither sent back to South India nor absorbed within the local population; (3) the rising independence of the Sinhalese nobility in relationship to the court at Anurādhapura, with Kālingan elements introduced by certain monarchs to offset Sinhalese aristocratic power; (4) economic insecurity arising out of political confusion and producing its own dynamics, which included peasant revolts and increasingly feudal structures "in which the topmost strata possessed extensive lands"; and (5) invasion and occupation by the Cholas, beginning in 993, which was largely enabled by the centrifugal tendencies preceding it and which furthered a momentum toward centralization anticipated in the reign of Vijayabāhu I (1055–1110 CE) and confirmed under Parākramabāhu I (1153–86 CE).

While Sri Lanka experienced several invasions from South India in its long history (foreign rule lasting sixty-six years, for example, in the second century CE), Sinhalese political history turned a corner during the reign of Kassapa V (914–23 CE), when its involvement in struggles abroad deepened further. Siding with the Pāndyas, with whom the Sinhalese had been at war twice in the previous century, Kassapa launched a policy of resistance to the emerging Chola kingdom and set into motion an era whose polity and economic changes were irreversible. While no single step in this development was responsible, the politics of Sri Lanka and South India had become so intertwined that by the early tenth century internal conflicts within Sri Lanka were all but inseparable from what was happening on the subcontinent. Whether cause or effect, these foreign dynastic entanglements led to increased numbers of mercenaries from abroad, to repeated internecine struggles among Sinhalese nobility complicated by their relations with Pāndyas and Kālingas and by the frequent involvement of bhikkhus (notably that of the Pamsukulin sect of the Abhayagirivihāra), and, above all, to threats to fundamental unity through continuing tensions between the court and factions based within Rohana to the south.

In his article about the first century of the Polonnaruva period, K. A. Nilakanta Sastri chronicles the events of Vijayabāhu I's career in mobilizing support that eventually ended the Chola occupation and in establishing an important but passing period of stability. His article also sheds light on the import of the Vēlaikkāras, who, as foreign mercenaries in Sri Lanka, exercised considerable influence throughout the eleventh century and beyond.[7] The generation following the death of Vijayabāhu in 1110 is not known in detail, but it was obviously one of political anarchy in which local princes protected their own fiefdoms. In the process, the people suffered. A sentence in the *Cūlavaṃsa* captures the mood: "In their insatiability and money lust they squeezed out the whole people as sugar cane in a sugar mill, by levying excessive taxes."[8] The remaining verses of the chapter cited (no. 53) provide a vivid picture of the chaos characterizing the period. The stage was now set for the emergence of the great hero-king and unifier, Parākramabāhu I.

Among the more suggestive discussions of internal developments in Sri Lanka society during this time is an essay by Keith Taylor, entitled "The Devolution of Kingship in Twelfth Century Ceylon." In this, he sees the thirteenth century (as the legacy of Parākramabāhu's policies) as "profoundly different from anything previously seen in Sri Lanka, in terms of its geography, economic base, and political organization."[9] In order to identify the causes, Taylor analyzes aspects of the previous four centuries, especially the reigns of Vijayabāhu I and Parākramabāhu I. He begins by offering three conclusions:

> First, the transition can be broadly identified as one which sees the end of the traditional organization of Ceylonese society and politics and the emergence of new, more fragmented, social and political patterns of which the imperial rule of Parakkamabāhu I is only the first and most successful example. Parakkamabāhu I's empire, though not an example of political fragmentation, was only possible by the destruction of the traditional order and the welding together of the resulting fragments through sheer physical force. Second, since the nature of Parakkamabāhu I's rule shows more continuity with what follows than with what went before, the breaking point of the transition must be placed prior to his accession. Finally, the central theme of the transition was the struggle of the Ceylonese monarchy to survive in the age of Chola power. Yet, while the continental pressures cannot be denied, they cannot be used as an excuse for the demise of the Ceylonese monarchy.[10]

Taylor's concept of *transition* provides the clue to his overall thesis. The era of dynastic warfare from the death of Vijayabāhu I in 1110 to the accession of Parākramabāhu I in 1153 is the breaking point of the transition. After this, "non-traditional patterns are the rule":[11] (1) the collapse of old feudal patterns with strongholds particularly in Rājarattha and Rohana and the shift to a pattern of personal loyalty on either the chieftain (*vanni*) or imperial level; (2) the shift from a predominantly peasant-based agriculture to one that was more diversified and included a rising merchant and artisan class; (3) the move toward isolating the Sangha from political involvement, coupled with either more imperial supervision of Sāsana affairs or, later, the creation of more organizational structures to guarantee self-regulation; and (4) the final crushing of Rohana-stimulated movements of political resistance, which facilitated momentary national unity under the aegis of Parākramabāhu I but rapidly undermined traditional centers of power and thus led to a distinct regionalizing of Sinhalese authority in the Southwest.

The post-Parākramabāhu I era, through the reign of Parākramabāhu II (1236–70 CE), has been explored by Amaradasa Liyanagamage in a book that examines the disintegration of the Polonnaruva kingdom, the founding of the Dambadeniya kingdom and the reign of Vijayabāhu III (1232–36 CE), the beginnings of Parākramabāhu II and the policies of Māgha (1215–36 CE), the Jāvaka and the Pāndya invasions, and the importance of the reign of Parākramabāhu II. As of this writing, no other treatment of comparable importance exists on this relatively neglected period in Sri Lankan history.[12]

Among the frequently debated topics about the Polonnaruva period is why it ended in the permanent shift of population away from this area and toward the so-called wet zone. A collection of papers edited by K. Indrapala, entitled *The Collapse of the Rājarata Civilization in Ceylon and the Drift to the Southwest,*[13] helps to suggest the complexity of the issues. Among the causative factors are the reliance on mercenaries, the steady influx of Tamil immigrants, the fact that trade was largely in foreign hands, the decay of the revenue system, and the breakdown of the old irrigation network. Several of the essays stress the collapse of the bureaucratic and administrative system that had previously maintained the dry-zone irrigation (followed eventually by widespread malaria, which discouraged reoccupation of the area), underscoring, among other factors, the breakdown of the local infrastructure (epitomized by the *kulīnas,* or local chiefs), which was stimulated by the trend toward centralization under Parākramabāhu I in particular.

This weakening of local administration and the resultant deterioration of the irrigation system (therefore, the entire economy) were inadvertent consequences of centripetal trends in the twelfth century and their aftermath. Not to be minimized, however, was the impact of foreign invasions, particularly that of Māgha in 1215, which led to the dislocation of the administrative machinery, hence the neglect of the irrigation system, hence the economic decline, and thus the resettlement of large numbers of people and the creation of two kingdoms (in Jaffna and the Southwest), though some believe that the collapse of the dry-zone reservoir system was a long process that cannot be attributed simply to the move toward centralization.

The debate continues, but its core relates to the main theme of this section, namely, the tension between the forces of centralization and provincial or localized autonomy. Further research bearing on the economic aspects of the tensions between centrifugal and centripetal forces within the Polonnaruva period, an age of immense pluralism, could prove instructive. Already, several studies on the irrigation system and on land tenure are noteworthy. Some show that while considerable advances were made (beginning in the first century CE) in tank size and technical achievement, the village tank system continued alongside the great reservoirs and canals.[14] This can be documented in the fifth century CE by regulations applying to reservoirs or tanks that were privately or corporately owned, indicating the importance of local networks alongside the system built and run by the state.[15] Other studies reveal how the construction and maintenance of major new irrigation ventures were intrinsic to the efforts, for instance, of Parākramabāhu I toward political and economic cohesion.[16] R. A. L. H. Gunawardana's article "Irrigation and Hydraulic Society in Medieval Ceylon" discusses the dynamism that existed in a society where the government did not have a monopoly on irrigation activity.[17] The economic power of the monastic estates is stressed (monastic officials often taking the place of royal officials), as is that of the increasingly independent gentry class that thrived in various parts of the country until the arrival of Māgha (1215 CE), who was ruthless both with that class and with the monasteries.

Gunawardana's thesis, namely, that "a multi-centered society with power devolving on the gentry and the monastic institutions in particular appears to be more true of the social structure of Ceylon than the concept of a centralized bureaucratic system of despotic rule" is an important one.[18] Finally, among various discussions on the nature of land tenure and of revenue in precolonial Sri Lanka one in particular bears mentioning. W. I. Siriweera maintains that while the king did not have sole ownership over land, he did have certain rights regarding the land—for example, taxation on grain and the right to unoccupied wasteland, abandoned land, land with no heirs, and various categories of royal land. Siriweera spells out the nature of service tenure (*rājakāriya*) to the king; the granting of immunities by the king to individuals, monasteries, or other groups; the nature and extent of temple lands; and the types and amount of taxation on or revenue from paddy land, trade, and irrigation water, as well as other sorts of royal revenue in medieval Sri Lanka (1000–1500 CE).[19]

This synopsis hints at the forces that were present in the Polonnaruva era; only a longer study could do justice to the details.[20] The primary point is that, because of increasing external pressures from South India, combined with a host of internal tensions, patterns of domestic disorder alternated with political centralization. The result was the establishment under Parākramabāhu I of a state that tended to monopolize power and create administrative structures that spelled the demise of long-existing regional authority. The justification for such a development, in light of foreign and domestic perils, is not difficult to see, but the results were ruinous to what had been a delicate but effective balancing of power over centuries.

In Keith Taylor's words, the effect was a "regionalizing of Sinhalese authority in the Southwest," creating over the next few centuries localized kingdoms that were remnants of the classical mode. The centripetal process, in response to exceedingly pluralistic and centrifugal forces, was paradoxically the cause of its own undoing. The very success of Parākramabāhu I, as registered in his administrative, military, economic, and religious attempts at reorganization, along with the devastation wrought by the Cholas earlier and by Māgha in the thirteenth century, destroyed the tissue that had composed the Sinhalese social structure and sustained its basic sense of cultural heritage. Despite numerous efforts at restoration, the destiny of this people had been permanently altered. Sri Lanka's destiny as the *Dhammadīpa,* the preserver of the true Dhamma, seemed mocked by its political fortunes after the collapse of Rājarattha. From this perspective, the glory of Polonnaruva as a ceremonial and a political complex, which had been considerable, seems more ironic than real, for the centripetalizing process increased the fragmentation of a society whose crises in ethnic identity had become acute long before the advent of colonialism.

The Threat of Disorder and the Legitimation of Power

Intrinsic to the centripetalizing process and to pressures resisting this process is the degree to which authority and power establish credibility in the eyes of power elites and, to some extent, the populace at large. Among other factors, sources of power depend on political and military strength, economic stability, personal charisma and influence, and the effective use of traditional symbols and ceremony. The task of interpreting the basis of authority necessitates reading between the lines of traditional documents, trying to distinguish between rhetoric and reality, and comparing materials from different sources.

The literature on this subject is considerable, but one needs to perceive the different norms that underwrite authority in Indian and Sri Lankan contexts.[21] From the formal establishment of Buddhism in Sri Lanka under Devānampiya Tissa, resulting from the mission of Mahinda (Aśoka's purported bhikkhu son), one can trace, on the one hand, a continuing tradition of close association between the Sangha and kingship and, on the other, a subtle but pervasive grafting into Sinhalese culture of Indian customs, institutions, symbols, and cosmology. Regardless of the actual fortunes of political authority and the steady infusion of new social and religious elements into Sri Lanka over the centuries, one sees impressive continuity from the early establishment of Anurādhapura as a ceremonial complex to its eventual collapse and replacement by Polonnaruva.

The grounds for legitimating power in Sri Lankan history is a subject on which considerable source material is available, yet few specific discussions exist of the historic tension between the religious basis for kingship and the tradition of secular statecraft (clearly present within the Polonnaruva period, but also before). While the dynamics of this tension are difficult to assess, it is useful to note the principal configurations of the *dhamma-danda* tension (perceivable in the *Cūlavaṃsa* particularly) as another approach to the theme of Sinhalese cultural identity and the dilemmas of pluralism.

Among the possible configurations, at least five are central to an understanding of the problem. The first concerns the basis on which legitimate power is acquired, maintained, and transferred; its preoccupation is not simply accession to the throne but accession undergirded by an ontological mandate. The second involves utilizing power either to maintain or reestablish basic order and stability; the monarch's role as protector of the realm is a sine qua non of legitimacy itself. The third is inseparable from the requirement of order and casts the king (indeed, the entire bureaucratic system) in the role of provider as well as protector, economic welfare being of one piece with political and military security. The fourth combines the previous two and directs the focus on the vocation of royal power (and all other powers by derivation) to promoting the well-being of the Buddha Sāsana. While patronage of other religious communities often accompanies patronage of the Dhamma, it cannot be at the latter's expense. And, fifth, there are symbolic, cosmological, and ritualistic aspects to the definition and enactment of legitimated power that are double-edged: they are as much a challenge to power as they are its reinforcement. When minimal stability and security are absent, legitimacy collapses. These five configurations will be discussed in sequence, though the fifth will be the primary focus of the chapter's third and final section.

Beginning with the reign of Sena I (833–53 CE) one can see the writing on the wall with respect to Indian mandala politics and to the Rohana-Rājarattha rivalry. After the seizure of Anurādhapura by the Pāndyas, who left "the splendid town in a state as if it had been plundered by yakkhas,"[22] and then through involvement in the internal politics of Rohana, Sena became the first king to establish a substantial base at Pulatthinagara (Polonnaruva) as a strategic post that was more remote from Indian attack and closer to the source of potential turbulence in the South. From this point in the mid-ninth century until the end of the Polonnaruva period the chronicle is filled with discussion about the balancing of power. Involved both with what transpires in South Indian politics and with the growing threat represented by Rohana and Dakkhinadesa, the monarchs of Rājarattha stand or fall on their ability to play the game of power (*danda*) and invest increasing resources in military expenditure. Predictable cycles unfold. With the growth of dynastic and regional factionalism comes the greater likelihood of foreign invasion and conquest. And with the tyranny and ignominy of conquest comes the invitation to strong-armed leadership to rid Lanka of the "blood-sucking yakkhas."

Authority is further legitimated as it proves capable of balancing power and containing the forces that would upset this. The Indian roots of this doctrine are ancient and, while apparent within the Anurādhapura period, became prominent from the ninth century on.[23] In figures such as Sena I, Sena II (853–87 CE), and Kassapa V (914–23 CE) one detects a finely honed instinct for survival based on the need to stave off greater threats by allying with lesser ones. The game of domestic and international realpolitik was a perilous one, but once pursued it became a normative element in the authority of kingship. The first great monarch of the Polonnaruva period, Vijayabāhu I (1055–1110 CE), was termed "wise in statecraft" as he applied with great skill the "four methods of warriors" (*caturo upāya*), long considered the means for political and military success.[24] His selection of wives (one Sinhalese, the other Kālingan) confirmed a growing trend toward political marriages with South Indian dynasties, a trend that often proved unfortunate within domestic politics throughout this era.

It was with the reign of Parākramabāhu I, however, that one senses increased association with the trappings and legitimizing authority of the Sanskritic tradition. For one thing, there is repeated evidence of *nītiśāstra* and *arthaśāstra* strands of material throughout the description in the *Cūlavaṃsa* of this king's reign. The early education of Parākramabāhu, his lifelong military exploits and the stratagems used, his political maneuverings (including his reorganization of the Sangha), and his basic policy of administrative centralization are evidence of this origin. The importance of this association cannot be overemphasized, for it is fundamental to what was then occurring in Sinhalese culture. The Brahmanic presence is unmistakable, though in a very different sense than within the Indian context. Here there is a deliberate use of that tradition and of the Buddhist tradition, both Indian and Sinhalese, for specific Sinhalese political and ideological ends. In this setting the Brahman-Kshatriya tension does not exist, even though Hindu ceremonies such as the *upanayana* and the *abhiśeka* are administered to princes and kings by royal *purohitas*.[25] Again, while not new in this era, the emphasis becomes more decided.

Equally prominent within the chronicle account is the increased weight given to auspicious signs and marks (*lakkhana*), as these foretell greatness and embody legitimacy itself.[26] While the *kāvya* and *praśasti* traditions in South Asia are clearly panegyric after the fact, the instances in which these are used attest to the meaning of genuine legitimacy. Those whom the chroniclers so honor fit the pattern of epic heroes. They are not only legitimated in the usual sense but are exemplars of kingship in the Sinhalese Buddhist mode. Regarding the young Prince Kitti (later Vijayabāhu I and easily one of Sri Lanka's great figures), an astrologer noted his marks of power, insight, and courage, saying: "Even in Jambudīpa he would, I believe, be capable of uniting the whole realm under one umbrella, how much more so in the Island of Laṅkā!"[27] More dramatic, though in obvious continuity, was the scene in which Vijayabāhu sees on his daughter Ratanāvalī signs auguring true greatness: "This thy body shall be the place for the birth of a son, who will surpass all former and future monarchs in glorious qualities, generosity, wisdom and heroism, who will be able to keep Laṅkā ever in safety and united under one umbrella, who will be in perfect wise a patron of the Order, and who will display an abundant and fine activity."[28]

The son in question was the future Parākramabāhu I, who ranks with Dutthagāmanī as Sri Lanka's epic king par excellence and who was born with marks on his hands and feet, which led the *purohita* and other *brāhmanas* to exclaim: "Apart from the island of Laṅkā he is able to unite under one umbrella and to rule even the whole of Jambudīpa."[29] The obvious extension of his potential domain and the resemblance of his birth story to that of Siddhattha Gotama link Parākramabāhu not only with the "pure dynasty of the Moon" but with the lineage of Cakkavatti kings. While dynastic lineage in the usual sense remains important for succession purposes, there is here an inflation of kingship and an association of the monarch with the Buddha, an association anticipated in the tenth-century document found in the Abhayagirivihāra in Anurādhapura, which claimed that only a bodhisattva could be king in Sri Lanka.

Within the Sri Lankan context the legitimation of authority goes beyond Brahmanic overtones and relates specifically to Sinhalese nationalism, the protection of the Sāsana, and the furtherance of the Dhamma.[30] Part of the process of centralization is the concern to bring all Sri Lanka under one umbrella. This is epitomized in the soliloquy of Parākramabāhu I in chapter 64 of the *Cūlavaṃsa,* as he weds statecraft with normative tradition in his determination to take possession of all Lanka and in associating himself with the claimed heroism of old. From his lips fall names from the Jātakas, the *Rāmāyana,* the *Mahābharata,* the Itihāsa tales, and the wisdom of Cānakka (Kautilya). Here in one canticle is *nīti* ethics solemnized and legitimated by association with the entirety of tradition. The king as protector, as the establisher of order, is being elevated by the Sāsana tradition. The Mahāsammata of old appears in new form and legitimates his power by protecting the powerless, by dispelling the forces of *adhamma,* whether yakkhas from abroad or rebels in Rohana. The influence of the *Arthaśāstra* is unmistakably present not just in this monarch's words but in his whole campaign to capture power, centralize the forces of government, establish a broad economic base, flex his military muscles abroad, unify the Sangha and disengage it from political involvement, and in his expansive artistic and cultural endowments. The clear blending of Indian and Sinhalese elements is nowhere more present in Sri Lanka's history than in this reign. The chronicle is replete with evidence. For one moment the tension between Sinhalese cultural identity and the forces of pluralism is exceedingly rich. An equilibrium is reached. The two wheels of Dhamma (*dhammacakka* and *ānācakka,* the wheel of righteousness and the wheel of power) appear to mesh. But the moment passes, and the yakkhas (the forces of disorder) return.

The story of this blending and of its fundamentally precarious nature is manifested in the importance of having the Buddha's relics (specifically the Tooth Relic and the Alms Bowl) in the possession of the monarch as legitimizers of authority. The saga of the Tooth Relic's fate, ever since it was brought to Sri Lanka in the fourth century, and of its intrinsic relationship to the king's role as protector, is central to Sinhalese identity. Parākramabāhu's resolve to unify the sacred isle, to bring it under one umbrella, necessitates the safekeeping of these regalia as talismans of power rooted in the Dhamma. The infamy of Vikkamabāhu I (1111–32 CE), who used these relics "as it pleased him" and incurred the wrath of the bhikkhus, stood as one among many examples of the relationship between political chaos and the loss of legitimacy.[31]

The next category stresses the king's role as provider, a role intrinsic to both Brahmanic and Buddhist traditions. This is so prevalent in discussions about the obligations of kingship that it becomes de rigueur. It is treated almost as a ritualistic act and presented frequently in that fashion within the chronicles. There is a deeper meaning, however. On the one hand, it is part of a reciprocal relationship with the Sangha, indeed part of a profound reciprocity between the social order and the cosmic order, between form and formlessness, to be discussed in the final section. On the other hand, it is a serious political commitment that is breached at the monarch's peril. As in most traditional societies, there is a perceived correspondence between legitimate sovereignty and economic well-being. When drought and famine strike, evil in high places is often seen to be its source. By whomever the mandate is given, it may be withdrawn for perceived cause.

It should be no wonder, then, that Sinhalese monarchs, along with kings elsewhere, draw attention to the bounty brought by their reign. A famous vow in this regard is that of Parākramabāhu the Great: "Truly in such a country not even a little water that comes from the rain must flow into the ocean without being made useful to man."[32] The greatness of monarchs in Sri Lanka is often measured by the extent of their irrigation projects, always a correlate of economic and social prosperity. While provision comes in many forms, there is a continuing suspicion that the elements of nature and the social order are bound together. In Buddhism, this suspicion stems, of course, from the Pāli canon, where kingly righteousness and unrighteousness affect the actions of other people. The nexus of merit or of infamy has what S. J. Tambiah calls a "multiplier effect," originating in the monarch but extending to all others in society.[33] The registers of meritorious works (*puññapot-*

takāni) of pious and beneficent kings acted as a stimulus not only to kings but potentially to all others. In summarizing the good works of Vijayabāhu I, the chronicler concludes by saying: "In the same way many courtiers and women of his harem amassed many merits in many ways."[34]

Beyond the king's role as provider is his symbolic identification with the powers of fecundity, specifically with the Vedic deity Varuna, guardian of the cosmic law and lord of the waters. Following the unification of Lanka, which was celebrated by his second consecration, Parākramabāhu I expresses his vow for the reign through this metaphor: "Those in search of help I would fain support by letting like a cloud overspreading the four quarters of the earth, a rich rain of gifts pour continually down upon them."[35] As the gods could grant or withhold the rains, so too righteous monarchs were thought to have special powers. At the high festival of the Tooth Relic, in celebration of its new temple (*dāthādhātughara*) in Polonnaruva and of the auspicious beginning of a new era, a great dark cloud threatened to dampen the occasion. With words of assurance, the king diverted the cloud around the procession. The chronicler records the people's cry: "In truth of great majesty is this Ruler of men, the foe-subduer; in consequence of his high merit he has appeared in Lanka. Here is merit, here is wisdom, here is pious devotion to the Tathāgata; here is fame and glory and exceeding great sublimity."[36]

While *kāvya* from start to finish, such encomia were used to associate the powers of righteous authority with the sources of power itself. As Wilhelm Geiger indicates in a footnote to the quote above, the Pāli term *bhatti* (Sanskrit, *bhakti*), or "pious devotion," used here suggests the influence of Hinduism, though there is no doubt about Buddhist devotion toward the relics, the Tathāgata himself, and the Dhamma, from at least the fifth century CE when the *Mahāvaṃsa* appeared and in all probability much earlier. The point here is what ensues when both kings and gods serve the Buddha. This is but one example of the confluence of Vedic, Brahmanic, Buddhist, Purānic, and popular religious traditions.[37] It is power empowered with ultimacy yet held accountable.

Beyond containing the forces of *adhamma* (starving off chaos) and beyond ensuring ample provision for the realm, those who wielded power and authority had special responsibility for the well-being of the Buddha Sāsana, particularly for the bhikkhu Sangha. Much has been written about this in recent literature, and certainly the chronicles attest to endless good and bad examples. Royal patronage and support from varied sectors and levels of society appear at the outset of Buddhist tradition in India and become deeply woven into the fabric of numerous cultures throughout Asia. Patronage of the Sangha inheres in the action of reciprocity, seen to exist between lay and monastic elements within the Sāsana. It is a mutuality in which both parties depend on each other in different ways and for different reasons. At the very least, the basic needs of monks are to be met through gifts to the Order. Beyond this minimal expectation, kings and pious laypeople compete to gain merit and receive monastic blessing through the building of stūpas, vihāras, pirivenas, and whole architectural complexes; through the support of elaborate festivals, including the symbolically important holding of robe-granting (*kathina*) ceremonies; through cultivation of learning, especially study and preservation of the canon; and through artistic embellishment edifying to the Dhamma's cause.

A crucial and unique feature of the royal vocation is the king's responsibility for reform of the Sāsana through regulative acts (*dhamma-kammena*) in which "the king is said to have purified the doctrine (*sodhesi sāsanam*)."[38] Taking their cue from the *Edicts of Aśoka,* Sinhalese monarchs from early days were involved in monastic disputes and at least since the early sixth century in Sāsana reforms. During the Polonnaruva period the most important occasions of this occurred in the reigns of Parākramabāhu I and Parākramabāhu II, in which codes of regulations (*katikāvatas*) agreed upon by the community of Buddhist monks were promulgated in 1165 and 1266/7, respectively.[39] While the monarch's role in assisting the Sangha to purify itself of corruption and disunity harkens back to Aśoka and was not uncommon in Sri Lanka, these particular regulations afford major clues not only into the condition of the Order at these times but also into changes that were emerging in the king-Sangha relationship. These changes, which accented the need for unity within the community of bhikkhus and prefigured later developments of organizational centralization, stemmed directly from political and social events of the twelfth and thirteenth centuries. The call for order and unity within the Sangha was clearly a response to the uncertain and confused nature of the times.

Another document, the *Nikāya Sangrahāwa,* written by Dhammakitti, who was *sangharāja* in the reign of Bhuvanekabāhu V (1372–1408 CE), is a concise history of the Sāsana from its beginnings in India through the middle of that monarch's reign.[40] It is especially interesting because of the focus on heretical movements within the Sāsana and again attests to concerns about unity. An entire history of ancient and medieval Sri Lanka could be written about the perceived correlation between sociopolitical unity and the unity of the Sangha.[41] Disunity in one is an implicit and often actual threat to the condition of the other. But it is equally true that power struggles within the body politic and/or within the Order attest to the delicacy of the tension that made up this reciprocity. In no sense was it a simple legitimation of power; it was more often than not a fragile balance in which various parties used each other.[42] If the chronicles are at times lyrical in their praise of righteous monarchs, they are also filled with admonition throughout. This will be referred to below.

A Ceremonial Complex: Enacting the Sacred through Rite, Symbol, and Cosmology

Alongside symbolic efforts at reintegration, psychic and communal forms of disorder persist. Indeed, a dialectical relationship exists between these countervailing forces. Enacting the sacred is at its core an attempted experiencing of oneness, of integration. Paradoxically, however, it occurs only through profound yet controlled forms of disintegration. These forms are preserved, renewed, and celebrated by vital communities in ways that are deeply religious, though they occur in all contexts of life, in the sociopolitical realm as well as elsewhere. What is at stake in genuine enactments of the sacred is not simply a recalling of a community to past visions of meaning but toward a deeper self-perception that generates new insight regarding the framework of existence. The recalling or anamnesis, at its deepest, is not simply to a past mode of the sacred but to a reality that transcends all modes of time and all forms of culture. At their best, symbols, myths, rituals, and cosmological perceptions serve to enhance the means by which clearer vision can transform experienced reality. Indeed, the essence of this experience is to allow for the disintegration of inappropriate images of reality and to welcome previously unknown forms of reality, which itself can never be captured by symbol, myth, or rite, let alone by doctrine.

The theme of Sinhalese cultural identity and the dilemmas of pluralism, therefore, reveal conflicts, stalemates, disintegration, and the possibility of renewal throughout its corporate history. Again, this is the nature of the classic relationship between continuity and transformation, between any ceremonial complex and its related components. At stake is a sustained tension between combinations of orthogenetic and heterogenetic elements within and among persons and communities. Among various possible motifs for exploring this tension, four will be noted here: those of transcendence, continuity, dialectic (or ambiguity), and combined disintegration/reintegration.

As Paul Wheatley's *The Pivot of the Four Quarters* makes clear, a basic characteristic of societies in early stages of urbanization is the vital function assumed by a ceremonial complex, a function that provides visions of transcendent unity and meaning beyond the obvious forms of social and ideological differentiation. While the long history of Anurādhapura as Sri Lanka's capital was frequently disrupted, with considerable diversity and dynamism among its many elements, the historic documents attest to the nation's basic identity and its continuing centricity. From the marking off of the original *sīmā* by Devānampiya Tissa, indicating the bounds of the Mahāvihāra and registering an identification between kingship and this monastic tradition, there was etched into Sinhalese consciousness a strain of continuity amid innumerable discontinuities and a perceived orthodoxy beyond all forms of heterogeneity.

The nature and character of Anurādhapura as a ceremonial complex is not at issue here. Rather, the concern is how Polonnaruva sought to replace it and to serve as a political and ideological rallying center in an era that became increasingly turbulent and was considerably more diverse. As the first part of this chapter indicates, the collapse of Anurādhapura revealed innumerable forces at work that threatened the fundamental existence of Sinhalese society as it had existed for centuries. Polonnaruva was therefore an attempt not only to salvage the nation politically but to rediscover the meaning of communal and religious self-consciousness. For this reason, establishment of the new capital was not simply a strategic relocation of power but a means of reestablishing in a fundamental sense the nation's identity. If Anurādhapura could take this identity for granted, despite its often storm-filled history, Polonnaruva had in fact to re-create it. What was basically implicit in the earlier period had to be made explicit again after the ninth century, as the society had become more complex and less unified.

It was thus not sentimentality that prompted Vijayabāhu I to choose Anurādhapura as the site for his consecration, even though Polonnaruva was by then clearly the permanent capital. Nor was it romanticism that motivated astute monarchs in the Polonnaruva era to restore the ruins of the old capital from time to time. It was instead sensitivity to the sacred, whether the motive was politically cynical or was deeply sincere.[43] In actuality, of course, the primary kings of Polonnaruva sought not simply to keep alive the past but to establish a new ceremonial and political center to replace the old. While continuity in art and architecture remained, among other features, the two cities were very different. The basic similarity was that each sought in its own era to manifest the transcendent within the ephemeral, to generate symbols of unity within the plural. As Wheatley puts it, to inquire into the nature of a city is a metaphysical question:[44] "For the ancients, who conceived the natural world as an extension of their own personalities and who consequently apprehended it in terms of human experience, the 'real' world transcended the pragmatic realm of textures and geometrical space, and was perceived schematically in terms of an extramundane, sacred experience. . . . Sacrality (which is synonymous with reality) is achieved through the imitation of a celestial archetype, as a result of which such religions can be powerful transformers of landscape."[45] "There is, however," adds Wheatley, "another aspect to this picture of centrality. The capital, the *axis mundi,* was also the point of ontological transition at which divine power entered the world and diffused outwards through the kingdom."[46]

While one becomes accustomed to poetic hyperbole in reading the chronicle accounts of royal munificence toward the Sangha particularly, one enters the realm of pure *kāvya* with the various descriptions of Pulatthinagara (Polonnaruva) under the building programs of Parākramabāhu I and, toward the end of its days, of Vijayabāhu IV (1270–72 CE). The *Cūlavaṃsa* reports: "By constructing in this way beautiful vihāras, gardens, tanks and the like he adorned with these numerous (works) the whole of Laṅkā."[47] In those terse words the efforts of Parākramabāhu I are summed up, but in many previous chapters one reads a catalog of an incredible program of construction, both secular and religious in nature. For one thing, the palace (*pāsādam*) in Polonnaruva was on a much grander scale than that in Anurādhapura, providing a clue to the conscious attempt to associate kingship and its authority with divine and cosmological models. Comparisons with the Indian godly abodes of Mount Kelāsa (Kailāsa) and Ālakamandā come easily to the chronicler. The earthly blends into the transcendent, providing the former with at least the semblance of lasting glory.

It is, of course, ironic that the final description we have of Polonnaruva was during the reign of Vijayabāhu IV, shortly before its ultimate collapse. Its majesty was claimed to exceed that of all the great Indian towns: "In this fashion the King had the town of Pulatthinagara—comparable to the city of Indra—restored, so that it surpassed Mithilā, subdued Kancīpurī, laughed to scorn Sāvatthī, subdued Madhurā, turned to shame Bārānasī, reduced Veśāli to nothing, and made Campāpurī tremble with her glory."[48] In Wheatley's words: "With the rise of secular, or rather secularly oriented, authority, there appeared also a new feature in the monumental architecture of the ceremonial city, namely the palace, a building which inevitably became the vehicle for conspicuous display, a distillation and projection of the glory and prestige of the territorially organized state over which the king ruled."[49]

One thinks immediately of another king (Kassapa, 473–91 CE) famous in Sinhalese history, who, it has been argued by Senarat Paranavitana, also sought to associate his rock-fortress architecturally with Ālakamandā, the dwelling place of Kuvera (Kubera, the god of wealth and lord of the yakkhas).[50] This imaginative though speculative interpretation is of Kassapa's intention to ingratiate himself with the populace and to gain legitimacy through association with the divine bestower of wealth. The comparison is not inappropriate when one considers that Parākramabāhu I was heralded as "ruler of the middle world, he filled the chief and the intermediary regions of the heavens with festive glory."[51] And his four generals are likened to the four protectors of the world, the *lokapālas* (Yama, Varuna, Indra, and Kubera), in the *Cūlavaṃsa*.[52]

Beyond the quest for a cosmological framework for the political order (by extension, the entire society) a deliberate connection was made with earlier ages in the Sāsana's history. This stress on continuity with sacred moments and figures in the past was basic to the process of enacting the sacred. So too was establishing a parallelism between macrocosm and microcosm. Among key examples of continuity certain ones stand out. Following the long struggle against the Cholas, Vijayabāhu I was quick to recognize that the Sangha was in desperate straits and enabled the Order to be revived through Burmese monks invited by the king to perform the rite of *upasampadā* (ordination), which established for the first time a religious connection between these two countries. Secondly, as mentioned before, the regalia needed by monarchs to authenticate their sovereignty included the Tooth Relic and the Alms Bowl Relic. Suspicions of dubious lineage arose whenever these were absent, spelling the promise of dire consequences. When appropriated by others, they were to be retrieved at any cost.

A third manner of accenting the heritage entailed preserving not only the Sangha but also the Dhamma in its written forms. Part of Sri Lanka's national pride lies with the fact that the canon was first committed to writing there in the first century BCE. This provides Sinhalese Buddhists with the claim to an unbroken tradition. While Dhammakitti's great history of the Sāsana, the *Saddhamma-saṅgaha,* was probably not written until a century after the collapse of Polonnaruva, it provided evidence of much earlier reverence paid to writing down and listening to the Dhamma. Along similar lines, it is recorded in the *Cūlavaṃsa* that Vijayabāhu III (1232–36 CE) had ordered the canon to be written down, as "so many books that dealt with the true doctrine had been destroyed by the alien foe" (i.e., Māgha). In fact, so bad were the consequences of that era that the very *devatās,* protectors of Lanka, had deserted the cause, implying that only the Dhamma could transmute chaos into order.[53]

By far the most noteworthy figure in this respect throughout the Polonnaruva period is Parākramabāhu II (1236–70 CE). While only forty pages are devoted to his reign in the *Cūlavaṃsa,* compared to six times that amount given to Parākramabāhu I, the former is depicted as having extraordinary liturgical insight, coupled with a sense of temporal continuity and spatial interrelatedness that were unparalleled in this age. How much truth lay behind the legends about him it is impossible to determine, but one detects a sensitivity that combined realistic politics with a profound vision of pluralistic order. He appeared at least to be in pursuit of some form of equilibrium that was not at the expense of diversity. Obviously, other kings evidenced similar sensitivity, but not to the same degree. Though an entire essay could be written on this topic, a few examples must suffice.[54]

While no less realistic than others about the military and political dangers of his day, Parākramabāhu II is featured as a reconciler and healer of divisions (e.g., his stance toward the *vanni* chieftains and toward political prisoners) and as having the ability to encourage local and national forms of popular religious expression alongside devout patronage of the Sangha. In fact, the impression is strong that he stimulated deeper levels of religious awareness among both bhikkhus and the laity. The lengths to which he went to facilitate pilgrimages to Sumantakūta to reverence the Buddha's footprint (Śrī Pāda) and also to honor the god Sumana attest, if nothing else, to his recognition that Sinhalese identity and self-consciousness required linking these two forms of piety and that liturgical expression of this assisted in restoring meaning to a people severely divided and lacking in vision.[55]

His awareness of the symbolic and liturgical significance of Devanagara (Sinhalese, Devundara) and also his decision to visit this site himself and to have its temple of Varuna (Vishnu) restored are of the same order.[56] His visit to Hatthavanagalla, where his own father had been cremated, and his reconstruction of the temple originally built by Gothābhaya (249–62 CE) on the site where the saint-king Sirisamghabodhi (247–49 CE) had sacrificed his life for his people express the same effort to identify his own reign with majesty and piety known in the past. The fact that the *Hatthavanagallavihāravaṃsa* was composed during Parākramabāhu's life and became an exceedingly popular text, translated into Sinhalese twice in the next two centuries, confirms the need for such association that was felt by an entire people. While doubtlessly political in part (note the solemn declaration at the start of his reign to rid Lanka of the Damilas and his cataloging of past kings who performed similar feats),[57] his sights extended beyond political security in search of the metaphysical basis on which the nation rests.

Much more could be said about his elevation of the Tooth Relic festival as a means of communal transformation, the importance he attached to pilgrimage to the sacred places visited by the Buddha (*pāribhogika*), and his ensuring that these forms of reverence continue well beyond his own time. Finally, it is no accident that two other chronicles of considerable importance were written during the thirteenth century (the former around 1200 CE, the latter during Parākramabāhu II's reign), namely, the *Dāthāvaṃsa,* which was translated into Pāli from a fourth-century Sinhalese (Elu) text and became in the Polonnaruva period an intrinsic part of the Tooth Relic cult and the *Thūpavaṃsa,* which is a history of the Mahāthūpa (the Ruvanvalī) in Anurādhapura constructed by the hero-king Dutthagāmanī, also based on earlier sources. The fact that the *Thūpavaṃsa* was translated again in the mid-thirteenth century, so soon after the passing of Parākramabāhu I, whose military and religious exploits were comparable to those of Dutthagāmanī, appears as a deliberate attempt to accent the continuity of greatness in an era when this was actually in doubt. Again, when threatened, authority doubles its claims. Thus, the Polonnaruva age was intentionally being woven not only into the fabric of classical Sinhalese history but into the wider cloth of the Dhamma.

If the quest for transcendence and the affirmation of historic continuity are central to the theme of enacting the sacred in this era, another ingredient is that of ambiguity. This appears especially in the career of Parākramabāhu I, to whom exhaustive attention is given in the *Cūlavaṃsa.* In its two volumes, covering a period from 301 CE to 1815, almost 40 percent of the text deals with him. One detects an attitude of ambivalence in the chronicle toward this remarkable and paradigmatic monarch. In an earlier essay I suggested that, while the chronicles of Sri Lanka are clearly didactic and while they are written from the perspective of the Mahāvihāra, one often finds within them a remarkable candor.[58] If righteous kings receive undiluted paeans, evil rulers are given their due. Throughout the chronicling of Sinhalese history, the moral of the lesson is made clear, including the note of ambivalence whenever the persons concerned are in fact held in question. This portrayal of reservation about particular figures is inherent in the relationship between the Sangha and the monarchy. While ideally a reciprocal and mutually supportive relation, it is inevitably open to abuse from either side. If part of the Sangha's function is to provide legitimation for kingship, this endorsement is always conditional. And, if central to society's expectation of the monarch is that he support and foster the Order, this puts certain obligations on the Sangha (hence the periodic need for purification). The deeper basis of the relationship is ontological, not simply social; it transcends historical accidents, but it is also fundamentally ambiguous because of the human capacity for evil.

Despite the seeming approbation of Parākramabāhu I and despite the frequent images by which he is associated with the Buddha, it appears plausible that the overriding mood of the depiction is fundamentally ambiguous, even ironic. It would take further research to explore the external factors behind that attitude, though one suspects that this monarch's purification of the Order and rather dramatic reorganization of the Sangha did not leave him without detractors, to put it mildly. The most prevalent trait he manifests is that of courage. His very name means "arm of courage" or "possessed of courageous arms." Repeatedly, he is referred to as lionhearted. His mission, indeed, can often be summed up as one who chases away the fear of others. The *abhaya mudrā* is evidenced in one form or another throughout his odyssey. His lion's roar sounds forth whenever he senses others to be afraid or when he wishes to instill fear into foes, whether human or beast. He proclaims:

"For the fearful I have no use, they may go where they like."[59] When he learns about his supporters' fear, he speaks in wrath: "Although they have witnessed my courage on diverse occasions and their own rescue over and over again by me from evil situations, their inborn cowardice doth not forsake these cravens."[60] Alternately, he is angry at their fear, amused at it, piteous of it, and all the more brazen because of it. The folly of his South Indian military policy, where he committed troops for years at immense expenditure and with no political gain, was evidence of considerable hubris.

How literally is one to take the image of the lion's roar (the *sihanāda*) in Buddhist terms? One suspects that it is not an image of profound courage per se but is, in fact, double-edged. The canonical *Sīhanāda Sutta* and the *Sampasādaniya Sutta*[61] call to mind the bravado of Sāriputta, the Buddha's disciple, when he emitted the lion's roar of faith in the Buddha, only to be exposed for what he was claiming to know. The image of Parākramabāhu I presented within the chronicle is of a devious, ambitious, relentless figure whose ends justify his means, yet he is clearly set upon a pedestal as a paradigm in some ways for later kings. The total portrait is thoroughly ambiguous, which deepens one's sense of the continuing dialectic between the Sangha and the political order. The contrast between this king and Parākramabāhu II is marked, but the full spectrum would include a marauder like Māgha. Compared with him, Parākramabāhu I would shine in splendor, but he would also represent the danger of unchecked power. A ceremonial complex thrives by the orchestrating of society's component parts. That these parts were so effectively silenced by this lion's roaring raises serious questions about the difficult task of balancing centripetal and centrifugal forces and how one fashions authentic unity or equilibrium out of pluralistic elements. The painful transition from a basically orthogenetic society to one deeply affected by outside influences was clearly in evidence.

Intrinsic to enacting the sacred is how particular forms of expressing sacrality (rite, symbol, myth, cosmology) engage persons and communities in a process that is both integrative and disintegrative. For authentic revitalization to occur there must be authentic dying. This is such a truism in the history of religions that it may often be taken for granted and thus seem to occur without pain and suffering. In actuality, the reverse is more true, namely, that growth in mind and spirit normally arises out of suffering; that is, the cleansing of individual and collective ego entails pain. Indeed, genuine forms of enacting the sacred are frequently as disruptive as they are recreative.

The motifs we have just discussed, namely, the experiencing of transcendence, historic continuity, and inherent ambiguity, have been chosen to suggest that the Polonnaruva era embodied a major struggle in the communal self-consciousness of the Sinhalese people. The abiding dilemma in question was how to embrace increasing pluralism (social, political, economic, and religious) without losing one's ancient sense of cultural identity. The problem is how to affirm that identity without imposing narrow and dated forms of it on a new age. In this case, the dilemma seems to have been intensified, not resolved. The political outcome of the collapse of Rājarattha civilization led to the demise of traditional Sinhalese culture as it had flourished for fifteen centuries. Other outcomes were more ambiguous, in that they revealed signs of renewal and promise as well.

As a way of understanding the ethos of this historical period and its aftermath, one thinks of other variants of this tension between disintegration and integration. One familiar example is Victor Turner's concept of *antistructure*, which exists in dialectical relationship with all forms of social structure. The essential task is to not only recapture a sense of the ultimate contingency of all social structures but to perceive their rootedness in a predifferentiated unity, which is the basis for any dynamic equilibrium. Rites expressing this promote the experience of what Turner calls "marginality," of being at the edges of the known. This quality of experience participates in the very act of disordering. The seriousness with which the antistructural dimension of reality is taken becomes the path toward or away from renewal and re-creation. Ironically, without the affirmation of antistructure a pluralistic community is impossible.[62] This is a crucial insight in human experience.

The basic thrust of this chapter on Polonnaruva has suggested that this is precisely what began to be experienced in a profound sense in Sinhalese self-consciousness. What was at stake was not merely political reversals and passing disorder but something more fundamental. The metaphor of exile is appropriate here. As Jonathan Smith notes, "To be exiled is to be in a state of chaos . . . to return from exile is to be re-created and reborn."[63] The psychic and spiritual necessity of this death can only be affirmed after the significance of chaos and disorder has been discovered. Symbolic of the perceived need to encounter the threat of chaos or disorder is the common recourse to *paritta* (Sinhalese, *pirit*) or protective chants. The chronicles and commentaries mention with some frequency the use of these chants, performed by monks for laypeople. Essentially, this rite may be seen as an instance of the fusing of both disintegration and integration. For example, whether one looks at the serious plague mentioned in the reign of Sena II[64] or at the famine in the days of Parākramabāhu II,[65] it is not simply the efficacy of the rite that is significant but the disordered condition of the community that gave rise to these threats. The heart of the issue here is what occurs symbolically in *paritta* ceremonies. A structural analysis would reveal that chaos itself (*adhamma*) is being recognized, confronted, and entered into.

An important analogy exists between encountering disorder of the sort just mentioned and encountering social and religious pluralism. Whenever psychic, social, or ideological crises arise, genuine community is threatened. Order is only reestablished as it allows itself to be transformed and enriched by the very forces that threaten it.[66] The combination, the interfusing of these two processes is powerfully suggested by Giuseppe Tucci: "In the physical world involution is redemption, a progressive process of reabsorption and of disappearance into the immediately preceding state until the complete elimination of the plane of māyā. In the Ego the process is one of reintegration, of return to the original unity after the subconscious has been overcome, after possession has been taken of it through symbols. Reintegration is not possible without this experience, this living in the midst of the world of māyā and then dissolving it, annihilating it with that conscious experience, since to know by testing means to dissolve."[67] In a way that is not easy to summarize, the struggles of the Polonnaruva period, its glory and its final ignominy, were of this order. They were an attempt to cope with powerfully centrifugal forces in a manner that tended toward centralization. They sought to fashion a new form of unity out of very diverse elements. As the problems were ambiguous, so too was their resolution. The period remains one that is fascinating in its own right and that calls for further study.

Just as interesting, this dialectic keeps vivid the constant influence and threat represented by Tamil culture and Tamil invaders throughout most of Sinhalese history. This presence is inevitably close to the surface in modern Sri Lanka as it wrestles with the problems of its diverse population, whose minority of Indian origin can neither be wished away by repatriation nor absorbed by conversion. And yet, it is in relationship to India as a nation, whose culture and politics have influenced most of Southeast Asia as well, that Sri Lanka's future intimately rests.

As a sequel to this, chapter 5 deals with the many-sided process and dilemmas within the evolving Sinhala quests for identity. Central to renewed quests for identity that constitute so much of today's social and political ferment is the necessity of coping with traditional and newly created definitions side by side. It is this combination that comprises the *problem of identity*, for definitions of self, community, and nation are forged out of situations where tradition and modernity make conflicting appeals, producing a rebirth of pride in one's heritage alongside a determination to benefit by more inclusive opportunities that were unimagined in the past.

5

Sinhalese Buddhism and Its Modern Quests for Identity

THE DILEMMAS OF A PLURALISTIC SOCIETY

In reference to the Sinhalese Buddhist *Mahāvaṃsa,* Wilhelm Geiger makes the important comment that a study of it "shows us how fallacious it is entirely to separate Buddhism from Brahamanism."[1] While the differences between these traditions are considerable, as is the diversity within each, Geiger's point is instructive for many reasons. First, it orients one immediately to the religious point of origin, the Brahmanical tradition, over against which early Buddhism emerged and grew. Second, it is a reminder of the sociopolitical framework validated by Brahmanism, providing the context on which the Sangha and its lay members depended in numberless ways. Third, ingredients of its mythology, art forms, rituals, and even its caste system are indelibly fused with the Buddhism of Sri Lanka, whose identity is unimaginable apart from this tradition. Fourth, it keeps vivid the constant influence and threat represented by Tamil culture and Tamil invaders throughout most of Sinhalese history. Fifth, it is inevitably close to the surface in modern Sri Lanka, which wrestles painfully with the problems of its diverse population, whose South Indian-origin minority can neither be wished away by repatriation nor absorbed by conversion. And, finally, it is in relationship to India as a nation, whose culture and politics have influenced most of Southeast Asia as well, that Sri Lanka's future intimately rests.

While the magnitude of these interconnections resembles Indra's Net in scope, only a few aspects bear mentioning in this context. The task is to assess the capacity of modern Sinhalese Buddhism to recognize that it exists within a culturally pluralistic context and to affirm that fact as an inherent part of its own reconceived and renewed identity. As one political scientist has asked, "Can religion, which served to legitimize relatively static traditional structures (political, social, economic), be reinterpreted to provide positive ideological support and legitimacy to the modernizing task which is widely understood to be the prime responsibility of the political system? Can reformulated religion [also] become an effective ally of a state committed to extensive socioeconomic change?"[2] Such a task begs a number of questions that will be explored throughout this chapter, although the principal effort here is to phrase the problem in a variety of ways and to suggest dilemmas and possibilities regarding the complexities of Sinhalese Buddhism within its present social contexts.

One of the clearer definitions of the modernization process depicts it as being "fundamentally one of differentiation, by which integralist sacral societies governed by religio-political systems are being transformed into pluralist desacralized societies directly by greatly expanded secular polities."[3] As a definition, this is a helpful assessment of a process evolving at different rates in different settings. Substantially, this asserts that men and women can and need to plan their societies for the welfare and education of all of their members and to develop relationships within a world community that are mutually constructive. Ideally, it is a concept of politics that combines concern for the well-being of each person with the awareness that governments are not only fallible but should be limited. A great deal could be said about how this does or does not work in practice, but the task in this chapter is to examine the role of Sinhalese Buddhism within the modernizing process in Sri Lanka.

The particular variants of this problem have historical as well as contemporary features that are necessarily related. To discuss modern structural and ideological components of any religious tradition apart from its development over centuries invites distortion. While no picture of Sinhalese Buddhism can be generalized to Theravada at large, there are features that have implications elsewhere. The topics selected for this purpose are fivefold: (1) the nature of sacro-political authority as perceivable from the classical to the modern period in India and Sri Lanka; (2) the nature and impact of Sinhalese Buddhist identity in ancient and current forms, in relationship to *Urbuddhismus* (that perceived essence of the early community) and to the continuing quest for national self-consciousness; (3) the Buddhist Sangha, its genius for creativity as well as endurance, its patterns of decay and reform, and its present organizational crisis; (4) the ongoing search for unity in the midst of pluralistic forces within the Sangha, within the Buddha Sāsana itself, and within diverse local, national, and wider settings; and (5) the primary vocation of Buddhism, as with every religious tradition, of keeping distinct yet continually relating the two domains, inadequately labeled "sacred" and "profane," encountered by each person and every community.

Sacro-Political Authority

In his *Kingship and Community in Early India,* Charles Drekmeier identifies "a central theme of Indian political speculation [as] the relationship between brahman legitimation and kshatriya authority."[4] While the legitimation-authority tension in Buddhism differs markedly from the normative Indian prototype, Brahmanic assumptions appropriated by the early Buddhist community gave rise to functional counterparts within the Sangha-monarch relationship in the Theravada tradition. Basic to this development was the sensed interdependence among power, authority, and legitimacy, in which "authority introduces the idea of 'right,' the legitimate use of power."[5] Within the Brahmanic tradition there is a rich intermingling of normative and pragmatic approaches to governance, providing notes of realism alongside canonical standards by which political activity is judged. As Heinz Bechert notes, "Indian culture . . . provided the tradition of divine kingship, but it gave also a tradition of purely secular statecraft which freed the ruler from all eventual restrictions resulting from divine kingship-dualism [and] which must be considered [in order] to understand state-Sangha relations."[6]

It is clear from the Sinhalese chronicles that the kings of Sri Lanka were as versed in the science of statecraft, depicted in the *Arthaśāstra* of Kautilya and conveyed by Brahmin priests within the court, as in prescriptions for righteousness stemming from both Hindu and Buddhist scripture and custom. This apparent dualism sustained an attitude of ambivalence toward political authority that remains as important now as at the outset of Buddhism. A proper awareness of its significance helps to correct fallacious images of Buddhism, let alone Hinduism, as being ahistorical by nature or as having little concern for socioeconomic conditions. In attempting to adjust these images, some interpreters suggest that both constitutional democracy and welfare state socialism were anticipated in original Buddhism. While these adjustments are equally fallacious, it is pertinent to identify the types of concern about the social order that are preserved in the records.

It is not surprising that the early Buddhist community, being a minority, should have felt somewhat differently about the power of the monarch than did their Brahmanic counterparts. Buddhist concern goes beyond this expected anxiety, however, questioning the very essence of power in a world of impermanence and self-seeking. In an article on this subject, B. G. Gokhale outlines three distinct attitudes that emerged in the first centuries of Buddhist presence in India: "Although the early Buddhists betray feelings of disquiet, bordering on fear, about the nature and functions of kingship as it existed in their times, they see no alternative to it and declare it to be absolutely essential to prevent humanity from lapsing into a state of anarchy. Finally, confronted with the fact of kingship and its absolute necessity for orderly human existence, they attempt to tame absolute political power by infusing into it a spirit of higher morality."[7] It is this apprehension about chaos that makes kingly power not only a less threatening alternative but a stabilizing influence as well, conducive to an atmosphere in which people may search for order and meaning both beyond and within the order of society. Many interpreters of the Theravada tradition (among them Gokhale, Mus, Sarkisyanz, Wijesekera, and Rahula) have noted an accompanying concern among early Buddhists and their successors for the social and economic well-being of all citizens.[8] It is not that the Buddha or his followers were social reformers, but that pursuit of the Dhamma depended no less on adequate economic welfare of the society at large than on stabilized political order. While similar ambivalence toward material goods existed in theory as existed toward power, the Sangha realized its dependence on the liberality of others as well as the threat to order represented by widespread privation. Emanuel Sarkisyanz notes, "Ideally kingship had, therefore, to guarantee such economic relationships as would ensure a sufficient livelihood for its subjects to allow them the leisure for meditation on which depended the achievement of Nirvana."[9] In correcting the impression of Max Weber that no social ethics were derivable from Theravada, Sarkisyanz appropriately distinguishes between what he calls the ethos of lay Buddhism and the ethos of the Buddhist order of monks, yet stressing as well the bridge that exists "between this 'Arhat' ideal and active social endeavor."[10]

It would be as great a mistake to see no connection between them as to miss the radical disjunction. The supreme tension was suggested first by the Buddhist monarch Aśoka, who, in explaining what lay behind his welfare measures, said, "I have done what I have primarily in order that people may follow the path of Dharma with faith and devotion."[11] While claiming no special merit for his policies, he underscored the motivation behind them. Whether one reads such statements cynically or accepts them at face value, one finds in Aśoka the paradigm of kingly prudence and virtue, a man whose own violence was said to have been converted into justice, *ahimsā*, and righteousness. The miracle believed by later Buddhists, as recorded in the legends about Aśoka (*Aśokāvadāna*), was that statecraft could be imbued with virtue, a belief that led them to term him as *dhammarājā* and to second Aśoka's own belief that *dhammavijaya* (conquest through righteousness, i.e., over attachment and ignorance) was possible.

The model of the Ideal King, however, makes little sense if one neglects in the reading of Sinhalese and Burmese history the continuing reappearance of cunning, violence, and self-assertion among kings and others. While the chronicles of both nations are clearly *heilsgeschichte,* heavily didactic in nature, they attest with extraordinary honesty to humanity's capacity for evil. The corruption of power, the misuse of authority, and the illegitimate exercise of kingship described in the records highlight the fragile yet essential relationship between legitimation and authority. In the person of kings whose exercise of power is tamed, either by their own conscience or by sanctions of the Sangha, whose political influence lay in accessibility to popular support, one finds a remarkable interdependence, or at least an ongoing balancing of power.

There have been many accounts of how this complex symbiosis benefitted the Sangha itself.[12] The *Mahāvaṃsa* records the extensiveness of kingly patronage, the monarch's role in settling disputes within the bhikkhu community, and the delicate yet crucial task of initiating reform (*sodhesi sāsanam*) within the Sangha whenever lack of discipline or heretical doctrine became issues. While one would expect any portrayal over centuries to include pictures of lawless monks and treacherous kings, the chronicles are also replete with testimonies about how power was in fact tamed.[13] Such kings became both in deed and in word *sāsana dāyakas,* that is, protectors and promoters of the faith, models not simply for other monarchs but for the community at large.

Unless the contemporary Sinhalese Buddhist scene is portrayed against this historical and ideological background, one comprehends inadequately the process of introspection and renewal occurring within this tradition. At whatever point one examines the picture within the past two hundred or more years, one may observe laypeople and bhikkhus wrestling with the fact that the former sacro-political authority was no longer extant. Some blame this on the British for "dishonoring" their agreement under the Kandyan Convention of 1815 to uphold the Buddhist religion. Some trace it to the beginnings of colonialism under the Portuguese in 1505, others to the decline of the Sinhalese civilization itself, starting in the thirteenth or fourteenth century.

What cannot be denied is that Sinhalese Buddhism, as every religious tradition, confronts a world in which entirely different assumptions, having social and political and economic implications, are presently operative. If past assumptions were diverse, though relatively stable, present ones are bewilderingly complex and in constant flux. If the task for religious institutions and their membership were simply to apply old teachings to new situations, the dilemma would be real enough. As one analyst put it, "The attack on traditional systems took various forms and moved at varying speeds, but everywhere it cracked open the integralist nature of society. Everywhere it separated the major component of the religio-political system. Religion could no longer legitimize political power in the convincing way it once had done, nor could governments confidently arrange ecclesiastical affairs in the traditional manner. The disruption of traditional systems left governments without legitimacy and autonomous religions with no prior experience of autonomy."[14]

Sinhalese Buddhist Identity and the Dilemmas of Reinterpretation

The manner in which a community in times of profound crisis reaches into the past to discover its identity and redefine itself in relationship to this past, even if only to dissociate itself from it, has considerable psychological and social importance. Frantz Fanon captures the essence of what had been occurring in a global sense during a prior generation: "In order to ensure his salvation and to escape from the supremacy of the white man's culture, the native feels the need to turn backward toward his unknown roots and to lose himself at whatever cost in his own barbarous people."[15] The humiliation of colonial status, the emergence into an incompletely prepared-for freedom, and the accelerating of a pace that destroys faster than it reconstructs breed insecurity and fear that not unsurprisingly issue in self-assertiveness, sometimes in hatred, often in further confusion about identity.[16] While not limited to transitional societies, the dilemmas behind national self-discovery are especially poignant in these contexts, as noted by Soedjatmoko:

> There is no doubt that nationalism has proven a potent force for national integration and for developing a new sense of purpose, helping to sweep away the anxieties and uncertainties resulting from the nation's shifting identity. In fact, the preoccupation with national identity itself is an inherent part of nationalism. The insistence on the uniqueness of one's own nation has occasionally, however, also led to the glorification of attitudes and values that were integral parts of the value system of the closed agricultural society from which it is emerging. Although the reconfirmation and elevation into permanent virtues of these values and attitudes undoubtedly contribute to greater self-confidence, they may at times make creative adjustment to the needs of modernization more difficult by prematurely freezing or fixing the self-image into a somewhat traditional cast.[17]

Attention has frequently been drawn to the involvement of Buddhist monks in anticolonial movements specifically, but the ingredients of nationalist sentiments in Sri Lanka need exploring if Sinhalese Buddhism's impact on future social change is to be anticipated in any sense. Heinz Bechert accurately observes that a critical study of the Sinhalese chronicles "reveals the part played by the political concept of the national identity of the Sinhalese in close connection with the religious tradition of Theravada Buddhism, i.e., the concept of the identity of the Sinhalese Buddhists."[18] The continuity of modern Sinhalese nationalism with its classical counterparts since the third century BCE is too important to go unmentioned. National and religious self-consciousness have been identified since that time, normally in moderate, though occasionally in virulent, form.

The national crisis of May 23–27, 1958, which issued in communal riots between Sinhalese and Tamils, killing several hundreds and requiring the declaration of a state of emergency, was only one major episode of violence between these two communities that, while coexisting within Sri Lanka in reasonable toleration of each other until modern times, also have a history of antipathy dating back to the ancient period. Sinnappah Arasaratnam notes: "The fact that the threat came mainly from the Tamil kingdoms across the straits served to keep alive the vision of the Tamils as the enemy of the Sinhalese people. . . . Thus it was that a people who had very close cultural relations with each other were cast politically in the role of antagonists."[19] While more modern forms of antagonism have stemmed principally from economic and social considerations (i.e., from the sizable Tamil immigrant labor force used in plantation estates and from the relatively higher proportion of Tamils in civil service positions and in commerce), the resultant communalism has carried racial and religious overtones that have further compounded the basic problems. Highly symbolic was the debate, during the middle and late 1950s especially, over the question of national language, as language and cultural identity can scarcely be separated.

To understand the dilemma felt by Sinhalese Buddhists, not to mention Tamils, it is helpful to perceive how their current crisis of identity had earlier manifestations and to relate current and historical forms to the claims both of their own uniqueness and of their uninterrupted continuity with the original Dhamma. These twin claims have clearly been opposite sides of the same coin and have served to justify their sense of a unique destiny as the primary recipient and conveyer of what the Buddha taught. The validation of their own future and of changes occurring within it depends in no small measure on their ability to reinterpret the meaning of their past identity in a religious sense.

In his depiction of the agonies faced by key figures in postindependence Burmese political and administrative echelons, Lucian Pye sketches the vicious cycle that "seems to develop in transitional societies: fears of failure in the adventure of nation building create deep anxieties, which tend to inhibit effective action; thus imagined problems become real and fears of failure become the realities of failure; and these failures further heighten anxieties."[20] As an ingredient of this, Pye underscored the deep-seated apprehension about chaos, the phobia of uncontrollable emotions, of running amok: "A latent fear of anarchy and a suspicion that all people must be controlled against dangerous and aggressive impulses are basic elements in Burmese political thought."[21]

While peculiar forces within Burmese society help to account for this, the phenomenon is discoverable in various forms in all societies. The recurring necessity of dealing with forces of disorder within and between people tends to blur the psychic and spiritual differences among so-called traditional, transitional, and modernized societies. The reversion to chaos is no respecter of time or place. A combined critical and sympathetic reading of the Sinhalese chronicles, juxtaposed against the events of more recent times, provides insight into the Sinhalese evolving and uncertain quests for identity and their implications for the future.

Lanka's self-image of being the "archetype of delusion" and the "paragon of enlightenment" reinforced its vocation as upholder of the Dhamma's purity, injecting into Sinhalese identity a comparable insistence on national purity. In the modern day, Dhammadīpa (the island of the teaching) embarks on exorcism of alien elements, whether through critiques of Christian influences from the colonial era and the Westernization of its urban elite, through the ignoring of all languages but Sinhala, or through repatriation plans for several hundred thousand Tamils.[22] While advocated primarily by extremists, large sections of the population were caught up in a renewed search for their Sinhalese self-consciousness. The preparations for the Buddha Jayānti (1956) and the installation of the first Buddhist governor general (1962) were both symptom and capstone, ceremonially speaking, of this quest.

This very uncertainty about identity is what drives a community to expel all elements from its presence that are seen to dilute its desired purity. Yet it is paradoxically in being enriched by differences within one's midst that a more secure identity can be forged. In fact, it may legitimately be argued that one of the factors helping to produce a creative and distinctive Sinhalese civilization was the very presence of Tamils, on the island and across the straits, throughout the centuries. As is frequently observed about Roman Catholicism, it is precisely in those situations where the church has not had a monopoly, so to speak, that it has been most alive and the least doctrinaire. Comparably, it may equally be true about Sinhalese Buddhism that part of its fortune has ironically been in having this Tamil thorn in the flesh. While the classic encounter between Dutthagāmanī and Elara, the Tamil king of Sri Lanka, restored the monarchy to Sinhalese Buddhist hands and marked the beginnings of Sinhalese nationalism, it could not quiet the fears that political chaos and the forces of *adhamma* were ever-present. The two millennia separating the monk Buddharākkhita's complicity in the 1959 assassination of Prime Minister S. W. R. D. Bandaranaike from the assurance given by eight arahants to Dutthagāmanī, who was distressed over slaughtering Elara's "great host numbering millions," were symbolically spanned.[23]

One additional aspect of Sinhalese Buddhist identity requires noting here, namely, the indissoluble connection with its Indian roots. The very mention of the Buddha himself, and of Vijaya, Aśoka, Mahinda, and Buddhaghosa, attests to Sinhalese dependence on its continental forebears. The continuance of apostolic succession and lineage (*ācariyaparamparā*) from Upāli in the Buddha's time to Mahinda and beyond, the implication of Sakka and innumerable named and unnamed Brahmanic deities in the many paradigmatic events of early Sinhalese culture,[24] and the involvement of Brahmin priests in coronation ceremonies (*abhiśeka*) of Buddhist kings all suggest how both orthodox and folk-religion elements of the Hindu tradition became merged with Sinhalese self-consciousness. Without question, the ambivalence toward things Indian needs resolving if temptations toward communalism are not to harden even further. Sinhalese Buddhist identity suffers no loss by acknowledging its Brahmanic heritage, while at the same time affirming that it had chosen a different path, in which case Tamils, too, might relax. The creative wrestling with religious self-awareness carries crucial import for social and political developments in the future. Lucian Pye has put the challenge as follows: "Fundamentally, the hope for transitional peoples resides in their quests for new collective as well as individual identities. Their development hinges on their capacity to find meaning in a fusion of what we have called traditional and modern modes of action, a fusion of world culture and their own historic cultures."[25] There is no culture to which those words do not apply.

The Sangha: Organizational Crisis

If the tradition and institutions of Theravada Buddhism have typically thrived on state support, we may be on the verge of seeing developments within Theravada having no precedent. While still the case in Thailand that the Sangha relates to the state in a traditional manner, this is no longer true in Myanmar and Sri Lanka. Though the history of British colonialism took different turns in Sri Lanka than in Myanmar, in both the state's connection with Buddhism became severed. It is no wonder that members of the Buddha Sāsana felt confused, betrayed, and irate with the loss of patron, defender, and arbitrator. If the symbiosis was not without its trials, in theory and frequently in fact the state's role as *sāsana dāyaka* was crucial for the Sangha. Without speculating on what this dislocation meant for the state, for the Sangha the word *crisis* is none too strong. While the nature of the crisis is varied, its principal element is organizational. Donald Smith has phrased it well: "Buddhism today is faced by serious problems of internal organization. Under the conditions of modern life, religion can function effectively only if organized coherently so that it can transmit its teaching to each new generation, protect its collective interests, and exert its moral influence on society and government. In Buddhism the laity is not organized into effective local units, the problem of indiscipline within the Sangha is very serious, and there is only the most tenuous connection between the laity and the Sangha."[26]

In order to grasp what role the Sangha might play as promoter of change in the future, it is essential to examine certain components of this organizational crisis, for without structural and ideological coherence there can be neither significant legitimizing, nor critique, of change. Among many components, five are singled out here: first, the problem of organizational unity in situations marked by immense fragmentation; second, the ongoing question of discipline within the bhikkhu community; third, the ironic but not unprecedented tension between the vow of poverty and monastic affluence; fourth, the dilemma of granting the laity more responsibility and influence without undermining the Sangha; and fifth, the insufficiently examined matter of maintaining a sensitive balance between what Heinz Bechert calls *Urbuddhismus* and *traditionalistischen Buddhismus* (i.e., between what was thought to be the canonical teachings of the Buddha and what has in fact been part of the Buddhist tradition over centuries).

At the heart of the problems affecting Sinhalese Buddhism today is the question of reform. There is no issue of importance to either the internal life of the Sangha, the relationship between bhikkhus and laypeople, or the impact of Buddhism on contemporary thought and society that is not centrally dependent on how and in what ways reform takes place. Inevitably hinging on reform is the matter of organizational coherence, the problem of unity. On the surface, the rejection by the Sangha of major reform measures suggested by the Buddha Sāsana Commission in its 1959 report was due to the measures' having become a political football. Beneath the surface, however, it was clear that what was being recommended was a totally new ecclesiastical polity, one that would reconstitute the operation of institutional Buddhism. Fundamental to these recommendations was the establishment of a bicameral deliberative body called the Buddha Sāsana Mandalaya, to be composed of two councils: one, of bhikkhus from all three *nikāyas* or sects, responsible only for internal matters within the Sangha; the other, of both bhikkhus and laypeople, "which would undertake to promote the general welfare of the Buddhists, meet the challenge to Buddhism from opposing forces, and deal with the state in regard to the rights of the Buddhists."[27]

There have been many accounts of why these efforts failed.[28] In essence, the Sangha obviously felt threatened; the disunity within the Buddhist community that the report sought to remedy was transcended only by uniform rejection of its measures. In fairness to the Sangha, it cannot be said that what was being rejected was the state's right to reform and purify the community. This right had been confirmed, by custom, at least from the time of Aśoka.[29] It would be more true to say that an attitude of trust had yet to be created toward a completely new kind of constitutional polity. To exist in interdependency with a Buddhist monarch is one thing; to entrust one's destiny in major ways to an untested conciliar body is quite another, particularly when it meant that state Buddhism was being rejected forever as a matter of policy.

On the other hand, the necessity of devising some sort of organizational clarity and corporate responsiveness to a host of human needs would be denied by few in Sri Lanka today. The extraordinary involvement of bhikkhus and laypeople in social and political activity during the past several decades is evidence of immense vitality, but the requirement for greater effectiveness appears even clearer. As Bechert notes, "The direct involvement of larger sections of the Sangha in political affairs in Sri Lanka as well as Burma in recent times was connected with an important change in its organizational structure, namely, the emergence of monks' associations outside the traditional structures of the nikāyas. . . . As a result, a new form of dualism in the life of the Sangha came into existence: for monastic and religious matters one had to stick to the traditional nikāya structures—for political and social activity the bhikkhus joined associations with no connection at all to the nikāya organization."[30] If the pyramidal system of the bhikkhu community in Thailand, with a Supreme Patriarch (*sangharāja*) at the head and an elaborate infrastructure as part of it, is not acceptable in either Myanmar or Sri Lanka, the development of some sort of functional equivalent would seem to be required.

No less dependent on Sāsana reform is the issue of discipline. While organizational restructuring may logically be prior, the very problem of indiscipline, coupled with the disappearance of state involvement in these matters, may become the primary catalyst toward establishing ecclesiastical tribunals, which were also part of the Buddha Sāsana Commission Report. To create jurisdictional bodies of this sort, however, without giving serious attention to Vinaya reform and the vocation of the bhikkhu in light of present needs is to miss central opportunities, even to betray Buddhism. The debates about reinterpreting the Vinaya date back at least to the Second Council (Vaiśālī, circa 377 BCE), leading to the emergence of the Mahāsaṅghikas and other sectarian developments later. As Rahula puts it, "the Vinaya was not ultimate truth, but only a convention agreed upon for the smooth conduct of a particular community."[31]

The *symptoms* of indiscipline reveal themselves in bhikkhu laxity of behavior, partisan political activity, occasional acts of violence, monastic landlordism, and even in sectarianism. The substance of indiscipline, however, goes far deeper. It relates inevitably to the vocation of the Sangha as preserver of the Dhamma, besides which all its activities are subsidiary. The qualitative distance between the average monk or layperson and the Buddha or the great exemplars through history cannot be measured in terms of centuries. To use the Vinaya as anything but a means toward this qualitative goal is, indeed, a betrayal of Buddhism. This is not to stress disproportionately Buddhism's social message,[32] which must derive from renewed quality of life within; it is only to distinguish substance from form, and end from means.

The sense of alarm and the cries for reform proceeding from public responses to Sinhalese bhikkhu political activity in the late 1950s were not only a reaction to excessive behavior, they were expressions of disenchantment and confusion about what a true bhikkhu should be. Without knowing it, these were not dissimilar to comparisons made by the Buddha. With a nice ironic touch, in sayings later called the *brāhmanavaggo* (Way of the Brahmin), the model bhikkhu was defined in terms which that earlier age could comprehend: "Him I call a Brahmin who is without hostility among those who are hostile, who is peaceful among those with uplifted staves, who is unattached among those who are attached. . . . Him I call a Brahmin whose wisdom is deep, who possesses knowledge, who discerns the right way and the wrong and who has attained the highest end."[33] Though an ideal was being described, it was not one without worldly implications. This will be discussed in the final section. Here it need only be said that for reform the Sangha must emancipate itself from dependence on external stimuli alone. While remaining sensitive to these stimuli, authentic reform efforts must proceed from within, though that is precisely the problem.

The necessity of new structures is not only to handle problems of disunity and indiscipline. C. D. S. Siriwardene adds:

> There is need also for organization to deal with the material needs of the Sangha. In the old village units the support and maintenance of the monks was a duty readily undertaken by all Buddhists. . . . However, the village no longer depends on the temple as it did in the past, and the bonds of interdependence have almost disappeared. . . . Unless the laity are able to ensure conditions that will enable the "bhikkhus" to live strict lives, it is useless to expect purity in the Sangha, and it is foolish to blame the monks for these violations of the Vinaya.[34]

The problems, however, are less simple than they sound; as with the other two instances a long history lies behind them. In fact, much of Sri Lanka's social history is involved with monastic *temporalia* and their administration. With the British period, separation of land from the Sangha began.

The Colebrook Reforms of 1832–34 and the enforcement of the 1856 Temple Land Registration Act during the years 1857–65 were the most prominent steps taken.

The primary anomaly is not extensive ownership of land by the Sangha but that it is principally held by up-country elements dominated by the Siam Nikāya, the largest and wealthiest of the three *nikāyas* in Sri Lanka.[35] And, at the same time, most temples on the island are marginally supported at best. This is not the place to discuss the complexities (legal, ecclesiastical, fiscal) of the situation but only to identify it among the more serious issues within the general organizational crisis of the Sangha, one that clearly complicates, even compromises its ability to deal effectively with other social and political concerns.

Siriwardene is correct, nevertheless, in stressing that guaranteed means of support must be found if the Sangha is to fulfill its basic vocation. Neither attachment to affluence nor the threat of involuntary poverty is conducive to spiritual well-being or to a healthy influence on society. The dilemma, of course, is how this support can be forthcoming from non-governmental sources or, if from the government, how it can be justified within a secular state concept. If funds are given to Buddhists, then Tamils, Christians, and Muslims will expect support as well. With Sri Lanka's marginal economy, there is little to spare, though one measure might be a guaranteed minimal income for all citizens. Whatever the solution, the problem for the Sangha is considerable, as with any monastic community where the vow of poverty competes with the generosity of pious laypeople, not to mention the responsible use of these gifts by clerical hands.

The fourth problem in organizational structure is also the greatest opportunity, namely, the relationship between bhikkhu and layperson and the need to reconceive this relationship in such a manner that neither be diminished and that both gain. In a traditional sense, the same kind of reciprocity existed between monk and laity as between king and Sangha, the latter in fact being the prototype for the former. Whatever distinctions existed among laypeople and among monks, the final dividing line between them was that "acquiring merit of various kinds was the motive underlying the religion of the laity, from the king down to the poor peasant," while monks were expected to tread the path to Nibbāna.[36] The term *dhamma-dāna* expresses vividly the nature of the reciprocity, that is, the giving of "spiritual, cultural and educational gifts" in return for material ones.[37]

Whatever can be said about the continuation of this pattern in urban areas, as well as in the villages, a social and a cultural revolution has been occurring that has begun to effect considerable changes. Not only the secularizing process, but the upgrading of education produces a population as sophisticated in most respects as their clerical counterparts. This makes available increasing numbers of people who can serve the Buddha Sāsana and society at large in new ways. Their role in education, in organizational activities, in "ecumenical" Buddhism, and even in Buddhist studies has already been immense. In fact, if not in theory, the role of the laity has undergone its own revolution. What is called for is a reconceived doctrine of the layperson, plus their inclusion in decision-making councils at local and national levels, enabling their service to be expressed in more thoughtful and responsible ways.

The consignment of laypeople to less than equal partnership was understandable in a traditionalist framework, but it will prove self-defeating if continued. Because of the continuing tendency in all religious traditions for false distinctions to exist between lay and clerical members, there is often an attempt made by laypeople to become diluted versions of ministers, priests, or monks and to conceive morality in narrow, often puritanical forms. What results is a version of religious thought and behavior that in no significant way analyzes, confronts, or transforms the culture. Consequently, secularism in its distorted forms goes unchallenged and the process of secularization as a legitimate enterprise is afforded no profound religious guidance. For laypeople to be given a vision of what real service to their fellow human beings through their loyalty to the Buddha Sāsana can mean, an entire transformation of perspective is required.

Finally, it is not inconsistent to say that at the same time renewed dignity must also be given to the monk and nun, as theirs is a role that the layperson cannot serve and that society clearly needs. Distinctions do exist between them, but these are of training, role, function, and opportunity—not necessarily of dedication, compassion, or wisdom. The latter distinctions do exist among persons, and Buddhism has a name for those who have attained high levels of spiritual growth (*sāvaka-saṅgha*), but it is always stressed that this community of attainment is spiritual in nature (i.e., supra-empirical) and is not restricted to monastic disciples of the Buddha.[38]

In both Myanmar and Sri Lanka the shift from a negative anti-colonialism to a more positive ideology created a vacuum into which rushed a resurgent but not reformed Buddhism. As Donald Smith notes, "Post-independence nationalism had to be nurtured on something which was both positive and indigenous."[39] The correspondence between national self-consciousness and the renascence of indigenous cultural forms is a worldwide phenomenon. Earlier we noted the present Sinhalese Buddhist attempt to rediscover dimensions of self-identity that had been stifled or ignored in recent experience. A similar development, in slightly less complex form, can be traced in Myanmar in the person of U Nu and others. It is generally characteristic of enduring religious traditions that they accommodate themselves to changing times and circumstances, absorbing and transforming various elements to which their members are exposed. The history of Buddhism reveals an extraordinary aptitude in this regard.

This does not mean either that the appropriation of indigenous beliefs, art forms, practices, or structures is indiscriminate or that important distinctions are not retained between local and indigenous on the one hand and orthodox or traditional on the other. In its Theravada modes especially, Buddhism maintains these distinctions carefully. Anthropological studies of locales in Thailand, Myanmar, and Sri Lanka are virtually unanimous in describing a basically two-tiered system, often with more precise refinements, of indigenous folk religious expressions superimposed by more or less canonical Theravada.[40]

What has happened during the past several decades in Myanmar and Sri Lanka is that political capital has been made of indigenous religion, of folk-Buddhism, and of orthodox Theravada, with the assistance of elements within the Sangha, by candidates seeking to ingratiate themselves both with the rural masses and the more sophisticated. The vital new ingredient in the picture is that through universal suffrage Buddhism becomes politicized in unprecedented ways, not infrequently resulting in disorder and communal violence. Here too, as with the four issues discussed above, the dilemma is compounded by the organizational crisis within Sinhalese Buddhism. What is called for is a sensitive distinguishing of *Urbuddhismus* Buddhism from its later cultural expressions, without either demeaning or glorifying the latter. This is an intellectual issue as much as an organizational one, since until the members of the Sangha are provided educational opportunities comparable to those of the laity, they cannot fully participate in the process. While there is obvious risk in this venture, there is ultimately much more to gain than to lose.

Out of Pluralism: New Forms of Unity

When the sun finally set on the British Empire, Westernized elites in places like Myanmar and Sri Lanka suddenly found themselves face to face with their own people. In Sri Lanka, unlike Myanmar, there had not been the kind of struggle for independence that tends to weld together differences within a population so that national consciousness begins to transcend communal differences. With the advent of universal adult franchise, through the Donoughmore Constitution of 1931, the active politicization of communal elements within the society became a possibility. In 1956, this possibility was actualized, making Ceylonese politics since that time bitterly partisan along religious lines. This problem of antipathy between Tamils and Buddhists, if not between Buddhists and Christians, had been foreseen by the royal commissioners who visited the island in 1927–28 in preparation for the 1931 constitution. Their report proved prescient, though their approved recommendation that representatives be chosen on regional, not communal, bases did not prevent increased discord. "Not only," the Report states, "is the population not homogeneous, but the diverse elements of which it is composed distrust and suspect each other. It is almost true to say that the conception of patriotism in Ceylon is as much racial as national and that the best interests of the country are at times regarded as synonymous with the welfare of a particular section of its people."[41]

The functional-valuational pluralism that develops through secularization is by definition not yet achieved in societies moving from traditional to modern patterns. In fact, it is often true that in the transitional stage simultaneous appeals to the past and to the future are unbearably strained. And also, where a society is diverse religiously, "the appeal to religious identity may prove severely disruptive to nationalism or may lead to the development of regionalist or separatist subnationalisms."[42] It was precisely this appeal in the mid-fifties that opened up old wounds in the Ceylonese body politic. Political and religious leaders seemed willing to risk this price in exchange for popular support and validation through the polls, though they were unable to contain the bitterness once it had been released. One of the continuing tests for Sinhalese Buddhism is its ability to effect constructive change without appealing to narrow communal interests.

The task, of course, is not for Buddhists alone, nor even primarily for religious groups. The task must be accomplished through effective political and economic means, though this may be obstructed or abetted by temple, church, and mosque. Perhaps the single most important assignment for religious communities in Sri Lanka and elsewhere is to facilitate the change from narrow to more inclusive definitions of human identity, in policy as well as in creed. In essence, this will mean the secularization of group identity, which may paradoxically release religious communities to serve in new ways. Both Myanmar and Sri Lanka are still in mid-stream in their efforts to achieve a new national self-consciousness that integrates substantive values from their traditions with the development of a modern nation state. As noted by W. Howard Wriggins, "The diverse demands and values of each group must in some measure be drawn into the political process, if large numbers are not to be in fact alienated from the political order."[43] The skills that are called for are immense—political, administrative, scientific, educational, industrial, economic, legal, among others. The temptation to substitute charisma and rhetoric for competence is never absent. The earlier example of U Nu in Burma (Myanmar) provides a grim reminder of how religious legitimacy can be misused and of how sectarian and separatist elements in a pluralist society thrive on politically promoted religion. The understandable fears of minority groups in such situations (e.g., Christian Karens in Myanmar and Hindu Tamils in Sri Lanka) not infrequently trigger potential succession movements, as Ne Win's March 2, 1962 coup to arrest this movement in Myanmar and as the Federal Party in Sri Lanka would indicate.

The need to develop adequate pressure-group channels, effective yet flexible party discipline, and a network of other organizations (political, economic, and social) to serve as infrastructure between the state and the society at large is transparent if the various sectors of the community are to feel represented and part of a larger whole. Besides, a number of studies on Sri Lanka have identified the economic factors behind communalism, which then are inevitably translated into political form. Part of the task of diversifying the economy, which is essential to the island's welfare, is to make available training and vocational opportunities on an open basis. The very clustering of ethnic or communal groups in certain areas of the economy and the pejorative attitude toward various kinds of work perpetuate stereotypes that Tamils and Sinhalese already have of each other. If religious institutions are to participate significantly in this process of changed attitudes and changed relationships through a reconstruction of organizational patterns and options, there is need for considerable reflection about which means best serve the goal of an open society. Donald Smith has stated it succinctly: "The most effective ideological reformulations, then, would be those which (1) evolve out of extensive multilateral ideological interaction, (2) are authenticated by established ecclesiastical authority, (3) are transmitted by a well-organized communications network, and (4) are associated with meaningful action programs."[44] Each context must create its own ways of meeting these criteria for the fostering of responsible change.

Intrinsic to a religious community's role in helping a society to fashion constructive unity out of pluralistic elements are its own efforts to blend unity and diversity within itself and in relationship to other religious traditions. While this is an ongoing task for all religions within a society, a special onus falls on those in the majority. The tensions among elements within the Sangha, the "tenuous" connection between bhikkhu and layperson, the deepening hostilities between Tamils and Buddhists (as well as between Buddhists and Christians or Buddhists and Muslims), and the lack of significant interchange with those who are hostile or indifferent toward religious values remain key items on the agenda in Sri Lanka. Thus far, it is more common for defensiveness and counterattack to dominate the exchanges, though there are examples to the contrary. What has been said about Indian nationalism applies, with appropriate changes, to its Sinhalese counterpart, namely, that it will not be secure if it "equates [Buddhist] glory with [Hindu] humiliation."[45]

One important development on the world scene that is bound to influence Sinhalese Buddhism in the long run, more than it already has, is the movement of international or ecumenical Buddhism. This is another instance of cultivating unity out of diversity. While part of the Mahayana canon, it is well known that the *Lotus Sutra* talks about *ekayāna* or one vehicle rather than two or three. This is what some Theravada Buddhists have been discussing and which neither promotes homogenization of Buddhism nor false syncretism with aspects of other religions. Rather, it encourages a *oneness of spirit* that enables persons who prefer to retain their differences but to be open toward each other. Joseph Kitagawa states the task as follows: "Basically, the question for world-wide Buddhism today is how to harmonize the various facets of Buddhism—the memory of Gautama Buddha, the authority of the canonical writings, the nebulous but real power of tradition, and the living experience of men and women in their particular cultural and historic situations."[46]

The harmonizing of the ingredients within Buddhism is inevitably of one piece with the existence of harmony between Buddhists and others, a harmony that honors differences of belief and practice but strives for oneness of spirit. That most politically astute of Buddhists, Aśoka, whose orthodoxy may not have been impeccable yet whose spirit of tolerance has often been noted, put it as follows: "King Priyadarsi honors men of all faiths, members of religious orders and laymen alike, with gifts and various marks of esteem. Yet he does not value either gifts or honor as much as growth in the qualities essential to men in all faiths. . . . The objective of these measures is the promotion of each man's particular faith and the glorification of the Dharma."[47]

Two Domains in Tension

The important sentence in that oft-quoted edict of Aśoka is the final one, in which the intent of all his policies is made clear. What he says about tolerance fits into that larger context. Tolerance is never an end in itself. Without it, people become closed to each other, but by itself settling for tolerance prevents deeper growth of mind and spirit. The Dharma that Aśoka sought to glorify has helped the Buddha Sāsana through centuries to maintain a balanced perspective, not simply about two domains of life but about two ways of looking at existence. Examining these helps to suggest how Theravada Buddhism could make the transition in its thinking about the political order from dependence on a framework presupposing a so-called *integralist* sacral society to one that is both pluralist and secular in nature.

In his several writings on the early Buddhist views of kingship, the state, and history, B. G. Gokhale has elaborated this theory of two domains or of "two wheels, two distinct realms of action" within the dominion of "two separate but equally important ideals of a *Cakkavatti,* the leader of the temporal realm, and the Bodhisattva, pre-eminent in the spiritual domain."[48] These domains are intended to reinforce each other, the state as protector and the Sangha as conscience of the state: "Affairs of this world and those of the next are like two wheels. Each has its own distinct identity but they are also like the wheels of the chariot, the axle on which they revolve, in this case, being the human society, its desires, aspirations and destiny. There is also the implication that Dhamma cannot operate in this world by itself as it needs the acquiescence, if not the support of *āṇā* or the state. The state and Order are separate in their own identities, but their interdependence cannot be ignored completely."[49]

To stop at that point would take one no further than the ancient Sinhalese symbiosis described in the first section of this chapter. In another context, however, Gokhale comments that "Buddhism views reality on two levels, ultimate and proximate or transcendental and phenomenal (*paramattha* and *sammuti*)."[50] It is this distinction, not one between "this life" and "the next life," that makes the substantive point. Clearly, Hinduism and Buddhism both talk about the next life; the whole theory of karma presupposes successive incarnations until one is released from *saṃsāra.* The implication here, on the other hand, is both a qualitative distinction between ways of viewing reality (this life or the next life) *and* an assertion that one therefore actually sees different levels of reality as one's state of consciousness deepens. To regard the domains mentioned above only in terms of state and Sangha (temporal and spiritual, even secular and sacred) is to treat superficially what is actually profound. Terms like *sacred* and *secular* become reified, with some things or ideas or institutions ending up in one category and some in the other.

It is not incidental that, as noted in chapter 1, in later Indian Mahayana Buddhism there was a deliberate merging of the two distinct but overlapping notions of sovereignty: the sociopolitical and that of the cosmos at large. The original choice of vocations put before the infant Siddhattha was later viewed as a false dichotomy, for as the Universal Ruler or Ideal King is also the Cakkavatti or Bodhisattva, so the Buddha is supreme monarch, the master of heaven and earth. What is implied is not a political but a spiritual sacralization, in which one who is fully enlightened sees the oneness in all reality. One sees the *dhammatā* or "principle of order that makes the world a cosmos and not a chaos."[51] This is comparable to what Edward Conze has said about Dharma, that while "it is the unconditioned One, it is not some barren remoteness, but infuses order into the multiple appearances of the conditioned world, and conformity to it is the basis of the spiritual life."[52]

By means of this binary orientation the Buddhist perspective can help provide meaning in the modern world where, despite the questioning of all ideologies, there is as much danger of fragmentation in a pluralist framework as of imposed order in an integralist one. In common with prophetic traditions within the West, there is within Buddhism a fundamental critique of all attempts to elevate partial truths into absolutes. Richard Robinson articulates this as follows: "The perfection of wisdom consists in the direct realization that all dharmas, whether conditioned or unconditioned, are empty."[53] He continues: "The teaching of emptiness [*śūnyatā*] repudiates dualities . . . between the relative and the absolute. It cannot be called monism, however, because it denies that reality is either a plurality or a unity. . . . This doctrine comes to terms with the early Buddhist quandary about the relationship between the nirvana-realm and the world. Not only is nirvana immanent in the world, but neither exists without the other."[54] And "Salvation from transmigration is to be found in the process of transmigration itself."[55]

The work of social welfare, even the reconstruction of society along more rational and just lines, is therefore crucial to the nirvanic quest, though not equatable with it. While a need clearly exists for the promotion of economic development, there is equal need not to define this as the good life. While valuational universalism would be an improvement over destructive communalism, its temptations may be blindness to particularity. Pluralist societies may provide opportunities their predecessors could not offer, but they are no less ambiguous in a qualitative sense. In short, "It is necessary to relate the purposes of the development process to other worthwhile purposes of human endeavor and of society."[56] Only after discussing the involvement of Buddhists in society is it appropriate to acknowledge that the Buddhist goal is a form of freedom to which ordinary social goals do not point. As much of recent activity on the part of bhikkhus and laypeople in Myanmar and Sri Lanka would suggest, there is danger that Buddhism may fall into the trap of equating social and political ends with genuine freedom. Again, while this freedom cannot be conceived in isolation from concern about the total welfare of human beings, the quest for it takes infinite paths, many of which are subtle and imperceptible.

At a conference titled "Religion and Progress in Modern Asia," held in 1963, Clifford Geertz made some comments that are as appropriate now as they were then: "There may be an intrinsic tension between the spiritual needs of man and the material needs of man, which can never be completely done away with no matter how clever one is or how much one manipulates institutions or anything else. The real problem in any state or in any religious tradition is . . . how to keep these two different things in balance,"[57] however precarious, difficult, and ongoing this balance may be.

Conclusion

Equal to the necessity of reexamining its past is Sinhala Buddhism's task of confronting an emerging world culture with its diverse yet many common features. As the past that one rediscovers is inevitably a mixed picture, so the future proves no less ambiguous. To exorcise the demons of colonialism, or of anything else, is not to avoid the dilemmas of renewed self-determination. As members of another religious order (Benedictines) have noted, "In such a climate an appeal to a venerable past can no longer be a guarantee of contemporary relevance. One of the effects of this heightened historical consciousness is a keener sense of the relativity of historical phenomena and a certain detachment from those currently occupying the scene."[58] With its stress on the continuing impermanence of all phenomena, its counsel of detachment toward all gain and loss, and its warnings about how easily attachment issues in possessiveness, fear, self-assertion, and suffering, it may be that the Buddhist tradition and its values do in fact promote fewer "dogmatic approaches to politics" than is generally the case.[59] If so, these may not only facilitate the adjustment to changes ahead but help to shape these very changes.

In this regard, three points are appropriate. First, as Wilfred Cantwell Smith has stressed, false images are sometimes conveyed about open, rapidly changing modern cultures in distinction to rigid, moribund religious traditions. While these images may be dead horses that few people are still beating, there has been a serious underestimating of "the dynamic, fluid quality of the so-called traditional religious systems. . . . If one is going to think in dichotomies at all, the proper picture is more nearly the confluence of two rivers, than the impact of one rushing river on a rock (or mud) citadel."[60] Donald Smith continues: "The case is not simply one of dynamic political processes acting upon static religious traditions."[61]

Second, while identifying change with progress is contrary to Buddhist thinking, as well as naive, it does not make one a cynic to disbelieve in progress theories or to regard change itself as ambiguous or to have serious reservations about what is *legitimized.* Neither need it prevent one from acting, nor from becoming better able to judge what changes may, in fact, improve particular situations. In the last analysis, progress is a matter of the spirit, though societies obviously fail if they remain unconcerned about the political and economic well-being of their members. Aśoka was not the only Buddhist to take this position; he was simply the most conspicuous political figure within Buddhist spheres of influence to do so.

And, third, for reasons not only of easing the transition from more traditional patterns of social organization to more modern ones, but also to help preserve the essence of historic cultures, it is important to emphasize continuity and not just change. In this regard, if one task of religious communities in years ahead is to support responsible change, there is need to cultivate a deeper awareness of how the past at its best may be reexperienced in the present (i.e., via modes of cultic *anamnesis*), providing channels for a more profound expression of both personal and corporate existence. The tension between "ambitions for new forms and tenacious adherence to old practices"[62] must be resolved by sensitive leaders who "want to modernize their country without destroying the fundamental values of their own traditions, for these are the source of their consciousness of self and their originality."[63]

It is inevitable that emerging cultural forms, like earlier ones, will combine new insights and values with new prejudices and limitations.[64] This does not demean the best of what is now becoming possible; it simply suggests that balanced validation of change is always tentative, never final. As with monarchs of old to whom extraordinary power and authority were granted, continuing legitimacy was not independent of how that power and authority were used. Among the more promising developments on the modern scene is the manner in which constitutional governments, industrial corporations, educational institutions, and elites within science and elsewhere are being held increasingly accountable by the body politic for the ends they serve and the means they employ. While it is still unclear what sorts of roles religious values and communities interpreting reality in religious ways will play in this development, it is inconceivable that they will be silent or that they will have no influence. In essence, what a religious community must do in order to develop new forms of viability is well put by Robert Bellah:

> It must be able to rephrase its religious symbol system to give meaning to cultural creativity in worldly pursuits. It must be able to channel motivation disciplined through religious obligation into worldly occupations. It must contribute to the development of a solidary and integrated national community, which it seeks neither to dominate nor to divide, although this necessity certainly does not imply sanctioning the nation as a religious ultimate. It must give positive meaning to the long-term process of social development and be able to value it highly as a social goal, again without necessarily taking social progress itself as a religious absolute. It must contribute to the ideal of a responsible and disciplined person. As part of the

> new balance between religious and secular in modern society, it must be able to accept its own role as a private voluntary association and recognize that this role is not incompatible with its role as bearer of the society's ultimate values.[65]

Specifically, about the role of Sinhalese Buddhism within the "modernizing" process in Sri Lanka, one may make the following comments.

First, while it is historically fallacious to assert that early Buddhism was socialistic in any recognizable sense, given the structuring of traditional societies, there is nothing in Buddhist doctrine or tradition that necessarily militates against the sharing of wealth or the means of production by socialistic legislation and practice. Indeed, though socialism is no more a guarantee of justice than other economic systems, the goal of distributed wealth is consistent with the intent and spirit of early Buddhism, if not its primary interest. It must be added that monastic landlordism in Sri Lanka would not be supportive of genuine socialism if this meant the loss of widespread temple holdings.

It is also true that similar assertions could not be made for the existence of democracy on the national level until recently, despite claims about republican forms of polity during the time of the Buddha. On the other hand, it is plausible to defend Buddhism's strong interest in the welfare of each person and, by extrapolation, to argue that widespread involvement in the political process is conducive to a more healthy social order. It must be recognized, however, that this would require not only stronger roles played by Buddhist laypeople but profoundly reinterpreted positions about the relative merits of political, social, and economic goals, within the general framework of a Nibbāna-centered orientation. While the compatibility of these elements is not impossible, it is rarely self-evident.

In addition, while historical Buddhism is not free from caste, sectarian, or communalistic elements, despite its tendencies to claim the contrary, it has been able to transcend these in many respects and to engage in significant Sāsana reform over the centuries. The future impact of laity and Sangha on political and social developments, nevertheless, will necessarily be related to their ability to overcome internal divisions and to resist temptations toward communal prejudices and separatist inclinations. In fact, the recent histories of Sri Lanka and Myanmar are sobering reminders that old wounds take more than time to heal.

Finally, while the beginnings of a fundamentally reinterpreted Buddhism, starting with the modernist movement of the nineteenth century, has often stressed its relationship to the social order (defined vaguely sometimes as Buddhist socialism) and while there have been immense increases in the political and social activity of Buddhists during the modern period, it remains true that the primary goal of Buddhism is not a stable order or a just society but the discovery of genuine freedom (or awakening) by each person. While it has never been asserted that the conditions of society are unimportant or unrelated to this goal, it is critical to stress the distinction between what is primary and what is not. For Buddhists to lose this distinction is to transform their tradition into something discontinuous with its original and historic essence. Even the vocation of the bodhisattva is not as social reformer but as a catalyst to personal transformation within society. The central task of Buddhism in the immediate future, however, is to display the reconcilability of what often but mistakenly appear to be diverging paths.

6

Identity Issues of Sinhalas and Tamils

DILEMMAS OF IDENTITY IN THE THROES OF SOCIAL CONFLICT

The political and social stalemate in contemporary Sri Lanka is composed of ethnic, class, religious, and other indicators of the elusive quality called "identity," in particular the differing interpretations of past and present grievances. The narrowness with which social identity is often defined and defended impairs efforts to imagine new possibilities. The Sinhalese have been portrayed as *a majority with a minority complex,* seeing itself threatened by the huge Tamil presence in the south of India. From an opposite perspective, Sri Lankan Tamils have seen themselves as victims of Sinhala self-aggrandizement and, in response, have as their goal becoming a plurality within an independent "nation" or homeland of Eelam in the northern and eastern provinces of the country. The failure to establish an inclusive and viable vision of identity acceptable to both sides and made credible through legislative enactment and equitable social policy generates a culture of disarray and mistrust, as well as a neglect of the country's political and economic needs for decades. This chapter addresses the aspects of and interrelationships among personal, communal, and national identities within the context of contemporary Sri Lanka and offers a vision of a larger, inclusive identity that surpasses the constraints and violence of fundamentalism.

Personal, Communal, and National Identities

In circumstances of ethnic communalism, and certainly in Sri Lanka, the grounds for sustained enmity include factors beyond those of ethnic background. Typically, these entail class issues, educational inequities, long-held historical grievances, a climate of confrontational politics, persistent recourse to violent engagement on both sides, and the relative absence of effective conflict resolution. At the center of recurring features of social conflict in contemporary Sri Lanka is the problem of personal and communal identity, arising in a variety of forms as social structures encounter, resist, or stimulate forces of change. To understand this development requires underscoring various aspects of the complexity of identity, each of which constitutes a significant part of the interplay between religious and social change in contemporary Sri Lanka.

The first attribute of identity may be visible in recurring features on the social, economic, and political landscape (e.g., those of status, leadership, law, and rising expectations) that comprise the impact of modernity on social and ideological structures. To cite these is not to imply that significant change was absent within earlier forms of society but simply that the extent, pace, and nature of change today are of a different order.

A second aspect of identity involves recognizing that peoples the world over, in all societies, are undergoing self-examination with regard to their roots, their heritage, and their ethnic, racial, and religious makeup. The ambivalence encountered within this experience lies in the prospect of continuing cultural diversity existing along with the potential threat of renewed ethnocentrism. While this fact makes the present moment of time confusing and volatile, it also provides the possibility for newly emerging forms of pluralism in which different traditions face each other afresh.

A third ingredient of newly experienced identity entails responding to whatever strategies that groups and communities use to advance their position, capture or influence power, and secure gains that are never permanently won. It is in this realm that one becomes particularly aware of social conflict, as power is sought and resisted, but the existence and causes of conflict need to be anticipated long before they are politically articulated and strategies are conceived.

A fourth element requires identifying continuing conflicts or dilemmas that arise from legal changes and power shifts, leading often to intensified communal rivalry and sometimes to the deterioration of circumstances that are already fragile. It is therefore important to see religious phenomena as inherently complex in order to gain insight into the roles that religious traditions play with respect to social conflict and to the more nuanced ways in which people perceive themselves.

Central to renewed quests for identity, constituting so much of social and political ferment today, is the necessity of coping with traditional and newly created definitions side by side. It is this duality that comprises the *problem of identity,* for definitions of self, community, and nation are being forged out of situations where tradition and modernity make conflicting appeals, producing a rebirth of pride in one's heritage along with the determination to benefit from opportunities unknown in the past.

At the heart of identity is what it means to be a person, as well as a community, which is a religious issue equally as much as it is a social, political, or ethnic issue. In fact, the crux of identity is religious to the degree that it takes seriously these other aspects of personhood (i.e., one's communal, national, and cultural roots) but does not bestow ultimate status on them. This notion of what authentically religious quests entail is foreign neither to ancient nor to modern concepts of being human. Indeed, these are quests that prompt societies to engage in self-criticism. In all these roles the social dynamic can be as much an agent provocateur as an agent of continuity, a disturber of peace no less than a provider of assurance.

Central among politically significant modern phenomena is the relationship between a community's self-image and the strategies it employs for effective social change. A spectrum of such strategies would run the gamut from violent attempts to seize power to assorted policies designed to abort substantial shifts in power. Any such spectrum contains overlapping positions, and central to what is at stake is the quest for a new identity, not simply access to power and its advantages. The role of religious loyalties and symbols among these tensions may be used to justify either radical or ultraconservative measures and policies. In fact, religious traditions lend themselves to a variety of ends (e.g., rise in status, political unification, legitimation of power), although religious quests unavoidably raise questions about values, goals, and procedures that have implications for political policy and action. In any case, religious affiliations are essential components in understanding the arenas of social conflict.

Arising from recent as well as ancient experiences of racial, religious, and ethnic forms of communalism there has emerged the dilemma of how to fashion local, national, and international cohesiveness (enabling communities to transcend more narrow definitions of identity) without creating forms of identification that do violence to how they construe themselves as persons and as social and ethnic entities. The more serious the political and economic problems, the greater is the temptation to fashion a basis of cooperation that does injustice to the diversity of ethnic and religious traditions. There is considerable evidence that forms of cohesiveness that disregard these traditions are short-lived. In fact, ignoring resources within social, cultural, and religious traditions invites an impoverishment of perspectives and stimulates the very communal antagonisms they seek to avoid.

The examples of dilemmas facing the world entail not only social conflict but also broader questions of communal and national identity. The increasingly interdependent nature of the modern world makes a cooperative approach to these dilemmas fundamental. However one addresses the dilemmas of ethnic identity, they remain intractable unless the goals become those that aspire to more inclusive forms of communal identity and find ways by which these become a reality.

Beyond Fundamentalism to a Larger Identity

Together with underscoring some of the main points in a collection of essays edited by Tessa Bartholomeusz and Chandra de Silva, titled *Buddhist Fundamentalism and Minority Identities in Sri Lanka,* this section identifies other elements in the complex mix of ethnic identity alongside traditional portrayals of Sri Lanka as a Sinhala Buddhist society.[1] The subtext of their volume is that the constructed images of Sri Lanka have been shaped and promoted over the past hundred years by a form of Buddhist fundamentalism that sees itself as the *curator* of true Buddhism but is still influenced by ethnically driven forms of historical, social, and cultural forces. The political policies emerging from this constructed image of identity have led to misrepresentations of the actual pluralistic nature of Sri Lankan identity and have thus fomented divisions among the many segments of this society.

From various angles, the contributors to this volume describe what they mean by "fundamentalism" and, in the process, identify a range of attitudes and positions in and among the minority groups in their relationship to the Sinhala majority. While John Holt questions using a term such as *fundamentalism,* he acknowledges that its use serves to underscore the evolving self-identification among Sinhala Buddhists over the past century. In the process, he shows in what ways this evolution has inspired similar quests for identity by other religious and ethnic communities and how it has issued in numerous forms of communalism. While the larger social movements of the late nineteenth century in Ceylon bound many religious and ethnic groups together in anticolonial and anti-Christian sentiments, the driving force, especially since the mid-1950s, has been nationalistic forms of Buddhism. These were "consciously invoked by politically motivated Sinhalas to advance their own empowerment (usually to the exclusion of other communities) or to rationalize their agendas for action taken against other communities in *post hoc* fashion."[2]

The aim of modern Sinhala Buddhist fundamentalism has been to achieve and maintain political power, through factors such as language, race, and ethnicity, and have thus generated "social identity and alienation between communities" in contemporary Sri Lanka.[3] By way of understanding the confluence of religion and political power as the core of Sinhala Buddhist fundamentalism, the tendency of many scholars, perhaps especially in the West, has been to locate the inception of this belief in the *Mahāvaṃsa,* a fifth-century postcanonical text. The Mahāvihāra position, as represented in this text and rearticulated in the late nineteenth century, was seen by critics of Sinhala ideology as a kind of apotheosis of Sinhala Buddhism. In the process, there were those who oversimplified the nature of the *Mahāvaṃsa,* tending to demonize it as the root and source of modern ethnocentrism. In my opinion, both apotheosis and demonization go too far.

In any case, the mythohistorical past as represented by this ancient work does reveal the interweaving of sacred and political power known as the two wheels of Dhamma. Behind images of reciprocity between these fundamental powers was an idealized vision of a precolonial, agrarian society, with its village life and temple at the symbolic center. It is this envisioned past that, however deeply the externals have changed, became paradigmatic for contemporary politicians seeking religious endorsement of their policies and for monks who look to the state for protection of the Dhamma and support of the Sangha. The reemergence of belief in Sri Lanka as the *dhammadīpa* (the unique island of the Dhamma) was intrinsic to the early stirrings of nationalism and became a political issue of great importance beginning with the 1956 elections. And it continues to be a unifying element among Sinhala people in the state's definition of Sri Lanka as a Buddhist nation and triggers animosity from the militant Tamils who regard this as coercive hegemony.

As De Silva and Bartholomeusz indicate in their separate essays,[4] the religious justification of violence in the twenty-six-year war against the militant Tamils created a major ethical dilemma that many Sinhala Buddhists, monks especially, continue to wrestle with. The issue of how to reconcile canonically specific Buddhist teachings against the use of violence together with the active endorsement of violence, even if seen as a defensive posture, is taken seriously by many monks in high positions. As Bartholomeusz writes in an article on just-war ideology in Buddhism published separately: "It must be stressed . . . that those who make arguments for war based on their interpretation of Buddhism—also maintain that Buddhism demands compassion and nonviolence. How to balance the demands of nonviolence with the protection of the entire island of Sri Lanka as a Buddhist territory has remained a constant feature of political and religious rhetoric in Sri Lanka since at least the 1890s, when archival resources allow for a comprehensive view."[5]

This conflicting obligation presents a critical dilemma to many, though to others the path is less ambiguous. A small though vocal minority see "quashing" the Tamils as an imperative if the country and Buddhism are to survive, while others believe that the way of nonviolence is the only one to be followed. Those who take this second path underscore the moral and spiritual danger for Buddhism whenever monks are "dragged into partisan politics," as some of De Silva's monk-informants put it.

The positions represented by these informants reveal the complexity of how the Sangha's relationship to social problems is viewed by monks and laypeople, specifically how more sensitive Buddhists react to ethnically narrow Sinhala attitudes about the Tamils, not just toward the Liberation Tigers of Tamil Eelam (LTTE). While strident forms of Sinhala-Buddhist fundamentalism do exist, one also finds moderate positions, as may be seen in the following comment by a respected bhikkhu. In response to then-President Kumaratunga's vow to provide special protection to Buddhism, this monk believes that giving *foremost place* to any one religion is "wrong because it is against Buddhist philosophy, it has no moral justification, and it is an infringement of the basic rights of other religions."[6]

As will be noted at the end of this chapter, this bhikkhu's reply is in accord with Emperor Aśoka's expression of tolerance toward other religious sects, in contrast to the views of some monks and laypeople who see no alternative but total elimination of militant Tamils, revealing how fierce the ideology of Sinhala-Buddhist fundamentalism can be at its worst. In response to such chauvinism one finds similar strains within militant Tamil ethnocentrism, although they are rarely legitimated by religious precepts.

An extended quote from John Holt's essay underscores the necessity of seeing the *otherness* of people who come from different communities not as aliens but as those whose participation is essential to the meaning of an inclusive society. He notes, however, how difficult this is:

> The dilemma is this: How to construct an inclusive nationalist discourse which recognizes the importance of a Buddhist *historical* past yet transcends its fundamentalistic myth-and-ritual function as a blueprint for the present and future. That is: How is it possible to transcend the sacred canopy of Buddhist nationalist discourse so that a new, more inclusive discourse can recognize the diversity of Sri Lanka's various communities? . . . For centuries, as I have argued elsewhere, the genius of Sinhala-Buddhist culture was expressed through its remarkable inclusivity and assimilations. . . . An inclusive discourse that celebrates recognition of difference has the potential power to marginalize fundamentalistic and totalistic persuasions on the one hand, and militant separatists on the other. . . . What Sri Lanka might discover is not so much its image as the *dhammadīpa*, but its lost and more recent "image" as a model multiethnic and multireligious society.[7]

This vision of an inclusive society is no more the brainchild of the modern world than Sinhala-Buddhist fundamentalism is a new entry within the past century. There are strong precedents for both of these conflicting visions. For the latter, one finds threaded throughout the Sinhala chronicles (*Mahāvaṃsa*), which after all represent the worldview of the powerful Mahāvihāra sect, a continuing inclination to reinforce the privileged position of this most influential of all religious groups in the society over a long period of time.

This is not to make light of this sect's contribution to Buddhist culture—its literature, its magnificent art forms, its understanding of Buddhist philosophy, its influence on political decision-making and social policy, and at many points in time its ability to coexist harmoniously with other religious sects. This is what Holt identifies as the "remarkable inclusivity and assimilations" that have been a prominent part of Sinhala Buddhist history.[8]

The problem has been this same group's temptation, as is often the case with long-empowered groups (in the religious as in the political order), to allocate to themselves power, authority, and privilege. This does not mean that countervailing powers were nonexistent in the Sangha as a whole in Sri Lanka over these long centuries. What it does mean is that the dominant ideology of Sinhala Buddhism, clearly a Mahāvihāra vision, tended to prevail, and when fortified by political power brooked no competition, especially in times when the Buddhist Order and the sociopolitical fabric were threatened. It is no accident that this ideology surfaced anew in the middle period of British colonial rule and that one of its main grievances was the proselytizing of the Sinhala people by Christians. What the Bartholomeusz and De Silva analysis makes clear is not only that Sinhala-Buddhist fundamentalism, which emerged in the late nineteenth century, is very much alive but that its resurgence stimulated sectarian movements within other religions and that this sectarian spirit exacerbated the tensions that have thrived in recent decades.

What is also evident is that the voices of *fundamentalism* in Sinhala Buddhism, as in other religious communities, are not the only voices, for it is clear that some groups in Sri Lanka are strongly advocating a multiethnic society. De Silva's conversations with many bhikkhus provide evidence of that. At this point, it is well to identify some of the primary points of Tamil and Sinhala self-interest.

The first and overriding concern of Sinhala Buddhists is *the preservation of national identity and the achievement of viable unity.* To be successful, such a vision cannot be couched in monolithic terms, nor one that excludes or minimizes the importance of other religious or ethnic groups. In other words, it would need to embrace the actual pluralism that constitutes Sri Lankan society and that has been fundamental to its long history. Because *identity* is a protean concept, however, individuals, communities, and nations are continually reconstructing the shifting borders within which to define themselves on the basis of experience.

Of equal importance is *the restoration of Sri Lanka's former ability to engage in and promote harmonious relationships between and among various ethnic groups.* While many models of this capacity exist in Sri Lankan history, as well as instances to the contrary, central to the process of deconstructing history and reconstructing it is the ability to understand how some forces have engendered inclusivity and why others have fought against it. For this reason, it is imperative that Sri Lankan history, as found in the chronicles, the commentaries, the inscriptions, and especially some of the newly unearthed archeological evidence, be studied with dispassion and impartiality. This has been central to the intent of the previous five chapters in this book.

There is equal need for *a clearer discernment of the essence of Buddhism as a teaching and practice of the path of wisdom and compassion.* This does not mean to homogenize Buddhism but to contrast it with efforts to promote an ideologically driven vision and a social structure that safeguards positions of privilege and self-interest. While a touchy subject in Sri Lanka, as the levels of defensiveness are close to the surface, the resources within Buddhist teachings and practices are infinitely more generous minded, and many models of these resources in the past and the present day remain available.

The possibility exists for Sri Lanka to become once more a model of pluralism that fosters harmony and well-being, not divisiveness. Sri Lankans taking on such a challenge would need to recognize that there is no ongoing health in separatist or narrow sectarian positions. While this vision may at present seem impossibly remote to many of the religious communities and to each of the political parties, it is nevertheless required if Sri Lanka is to emerge from the rancor that has continued to suffocate it.

Among fundamental Tamil concerns and challenges, one might identify the following:

The right to and possibility of self-determination and self-empowerment within a larger Sri Lankan nation and body politic. Such a scenario would be one in which not only Tamils but all other ethnic groups are given voice, recognition, and adequate political representation. While this would mean the preponderance of Tamil influence in the northern and eastern regions, the same rights and opportunities for minority groups in these same areas would be required for minorities throughout the country. As a work in progress, the intent would be to foster strong unity among the many parts and at the same time realize the actual interdependence as both a fact and, in the long run, a much more expansive goal.

Guaranteeing the importance of human rights by means of adequate structures and an open and responsive process. It seems clear that Sri Lanka could learn from the struggles to achieve and protect such rights in other societies. The difficulty of approximating this goal is exceeded only by the necessity of aspiring to it. There is perhaps no more crucial task in the modern world than this, though it is naturally interconnected with other issues, such as the problems of overpopulation, threats to the environment, nuclear proliferation, ethnic communalism, and economic disparities, to mention but a few.

The continuing recognition and the strong encouragement of the best in Tamil cultural and religious traditions as a way of adding to the richness of Sri Lankan society. This would need to occur alongside similar forms of appreciating and encouraging Muslim, Christian, and Buddhist contributions to the social and cultural fabric of the society. There are increasing models of this around the world, though the counterexamples of religious prejudice and self-righteousness continue to abound.

The value of maintaining kinship with Tamils in South India in religion, culture, and history while at the same time making the effort to play a constructive role within the larger Sri Lankan mix. The fact that this sense of a larger identity has existed in the past is crucial to its being renewed in the future, though it can only occur within an ethos of trust. In the meantime, for understandable reasons, the lot of militant Tamils is cast primarily with their racial and historical ties with South India and with Tamils in diaspora. While models for a healthy sense of dual or multiple identities may be found elsewhere, for example, among the huge numbers of immigrants to the United States over two centuries and among more recent immigrants to parts of Europe and Canada, and while expanding the limits of one's self-identity is hardly free of tension, the process of stretching these boundaries helps to foster among individuals and within communities a greater capacity for openness, appreciation of diversity, and engagement with a process of inclusivity.

Among the world's remarkable examples of generosity of spirit and open-mindedness, combined with pragmatic good sense, is the 12th Rock Edict of the Emperor Aśoka, from the mid-third century BCE. The words in that proclamation provide a deeply humane perspective and are in contrast to the sectarian position of Sinhala-Buddhist fundamentalism. As Romila Thapar suggests, Aśoka's statement may have been inspired or prompted as a result of criticism from leaders of other sects. Even if this were the case, the nature of Aśoka's response is itself impressive. As Thapar says, it is "a direct and emphatic plea for toleration amongst the various sects . . . [not to be viewed as] a passive co-existence but an active frame of mind."[9] She is perceptive both in seeing Aśoka's view of Dhamma as a "policy of social responsibility" rather than an attempt to impose Buddhism on others in his empire and in regarding his motives as essentially "a plea for the recognition of the dignity of man, and for a humanistic spirit in the activities of society."[10]

Because Sinhala Buddhism recognizes Aśoka as the supreme paradigm of political wisdom and compassion, his words have often been taken with great seriousness. The fact that they are in contrast to the spirit with which many Buddhists in Sri Lanka have regarded people of other religious or ethnic traditions represents a significant departure from Buddhist tradition. The harshness in which fundamentalist judgment is sometimes couched has been justified by the claim that it is not Tamil religion or even Tamils as a people who are the problem but the terrorists among the Tamils, specifically the LTTE.

While this kind of distinction is important, it raises the question of how sectarian views and the politicizing of ethnic identity have contributed to recriminations by militant Tamils out of frustration with the frequent nonresponsiveness to expressed grievances. This is not to justify resorts to terrorist activity, but it does signal a lack of self-criticism and an inability to comprehend how one contributes to the kind of social climate and responsive order that the following of Aśoka's words envision:

> This progress of the essential doctrine takes many forms, but its basis is the control of one's speech, so as not to extoll one's own sect or disparage another's on unsuitable occasions, or at least to do so only mildly on certain occasions. On each occasion one should honour another man's sect, for by doing so one increases the influence of one's own sect and benefits that of the other man; while by doing otherwise one diminishes the influence of one's own sect and harms that of another man. Again, whosoever honours his own sect or disparages that of another man, wholly out of devotion to his own, with a view to showing it in a favorable light, harms his own sect even more seriously. Therefore, concord is to be commended, so that men may hear one another's principles and obey them. This is the desire of the Beloved of the Gods [Piyadassi], that all sects should be well-informed, and should teach that which is good, and that everywhere their adherents should be told, "The Beloved of the Gods does not consider gifts or honour to be as important as the progress of the essential doctrine of all sects."[11]

Clearly, these are words of aspiration; they are not descriptive of how religious communities typically relate to each other in the social order. And yet it was out of sobriety from seeing how his own troops had devastated another army that the powerful Aśoka envisioned another means of *conquest*, one referred to in this book's preface as a "conquest by Dhamma." In a sense, these are the words of a political realist who comes to an awareness that decimation of an enemy may as an ironic consequence wreak havoc on one's own people. It was not only a turning point in his life; it was the generating of a vision which, however rarely followed, remains a viable counterpoint to both cynicism and despair.

EPILOGUE

A VISION OF PLURALISM ENACTED

Jerri Hurlbutt

One spring morning, during a month-long stay at the Asian Rural Institute (ARI) in Tochigi, Japan, Bardwell L. Smith, distinguished professor of religion and Asian studies, was intently watching a very large sow who had just given birth to a squirming mass of piglets. His job was to alert someone immediately if she started to roll over onto her young, to prevent her from killing them with her weight. Over his long career in academia, Bardwell had traveled to Sri Lanka, Myanmar, Thailand, China, Japan, and most countries in Europe; led numerous student groups to programs in Asia; and been dean of the college. He had never, however, had this job, protecting a sow's young, which he took very seriously. His wife, Charlotte, across ARI's grounds, had also never had the job of shoveling chicken manure, but she, too, performed her task dutifully.

These were among Bardwell's recollections of his and Charlotte's time at ARI. While perhaps not exhibiting a direct relation to Sinhalese Buddhism and Sri Lankan history nor on the scale of scholarship covering centuries of these topics, the tasks that Bardwell and Charlotte performed reflect the everyday practice of a place Bardwell believes succeeds in carrying out a mission that remains elusive in contemporary Sri Lanka and, indeed, around the world: the fostering of inclusive, pluralistic community, where differences are valued, not a source of enmity and violence. Bardwell turned to his experiences at ARI and what this organization represents and practices as he was wrapping up the manuscript for this book, *Precarious Balance.*

Bardwell met the future founder of ARI, Toshihiro Takami, at Yale Divinity School, in 1960, when Takami was a student there and Bardwell a graduate-school tutor in Christian ethics. Rev. Dr. Takami returned to Japan and later founded ARI, in 1973. With the slogan "That We May Live Together," ARI exists to train women and men, primarily from Asia, Africa, and the Pacific region, "for a life of sharing." The institute offers instruction and practice, through community-based learning, in sustainable agriculture, rural leadership, and community building. It values the deep connections between food and life, spiritual growth, the dignity of labor, and the experience of sharing and growing food together.

To Bardwell, ARI is the example of successful interreligious pluralism; its founding included joint efforts by the National Christian Council in Japan and CARITAS Japan and the Buddhist group Rissho-Kosei-kai, a group Bardwell knew for its practical concerns regarding the well-being of the group and others in the community, working in poor urban areas, and with members of other religions. In addition, as described by Richard Gardner, in an article about ARI, the pluralism at the heart of ARI's mission has historical roots: "There is a sense . . . in which ARI may be trying to revive a form of tolerance and community that has little to do with humanism understood as a way of thought emerging in the West during the course of the Renaissance. Prior to the emergence of modern nation states, people of different faiths in many traditional societies lived together in communities that valued religious tolerance and mutual respect. Included here are many traditional societies . . . that are . . . now associated with violence rather than tolerance."[1]

Likewise, *Precarious Balance* traces the history of such pluralistic roots in Sri Lanka, with the hope that they can again be a resource for resolving conflicts on a larger scale that encompasses social, political, historical, and religious differences and experiences.

The pluralism at ARI is reflected not only in its founding but among the people who attend ARI. One attendee Bardwell met was a man from East Africa, a Muslim who had heard of ARI through a friend who had gone there. Bardwell asked him why he would be attracted to ARI, and he answered that people were welcoming of Muslims at ARI, unlike in East Africa. He related that his experience at ARI transcended previous interreligious encounters and was one he thought couldn't exist. Teaching there was practical and accepting of all forms of Christianity and Islam; people were genuinely open, kind, and respectful. This man's stay at ARI was made possible through others' financial donations, and others like him were able to attend through this generosity.

Bardwell stressed that what is important at ARI is the life experience of people—for example, dealing with animals and farming (as in his and Charlotte's tasks), not doctrine. People of all religious backgrounds, from all over the world, come to ARI. For Bardwell, ARI has one of the most expansive views of community he has witnessed, one the world is in desperate need of. While on a smaller scale than resolving centuries of political conflict, it gives one the experience of what he references in the preface: the "vision of an inclusive society."

In interviewing Bardwell for the epilogue to this book, it struck me that, whether in Sri Lanka or while at ARI in Japan, the common thread for him was not just this vision but the enactment—at ground level—of bridging differences between people, for the common good, without attempting to homogenize or eliminate such differences. The specifics of place, history, religion, and social and political status are inherent to and must be acknowledged in this pragmatic vision, but the goal is the same: the welfare of all, through our undeniable interdependence.

NOTES

1. Concepts of an Ideal Social Order as Portrayed in the Chronicles of Ceylon

1. The Venerable Walpola Rahula cites the main sources on which he based his *History of Buddhism in Ceylon:* namely, the Pāli Scriptures, the Aśokan Edicts, the Ceylon Inscriptions, the Pāli Commentaries, Sinhalese folktales, and miscellaneous works in Pāli and Sinhalese. Besides his work, most of the secondary sources used in this chapter also deal extensively with this material. While considerable work remains to be done on the whole period in question, present scholarship is based on a wealth of sources that corroborate and supplement the story told within the chronicles. See Rahula, *History of Buddhism in Ceylon,* xix.
2. Law, *On the Chronicles of Ceylon,* 43.
3. "For more than two thousand years the Sinhalese have been inspired by the ideal that they were a nation brought into being for the definite purpose of carrying the torch lit by the Buddha." Wijewardena, *The Revolt in the Temple, Dharma-Vijaya (Triumph of Righteousness),* 3.
4. Rahula, *History of Buddhism in Ceylon,* xxiv.
5. Law, introduction to the *Dīpavaṃsa,* 5.
6. Ludowyk, *The Footprint of the Buddha,* 11.
7. The discontinuities are no less apparent, but by comparison during the classical period they seem subdued. One observes them in the breakdown of dynasties, in the resolute but abortive resistance by orthodoxy to heretical doctrines, in the gradual decline of Sinhalese civilization itself beginning in the thirteenth century, to mention only three.
8. In an essay dealing in part with the influence of Indian thought on Sinhalese it is inevitable that both Sanskrit and Pāli terms be used and that occasionally the same term be rendered first in one, then in the other (e.g., *Dharma, Dhamma*). The spelling used depends on the context.
9. "Thus it was that a people who had very close cultural relations with each other were cast politically in the role of antagonists. By retaining their independence, the Sinhalese were enabled to develop their distinctive strand of civilization, though they owed much to Dravidian influences." Arasaratnam, *Ceylon,* 60.
10. Geiger, *Culture of Ceylon in Medieval Times,* 176.
11. The attainment of arahantship through beholding the miraculous, "with believing and joyous heart," need not be held inconsistent with the above, as this stage precedes that of final extinction. It should be noted, however, that the chronicles frequently record the mass attainment of arahantship in this manner. See *Mahāvaṃsa,* 217, for one example.

12. The locus classicus of this is the *Mahāparinibbāna Sutta* of the *Dīgha Nikāya;* see *Dialogues of the Buddha,* 2:108–9.
13. *Mahāvaṃsa,* 7:1–4, trans. 55. The responsibility is then delegated by Sakka to Vishnu.
14. Several studies have dealt with this subject in part, though no exhaustive treatment has yet appeared (as of this writing). Geiger's work mentioned above and an interesting article by Gokhale, "Early Buddhist Kingship," are two among many. The latter will be discussed later.
15. Paul Mus, preface to Sarkisyanz, *Buddhist Backgrounds of the Burmese Revolution,* vii.
16. *Cūlavaṃsa,* 38:19–28, trans. 29–31.
17. As we shall see later, through Mahayana influence he becomes both.
18. *Mahāvaṃsa,* 2:2, trans. 10.
19. Ludowyk, *Footprint of the Buddha,* 88.
20. Ludowyk, *Footprint of the Buddha,* 88. E. W. Adikaram shows how bhikkhus are encouraged in their efforts to lead a pure life by being reminded that they are "descended from the unbroken line of Mahāsammata," are grandsons of "the great king Suddhodana," and are younger brothers of Rāhulabhadda. See Adikaram, *Early History of Buddhism in Ceylon,* 126.
21. *Mahāvaṃsa,* 5:276, trans. 49.
22. Malalasekera, *The Pāli Literature of Ceylon,* 54. He goes on to document the measures used to suppress this dissent. It is only fair to indicate that the attacks were reciprocal.
23. *Mahāvaṃsa,* 17:3, trans. 116.
24. 377 BCE–1029 CE.
25. *Mahāvaṃsa* 31:89–90, trans. 216.
26. *Mahāvaṃsa,* 11:8–16, trans. 77–78.
27. *Mahāvaṃsa,* 11:32–35, trans. 80.
28. *Mahāvaṃsa,* 11:36, trans. 80. Rahula makes the point that it was Aśoka who also conferred the honorific term *Devānampiya* ("beloved of the gods") upon the Sinhalese king. While used in India even before Aśoka, it was probably not used as an honorific in Sri Lanka prior to this time. It was a term used of Aśoka himself and therefore reinforces the sense of continuity. See Rahula, *History of Buddhism in Ceylon,* 27.
29. Rahula, *History of Buddhism in Ceylon,* 59–60. Seven centuries later, the tide had reversed itself and various figures like Buddhaghosa in the fifth century CE made their way to Sri Lanka to translate the Sinhalese commentaries into Pāli and made their insight available beyond Lanka. With this event, symbolically, the wheel had turned full circle, so to speak.
30. Strong, *The Legend of King Aśoka,* 40.
31. Ludowyk, *Footprint of the Buddha* 23. The reference in the first sentence is to the Buddha's footprint on Adam's Peak in south central Sri Lanka.
32. Ludowyk, *Footprint of the Buddha,* 61.
33. *Mahāvaṃsa,* 5:188–89, trans. 42. As we shall see later when considering the concept of an ideal king, the epithets for such a figure are myriad. *Dhammarāja* is one; *priya-*

darsi rāja is another. The latter means "one who sees to the good of others" (i.e., the prototype of benevolence, apparently used only in reference to Aśoka). See Nikam and McKeon, eds. and trans., *The Edicts of Asoka,* 25–26.

34. Set into the poetic framework of the four cycles of history (the four *yugas*) we find the beginnings of a historiography that, while retaining much of the Brahmanic perspective, points forward to the expectation of the Buddha Metteyya and time's fulfillment, not unlike what occurred in later Hinduism in the *bhakti-mārga* of Rāmānuja and others.
35. *Mahāvaṃsa,* 1:3, trans. 1.
36. Rahula, *History of Buddhism in Ceylon,* 162.
37. Ludowyk, *Footprint of the Buddha,* 107–8.
38. Mark 5:1–20.
39. *Mahāvaṃsa,* 1:25, trans. 4.
40. *Dīpavaṃsa,* 12:32, trans. 201.
41. *Dīpavaṃsa,* 9:28–37, trans. 191. For a thorough discussion of the symbolism of the *yakkha* (Sanskrit, *yaksa*) motif, primarily in its Indian setting, see Coomaraswamy, *Yaksas.* The earliest edition was published in 1928.
42. According to Adikaram, the recitation of the *Parittas* (Protection Suttas) in Sri Lanka dates back at least to the late fourth century CE, though they are part of the Pāli canon itself. They are still used extensively. Originally, they had a public import and were chanted in times of famine, plague, or other ill. See Adikaram, *Early History of Buddhism in Ceylon,* 143–44.
43. *Mahāvaṃsa,* 36:133, trans. 266.
44. *Mahāvaṃsa,* 25:101–103, trans. 177. "Sitting then on the terrace of the royal palace, adorned, lighted with fragrant lamps and filled with many a perfume, magnificent with nymphs in the guise of dancing-girls, while he rested on his soft and fair couch, covered with costly draperies, he, looking back upon his victory, great though it was, knew no joy, remembering that thereby was wrought the destruction of millions (of beings)."
45. *Mahāvaṃsa,* 25:17, trans. 171.
46. *Mahāvaṃsa,* 25:109–112, trans. 178. Regarding the one and a half: "The one had come into the (three) refuges, the other had taken on himself the five precepts." A perceptive way of examining the several Dutthagāmanī myths and of seeing how mythic narratives influence written texts may be found in Gananath Obeyesekere's essay "Duṭṭhagāmaṇī and the Buddhist Conscience": "In other words, one could argue that the historical conditions of a period affect the myth—its forgetting, its recreation, its revival or the proliferation of its versions. However, the oral traditions are more vulnerable to social and historical change than written texts. When texts get written, they are frozen in time, and when they deal with issues of moral and cultural significance they take on a life of their own, becoming a part of a dialectic that may exist independent of historical context, dependent on a moral and political ideology. The moral significance of a myth helps it transcend a specific historical rootedness. Myth or versions thereof that arise in particular periods, especially if they are written, continue to coexist with others from earlier periods. This situation

naturally produces contradictions, differing or opposed versions that then produce more debates and newer versions of myths, or newer interpretations of old myths" (146–47).

47. Ludowyk, *Footprint of the Buddha,* 101.
48. Geiger, *Culture of Ceylon in Medieval Times,* 204.
49. *Dīpavaṃsa,* 3:53–54, trans. 151. The "norm" referred to is, of course, the Dhamma.
50. *Dīpavaṃsa,* 6:27–32, trans. 172–73.
51. *Dīpavaṃsa,* 6:44–45, trans. 174.
52. *Dīpavaṃsa,* 6:51, trans. 175. The *Mahāvaṃsa* likewise describes this scene and adds an account of how the paths of these two had crossed in an earlier life, confirming the destined nature of their meeting and of Nigrodha's preeminence. See *Mahāvaṃsa,* 5:37–72, trans. 29–32.
53. *Dīpavaṃsa,* 6:84–85, trans. 178. The story of royal support for the economic needs of the Sangha has been told by many; Geiger's book referred to above is one example. Through the tax structure, through land grants, through sizable endowments, among other measures, the Order received considerable fiscal assistance. Grants made to the bhikkhu community were known as *saṅgha-bhoga.* There also grew up the practice that whatever was produced in certain locales was for the *vihāra,* a practice known as *lābha-sīmā,* related as it was to the whole concept of *sīmā,* where boundaries of the Sangha are coextensive with the boundaries of the state. This kind of economic, social, and political power granted to the Order made it in time influential in the making of policy. It was a secular force, let alone a moral power of substance, that no king could ignore.
54. *Mahāvaṃsa,* 5:191–97, trans. 42–43. The immediate son and daughter in question were, of course, Mahinda and Samghamitta, who received the *pabbajjā,* or ordination into the Order, but by extension the same criterion of kinship applies to all parents.
55. The later section on the ideal king will sketch further aspects of the monarch's role as patron.
56. See Rahula, *History of Buddhism in Ceylon,* 75. The antiphonal nature of the oblation is caught in the *Cūlavaṃsa* description of Moggallāna's ascent to the throne: "He approached the community, greeted it respectfully and pleased with this community, he as a mark of distinction, presented it with his umbrella. The community returned it to him" (*Cūlavaṃsa,* 39:31–32, trans. 1, 46). The white parasol or umbrella (*seta chatta*) was traditionally the prime symbol of royal authority.
57. Malalasekera, *Pāli Literature of Ceylon,* 38.
58. Gokhale, "Early Buddhist Kingship," 15.
59. Gokhale, "Early Buddhist Kingship," 21.
60. Nikam and McKeon, *The Edicts of Asoka,* 64. Joseph M. Kitagawa has put it this way: "Asoka found in the Dharma a Universal principle, applicable both to religious and secular domains, as well as to all men, Buddhist and non-Buddhist alike." See his article "Buddhism and Asian Politics," *Asian Survey* 2, no. 5 (1962): 2.
61. Sarkisyanz, *Buddhist Backgrounds of the Burmese Revolution,* 56.

62. Nikam and McKeon, *The Edicts of Asoka,* 48.
63. Nikam and McKeon, *The Edicts of Asoka,* 48.
64. It goes without saying that these convictions are not developed "conceptually" either within the chronicles or within ancient Buddhist tradition. It is true, nonetheless, that the raw material for them may be found throughout the writings.
65. See Conze, "Dharma as a Spiritual, Social and Cosmic Force," in which he sees the same tripodic nature of the Buddhist orientation but develops it in a different direction.
66. Sarkisyanz, *Buddhist Backgrounds of the Burmese Revolution,* 41.
67. *Mahāvaṃsa,* 5:23, trans. 28.
68. *Mahāvaṃsa,* 28n1.
69. *Mahāvaṃsa,* 5:25–32, trans. 28.
70. *Mahāvaṃsa,* 11:8, trans. 77–78.
71. *Cūlavaṃsa,* 72:310–29, trans. 1, 347–48.
72. *Mahāvaṃsa,* 34:94, trans. 245.
73. *Mahāvaṃsa,* 21:34, trans. 145.
74. *Mahāvaṃsa,* 17:56, trans. 120; 31:125, trans. 219.
75. Admittedly a Mahayana claim, but made in other ways by Theravada.
76. *Mahāvaṃsa,* 29:18, trans. 192. See also 34:51–57, trans. 242. This has a connotation similar to that of the Old English word *weorthscipe* (worthiness), from which "worship" (or paying reverence to that which is worthy) is derived.
77. *Cūlavaṃsa,* 37:109, trans. 1, 10.
78. *Cūlavaṃsa,* 27:105–78, trans. 1, 9–17.
79. *Mahāvaṃsa,* 36:71–97, trans. 261–63.
80. *Cūlavaṃsa,* 37:108, trans. 1, 10.
81. *Cūlavaṃsa,* 37:180–81, trans. 1, 17.
82. *Cūlavaṃsa,* 51:124, trans. 1, 159.
83. Geiger, *Culture of Ceylon in Mediaeval Times,* 133.
84. *Cūlavaṃsa* 51:2–5, trans. 1, 147.
85. *Cūlavaṃsa,* 49:51–61, trans. 1, 132–33.
86. *Cūlavaṃsa,* 48:97, trans. 1, 119.
87. *Cūlavaṃsa,* 46:25–26, trans. 1, 100.
88. *Cūlavaṃsa,* 46:18, trans. 1, 99.
89. *Cūlavaṃsa,* 48:11, trans. 1, 111. He continues: "Therefore should a wise king ever practice piety; in every place where men dwell he will become renowned and finally, surrounded by his companions, he enters Nirvana." In a note (*Cūlavaṃsa,* trans. 1, 111n3) Geiger suggests the pragmatic advantages to a king to educate his people to piety, as it ensures order in the realm. No doubt there were monarchs who practiced piety for just this reason, as well as those whose practice was otherwise motivated.
90. *Mahāvaṃsa,* 31:126, trans. 219.
91. Mus, preface to Sarkisyanz, *Buddhist Backgrounds of the Burmese Revolution,* xviii.
92. Rahula, *History of Buddhism in Ceylon,* 62.
93. Sarkisyanz, *Buddhist Backgrounds of the Burmese Revolution,* 42.

94. Sarkisyanz, *Buddhist Backgrounds of the Burmese Revolution,* 42, quotes Mus, *Esquisse d'une Histoire du Bouddhisme,* 650, as saying that it was largely through the bodhisattva ethos that "Buddhism developed from an ethical sect into one of the *politically* most effective ethical systems in the world."
95. Sarkisyanz, *Buddhist Backgrounds of the Burmese Revolution,* 44.
96. For example, *Dhammarāja, Dhammiko Dhammarāja, Mahādhammarāja, Mahāsudassana, Mahāsattva, Bodhisattva, Cakkavatti (Cakravartin), Bodhisattvavātāra, Metteyya (Maitreya), Buddharāja,* etc.
97. Gokhale, "Early Buddhist Kingship," 22.
98. For a discussion of this concept, which may be compared with that of the New Jerusalem, see *The Questions of King Milinda,* trans. T. W. Rhys-Davids (New York: Dover, 1963), part 2, 208–43.
99. *Mahāvaṃsa,* 19:44, trans. 132.
100. *Mahāvaṃsa,* 19:58, trans. 133.

2. Kingship, the Sangha, and the Process of Legitimation in the Anurādhapura Period, Third Century BCE to Tenth Century CE

1. I am indebted to Peter Berger's discussion of the process of legitimation in his book *The Sacred Canopy: Elements of a Sociological Theory of Religion* (New York: Anchor Books, 1990); see especially 29–51. For an astute critique of broader aspects of Berger's thought, see Van A. Harvey, "Some Problematical Aspects of Berger's Theory of Religion," *Journal of the American Academy of Religion* 41, no. 1 (March 1973): 75–93.
2. *Dīgha Nikāya* (PTS ed. 3:80–98, trans. *Dialogues of the Buddha,* 3:76–89). See also Vishwanath Prasad Varma, "Studies in Hindu Political Thought and Its Metaphysical Foundations," *Journal of the Bihar Research Society* 38, parts 3–4 (1965): 454–66. As Varma says, "The 'law of the fishes' symbolizes the sheer prevalence of the cult of naked and unashamed force" (466). Or, from the *Rāmāyana,* trans. Ralph T. H. Griffith (London: Trübner, 1870–74), book ii, canto lxvii, p. 612: "In kingless lands no law is known, / And none may call his wealth his own; / Each preys on each from hour to hour, / As fish the weaker fish devour."
3. *The Laws of Manu,* trans. Georg Buhler (Oxford: Clarendon, 1886), 238. See also Jan Gonda, *Ancient Indian Kingship from the Religious Point of View* (Leiden: E. J. Brill, 1969), 3–6, 17–19.
4. *Mahāvaṃsa,* 4:1–44, trans. 19–23. The transliteration of Dharma (Sanskrit) or Dhamma (Pāli) will vary here according to the context referred to or the text cited.
5. *Mahāvaṃsa,* 7:1–5, trans. 55. The person referred to is Vijaya, who is said to have landed on Sri Lanka that same day, that of the Buddha's *parinibbāna.* Sakka (Indra) then handed over the guardianship to Vishnu (Upulvan). Indra is also seen as the god who makes possible the fecundity of nature, as he supplies both light and water. Kingship in association with Indra becomes, therefore, the bestower of blessings.
6. *Dīpavaṃsa,* 1:46–47, trans. 135. Also, *Mahāvaṃsa,* 15:160–65, trans. 108–9.
7. *Dīpavaṃsa,* 2:5, trans. 139. These mythic beings are to be seen not literally as beasts, but as symbols of disorder, whose power is sought in the Dhamma's behalf.

8. *Majjhima Nikāya* sutta 86 (PTS ed. 2:102), trans. *The Book of Middle Length Sayings,* trans. I. B. Horner (Bristol, UK: Pali Text Society, 1954–59), 2:288.
9. See Rahula, *History of Buddhism in Ceylon,* 39–41, for other examples in India and Sri Lanka of conquering and controlling "yaksas and nāgas." See also Edward Conze's essay "Dharma as a Spiritual, Social and Cosmic Force," in his *Further Buddhist Studies* (London: Bruno Cassirer, 1975). He writes: "Those parts of the world which have escaped the control of Dharma are marked by strife (*rana*) and turmoil (*damara*). On a more or less poetical and allegorical level this is often shown in the scriptures by contrasting the serenity, peace and harmony of the world which is dominated by the Buddhas and Bodhisattvas (who are channels through which the transcendental Dharma reaches the world) with what is going on in the hells or among Mara's hosts" (241).
10. *Mahāvaṃsa,* 15:56–172, trans. 101–9.
11. *Mahāvaṃsa,* 15:180–94, trans. 110–11.
12. *Cūlavaṃsa,* 37:105–98, trans. 1, 9–19.
13. Berger, *The Sacred Canopy,* 39.
14. *Mahāvaṃsa,* 1:3–4, trans. 1. See the section "The Extent and Legitimation of Power" later in this chapter for the way in which Sinhalese Buddhist ideology during this long period was strongly political in nature. See also chapter 1.
15. Berger, *The Sacred Canopy,* 33.
16. Berger, *The Sacred Canopy,* 36–37.
17. *Mahāvaṃsa,* 5:23, trans. 28. The verses that follow (24–33) are a delightful depiction of this organic harmony within the natural world.
18. *Mahāvaṃsa,* trans. 28n1.
19. *Mahāvaṃsa,* 15:38–40, trans. 94. Besides the devatās, the nāgas and their mortal foes (the *supannas*) also heard and were converted.
20. *Mahāvaṃsa,* 31:84, trans. 216.
21. *Mahāvaṃsa,* 30:99, trans. 208.
22. *Udāna,* 8.3; trans. *The Minor Anthologies of the Pali Canon,* part 2, *Udāna: Verses of Uplift and Itivuttaka: As It Was Said,* trans. F. W. Woodward (London: Geoffrey Cumberlege, 1948), 98.
23. Senarat Paranavitana, *Sinhalayo,* 2nd ed. (Colombo: Department of Archaeology, 1970), 20.
24. A. D. T. E. Perera, "Buddha on the Sacred Seat of Brahma" *World Buddhism* 21 (May 1973): 38.
25. A. D. T. E. Perera, "Buddha on the Sacred Seat of Brahma," 43. Kailāsa is the mountain paradise of Shiva, lying in Hindu cosmography to the east of Mount Meru. See Himansu Bhusan Sarkar, "The Evolution of Śiva-Buddha Cult in Java," *Journal of Indian History* 45 (1967): 637–46, for the opposite process, that is, the adoption of Buddha into the Hindu pantheon as one of the ten Avatāras of Vishnu. This happened by the eleventh century CE, if not earlier. See Senarat Paranavitana, *Ceylon and Malaysia* (Colombo: Lake House Investments, 1966), 202–3, for an interesting statement on the development of the cosmic mountain theme in Southeast Asian Buddhist art.

26. Rahula, *History of Buddhism in Ceylon,* 62.
27. *Dīgha Nikāya* sutta 17, PTS ed. 2:169–99, trans. *Dialogues of the Buddha* 2:199–232; and sutta 30, PTS ed. 3:142–79, trans. *Dialogues of the Buddha,* 3:137–67.
28. U. N. Ghoshal, "Principle of the King's Righteousness," *Indian Historical Quarterly* 32 (1956): 309. One ruling over the four quarters was called *digvijayin.*
29. Paranavitana, *Ceylon and Malaysia,* 26. Kuvera (Kubera) is the god of wealth, whose paradise is Alaka.
30. Senarat Paranavitana, *The Story of Sigiri* (Colombo: Lake House Investments, 1972), 22. In general, both the Buddhists and the Jains rejected the divinity of kings, though the evidence is less clear than orthodoxy implies. Paranavitana's speculations on this topic have been subject to much criticism. See Sirima Kiribamune, "Some Reflections on Professor Paranavitana's Contribution to History," *Ceylon Journal of the Humanities* 1, no. 1 (January 1970): 76–92.
31. *The Laws of Manu,* 396.
32. Balakrishna, "The Evolution of the State," *Indian Historical Quarterly* 3 (1927): 325. The passage referred to is *Śukranīti,* 1:375.
33. Berger, *The Sacred Canopy,* 35–36.
34. This is fully discussed in a number of studies. See Hettiarachchy, *History of Kingship in Ceylon,* 6–64; Geiger, *Culture of Ceylon in Medieval Times,* 111–32; Paranavitana, *The University of Ceylon History of Ceylon;* Ellawala, *Social History of Early Ceylon,* 11–27.
35. See Indrapala, *The Collapse of the Rajarata Civilization and the Drift to the South-West.*
36. As expressed in one famous maxim: "Watch for the weaknesses of others as a hawk watches its prey. And conceal your own weaknesses as a tortoise hides its soft body."
37. *Cūlavaṃsa,* 66:126–581, trans. 1, 263–66. See also pages vi and xiv.
38. See *Cūlavaṃsa,* 52:37–41, trans. 1, 165–66, where it is said that Kassapa was "versed in statecraft" as well as being "a mine of virtues." Regarding Dhātusena, see *Cūlavaṃsa,* 38:14–28, trans. 1, 29–31, in which his uncle perceives that the boy Dhātusena "must be made a master in state-craft." The political aim of the chroniclers has been capably discussed by Heinz Bechert, who writes in his essay, "The Beginnings of Buddhist Historiography" that "the basic idea of this ideology was that of the unity of nation and religion" (7).
39. *Cūlavaṃsa,* 1, 67n8.
40. *Mahāvaṃsa,* 36 :110–37:31, trans. 264–69.
41. Extension of royal power came also through capable administration of justice, through the regular process of succession to the throne and through the power to make appointments to important positions and to make summary dismissals.
42. U. D. Jayasekera, *Early History of Education in Ceylon* (Colombo: Department of Government Affairs, Government of Ceylon, 1969), 53.
43. Ghoshal, "Principle of the King's Righteousness," 306–7. See also John W. Spellman, *Political Theory of Ancient India: A Study of Kingship from the Earliest Times to circa A.D 300* (Oxford: Clarendon Press, 1964), 211–219. Also, the *Cakkavatti-Sīhanāda Sutta Dīgha Nikāya* sutta 26 (PTS ed. 4:59–76, trans. *Dialogues of the Buddha,* sutta

26, 3:53–76); and *The Sutra of Golden Light [Suvarṇaprabhāsa Sūtra]*, trans. R. E. Emmerick (London: Luzac and Co., 1970), 57–62.

44. See B. P. Sinha, "The King in the Kautilyan State," *Journal of the Bihar Research Society* 40 (1954): 291–308, and U. N. Ghoshal, "An Aspect of State Administration in the Pre-Maurya Period-Influence of Public Opinion on Kingly Governments," *Journal of Indian History* 40 (1962): 551–55.
45. Hettiarachchy, *History of Kingship in Ceylon*, 143. This is a capable study of this subject. Especially excellent is his chapter "The Relationship between the King and the Sangha," 116–43, which is one of the more perceptive analyses of this topic that exists. It restricts itself, however, to the period before the fourth century CE.
46. Berger, *The Sacred Canopy*, 32.
47. Ping-ti Ho and Tang Tsou, eds., *China in Crisis*, vol. 1, *China's Heritage and the Communist Political System* (Chicago: University of Chicago Press, 1968), 279.
48. Rahula, *History of Buddhism in Ceylon*, 251–52. The reference here is to the *Sigālovada Sutta* of the *Dīgha-Nikāya* (sutta 31, PTS ed. 3:180–93, trans. *Dialogues of the Buddha*, 3:173–84). The Sigāla Homily is, of course, among the most important suttas for expressing the nature of true reciprocity, though it focuses on what it means for the layperson in the relationships of the "six quarters" (i.e., between parents and children, teachers and pupils, husband and wife, friend and friend, master and servant, laypeople and religious "recluses and brahmins").
49. S. J. Tambiah, "The Ideology of Merit," in *Dialectic in Practical Religion*, ed. E. R. Leach (Cambridge: University of Cambridge Press, 1968), 116. For the growth of the concept of merit in postcanonical Theravada texts, see the article by Heinz Bechert, "Notes on the Formation of Buddhist Sects and the Origins of Mahāyāna," in *German Scholars on India: Contributions to Indian Studies*, vol. 1, especially 16–17 (Varanasi: Chowkhamba Sanskrit Series Office, 1973).
50. *Dīpavaṃsa*, 6:84–85, trans. 178. The gift in that particular instance, apparently unsolicited from the monks, was said to be eighty-four thousand monasteries, a figure merely symbolic of his attested munificence.
51. *Mahāvaṃsa*, 5:193–97, trans. 43.
52. *Mahāvaṃsa*, 28:44, trans. 190.
53. *Mahāvaṃsa*, 31:126, trans. 219; cf. 27:48, trans. 186.
54. *Cūlavaṃsa*, 1, 10nn1–2.
55. *Mahāvaṃsa*, 36:38, trans. 258. See also Malalasekera, *The Pāli Literature of Ceylon*, 51, who says that this custom existed before this time and also continues to be practiced today. As he was dying, Dutthagāmanī expressed his fear of death to the bhikkhu Therasutābhaya, who comforted him and assured him of his great merit. The catalog of his good deeds was then read to him out of the "Merit Book" (*puññapotthaka*), which kings and other laypeople often kept. As Geiger indicates in his introduction to the *Cūlavaṃsa* (iv–v), the source materials available to the compiler were mainly *puññapotthakāni*, that is, "registers of meritorious works by which the prince had furthered the Church (*sāsana*) and the laity (*loka*)."
56. Nikam and McKeon, *The Edicts of Asoka*, 46–47.
57. Berger, *The Sacred Canopy*, 40–41.

58. Rahula, *History of Buddhism in Ceylon*, 74.
59. Senarat Paranavitana, "Civilisation of the Polonnaru Period: Religion, Literature and Art," in *History of Ceylon*, ed. H. C. Ray, vol. 1, part 1 (Colombo: Ceylon University Press, 1959), 384.
60. For a suggestive interpretation of the protection ceremonies and the cosmic calendrical rites, which aim to ensure both public and private benefits, see Tambiah, "The Ideology of Merit," 118–20. In this section he writes: "Man, too, subjects himself to the moral order in these cosmic rites; his merit-making and selfless giving of gifts express this subjection; the Buddhist monk, through his form of ascetic subjection, appropriately chants and preaches about the Buddha's conquest of desire, pain and death. Perhaps at the back of these religious actions are the basic ethical ideas that man transcends his limitations by subjecting his animal nature, that it is by freely giving that he receives bountifully, that by refusing the grosser things in life he measures the value of life, and that by harnessing and releasing ethical energy, nature and agencies external to man can be brought into a single harmonious order. It is in this sense that Buddhist cosmic rites are not manipulative or instrumental in the manner of spirit cults or 'magical' rites. And this is why Buddhist values and action necessarily have a higher place in the hierarchy of values and acts that comprise the universe of religious action. . . . On the other hand, a coercive relationship of bargaining with spirits, their placation or domination, is again a statement of power relations that are an extension of and a contrast to the socially normal manipulative behavior. . . . However ethically valued, both are stubbornly present in real life—for if either gains supremacy life will be heaven on earth or pure hell; both are improbable."
61. Conze, "Dharma as a Spiritual, Social and Cosmic Force," 250.
62. Hans-Dieter Evers, *Monks, Priests and Peasants: A Study of Buddhism and Social Structure in Central Ceylon* (Leiden: E. J. Brill), 1972.

3. Varieties of Religious Assimilation in Early Medieval Sri Lanka

1. Dirian K. Dohanian, "Prolegomena to the Study of the Mahāyāna in Ancient Ceylon," in *India's Contribution to World Thought and Culture* (Vivekananda Commemoration Volume), ed. S. Vivekananda and L Chandra (Madras: Vivekananda Rocke Memorial Committee, 1970), 433.
2. R.A. L. H. Gunawardana, "Before the State: An Early Phase in the Evolution of Political Institutions in Ancient Sri Lanka," *Studies in History* 4, no. 2 (1982): 200.
3. Edward Shils, "Centre and Periphery," in *The Logic of Personal Knowledge: Essays Presented to Michael Polanyi on His Seventieth Birthday*, edited by Polanyi Festschrift Committee (London: Routledge and Kegan Paul, 1961): 117.
4. Shils, "Centre and Periphery," 123–24. His entire essay is germane to this particular issue.
5. S. N. Eisenstadt, "Some Observations on the Dynamic of Traditions," *Comparative Studies in Society and History: An International Quarterly* 2 (1969): 458. This essay is

reprinted in Bardwell L. Smith, ed., *Religion and Legitimation of Power in Thailand, Laos and Burma* (Chambersburg, PA: Wilson Books, 1977).

6. To those familiar with H. Richard Niebuhr's typological study entitled *Christ and Culture* (New York: Harper and Brothers, 1951), in which he develops brilliantly a spectrum involving five primary positions, my indebtedness to his approach will be clear. For many reasons, the same kind of approach would not work with Sinhalese Buddhism, but I have deliberately used his categories, adding one more, as a way of depicting the diversity of stances within a completely different religious tradition.
7. See Sukumar Dutt, *The Buddha and the Five After-Centuries* (London: Luzac, 1957) for a stimulating but inconclusive approach to this subject.
8. *Cūlavaṃsa*, 41:38–39, trans. 1, 55.
9. See *Nikāya Sangrahāwa, Being A History of Buddhism in India and Ceylon,* trans. C. M. Fernando, rev. and ed. W. F. Gunawardhana (Colombo: H. C. Cottle, 1908). Also *A Manual of Buddhist Historical Literature (Saddhamma-Samgaha),* trans. Bimala Churn Law (Calcutta: University of Calcutta, 1941).
10. For fuller discussion of this, one may consult the following: Adikaram, *Early History of Buddhism in Ceylon;* Rahula, *History of Buddhism in Ceylon;* Malalasekera, *The Pāli Literature of Ceylon;* Godakumbura, *Sinhalese Literature.*
11. *Nikāya Sangrahāwa,* xxx–xxxi. For a more sophisticated and extended explanation of what happened to the structure of the Sangha and its sectarian nature, see R. A. L. H. Gunawardana, *Robe and Plough: Monasticism and Economic Interest in Early Medieval Sri Lanka* (Tucson: University of Arizona Press, 1979).
12. See *The Katikāvatas: Laws of the Buddhist Order of Ceylon from the 12th to the 18th Century,* translated and edited by Nandasena Ratnapala (Munich: Kitzinger, 1971). An important distinction exists between *sāsana katikāvatas* and *vihāra katikāvatas* in that the latter apply only to local or sectarian branches of the Sangha.
13. For an analysis of this interesting movement, see Steven E. G. Kemper, "Buddhism without Bhikkhus: The Sri Lanka Vinaya Vardena Society," in *Religion and Legitimation of Power in Sri Lanka,* ed. Bardwell L. Smith, 212–35 (Chambersburg, PA: Anima Books, 1978). For an excellent study of the forest monks, see Michael Carrithers, *The Forest Monks of Sri Lanka: An Anthropological and Historical Study* (Delhi: Oxford University Press, 1983).
14. *Cūlavaṃsa* 37:51, trans. 1, 1.
15. For a survey of the "evolution of Sinhalese sculpture," which sheds light on the repeated Indian artistic influences, see Nandadeva Wijesekera, *Early Sinhalese Sculpture* (Colombo: M. D. Gunasena, 1962), 121–74.
16. Panditha, "Buddhism during the Polonnaruva Period," in "The Polonnaruva Period," special issue, *Ceylon Historical Journal* 4, nos. 1–4 (July 1954–April 1955), 125. See also Paranavitana's article "The Art and Architecture of the Polonnaruva Period" (plus numerous plates) in the same special issue on "The Polonnaruva Period," *Ceylon Historical Journal* 4, nos. 1–4 (July 1954–April 1955). For bronze images especially, see P. Sarvesvara Iyer, "Puranic Saivism in Ceylon during the Polonnaruwa Period", in *Proceedings of the 1st Conference-Seminar of Tamil Studies, University of*

Malaya, Kuala Lumpur. International Association of Tamil Research 1 (1968): 462–74; and Sir P. Arunachalam, "Polonnaruwa Bronzes and Siva Worship and Symbolism," *Journal of the Royal Asiatic Society (Ceylon Branch)* 24, no. 68 (1915–16): 189–222 (plus numerous plates).

17. Nandasena Mudiyanse, *Mahāyāna Monuments in Ceylon* (Colombo: M. D. Gunasena, 1967), 11. See also P. E. E. Fernando, "Tantric Influence on the Sculptures at Gal Vihāra, Polonnaruva," *University of Ceylon Review* 18 (1960): 50–66; and S. Paranavitana, "Mahayanism in Ceylon," *Ceylon Journal of Science* 2 (1928): 35–71, in which he first gives a historical sketch of Mahayana in Sri Lanka (noting its particular strength in the third, sixth, and ninth centuries because of Indian influences) and then focuses on the bodhisattva cults (especially those of Nātha or Avalokiteśvara and of Sumana or Samantabhadra) that emerged in the Polonnaruva period, or slightly before, and thrived through the fifteenth century.

18. O. H. de A. Wijesekera, "Sanskrit Civilization among the Ancient Sinhalese," *Ceylon Historical Journal* 1, no.1 (1951): 23–29.

19. Dohanian, "Prolegomena to the Study of the Mahāyāna in Ancient Ceylon," in *India's Contribution to World Thought and Culture,* edited by Lokesh Chandra (New Delhi: Archaeological Survey of India, 1970), 428.

20. *The Dāthāvaṃsa: A History of the Tooth-Relic of the Buddha,* ed. and trans. Bimala Churn Law (Lahore: Motilal Banarsidas, 1925).

21. *The Chronicle of the Thūpa and the Thūpavaṃsa,* edited and translated by N. A. Jayawickrama (London: Luzac, 1971). In a similar way, another chronicle written during this same reign, the *Hatthavanagallavihāravaṃsa,* serves to associate the saint-king Sirisamghabodhi (247–49 CE), the account of whose short reign comprises two-thirds of the text, with Parākramabāhu II, the high point of whose pious career is the miracle of the Tooth Relic described in the final chapter of this chronicle (as well as in chapter 82 of the *Cūlavaṃsa,* translated at 2, 143–47). See *Hatthavanagallavihāravaṃsa,* edited by C. E. Godakumbura, translated by James d'Alwis (London: Luzac, 1956).

22. See *Cūlavaṃsa,* 74:243, trans. 2, 43, along with Geiger's note 2; as well as 85:33, trans. 2, 162; 85:121, trans. 2, 170.

23. Senarat Paranavitana, *The God of Adam's Peak* (Ascona, Switzerland: Artibus Asiae, 1958), 71–73. Other important treatments of the fusing of Buddhist belief and practice with both indigenous and Brahmanic or Hindu traditions are the following: Paranavitana, *The Shrine of Upulvan at Devundara* (Colombo: Ceylon Government Press, 1953); Coomaraswamy, *Yaksas;* Richard F. Gombrich, *Precept and Practice: Traditional Buddhism in the Rural Highlands of Ceylon* (Oxford: Clarendon, 1971), especially his chapters "The Buddha," 80–143, and "A Sketch of the Universe as Seen from Mīgala," 144–213, in which he depicts the rich composite of traditional Buddhist practices and beliefs alongside the coexistence of folk religion, Hindu ingredients, and diverse forms of Buddhist ritual and belief that constitute the Sinhalese tradition; M. B. Ariyapala, *Society in Mediaeval Ceylon: The State of Society in Ceylon as Depicted in the Saddharmaratnavaliya and Other Literature of the Thirteenth Century* (Colombo: Department of Cultural Affairs, 1956), 179–249; and Senarat Pa-

ranavitana, "Pre-Buddhist Religious Beliefs in Ceylon," *Journal of the Royal Asiatic Society (Ceylon Branch)* 31, no. 82 (1929): 302–27.

24. Hans-Dieter Evers, *Monks, Priests and Peasants: A Study of Buddhism and Social Structure in Central Ceylon* (Leiden: E. J. Brill, 1970).
25. Obeyesekere, "The Buddhist Pantheon in Ceylon and Its Extensions," in *Anthropological Studies in Theravada Buddhism*, ed. Manning Nash (New Haven, CT: Yale University Press, 1966), 1–26.
26. Obeyesekere, "The Great Tradition and the Little in the Perspective of Sinhalese Buddhism," *Journal of Asian Studies* 22, no. 2 (February 1963): 144.
27. Obeyesekere, "The Great Tradition," 144. See also Michael M. Ames, "Ritual Prestations and the Structure of the Sinhalese Pantheon" in Nash, *Anthropological Studies in Theravada Buddhism*, 27–50; Edmund R. Leach, "Pulleyar and the Lord Buddha: An Aspect of Religious Syncretism in Ceylon," *Psychoanalysis and the Psychoanalytical Review* 49 (1962): 80–102, which shows how the Hindu god Ganesha (son of Shiva and brother of Skanda) becomes Pulleyar, a feudal dependent of the Lord Buddha among Buddhists in North Ceylon; Nur Yalman, "The Structure of Sinhalese Healing Rituals," *Journal of Asian Studies* 23 (June 1964): 115–50; Michael M. Ames, "Buddha and the Dancing Goblins: A Theory of Magic and Religion," *American Anthropologist* 66 (1964): 75–82; and Richard Gombrich, "The Consecration of a Buddhist Image," *Journal of Asian Studies* 26, no. 1 (November 1966): 23–36.
28. Obeyesekere, "The Great Tradition," 145–46. Another interesting paper by Obeyesekere, "Social Change and the Deities: The Rise and Fall of Deities in the Sinhalese Buddhist Pantheon," unpublished manuscript, read at a symposium held at Swarthmore College (April 1972), traces, among other things, the dramatic rise in the influence of Skanda (the god of Kataragama) in recent times and analyzes some of the factors behind this.
29. Aside from the several titles mentioned in note 22, see the following: (1) Heinz Bechert, "Eine alte Gottheit in Ceylon and Südindien," *Beitraäge zur Geistesgeschichte Indiens, Wiener Zeitschrift fur die Kunde Süd- und Ostasiens* 12–13 (1968–69): 33–42, which examines with great care the evolving identification of the North Indian god Skandakumāra with South Indian and Ceylonese gods of a similar nature from the fourteenth century on; (2) Gananath Obeyesekere, "The Pataha Ritual: Genesis and Function," *Spolia Zeylanica* 30, part 2 (1965): 279–96, spells out the nature of a ceremony of first fruits after the harvest or "in times of crisis like pestilence, famine and drought" (with the goddess Pattini presiding) in which a major theme is the tension between kingship as traditionally legitimated and kingship gone astray, a theme fitting into the *danda-dhamma* tension but also showing how ritual often inverts the meaning of myth, exposes its nonconformance with reality, and acts as an assimilating agency of new ingredients over time; (3) Gananath Obeyesekere, "Gajabāhu and the Gajabāhu Synchronism: An Inquiry into the Relationship between Myth and History," *Ceylon Journal of the Humanities* 1, no. 1 (January 1970): 25–56, reprinted in *Religion and Legitimation of Power in Sri Lanka*, ed. Bardwell L. Smith, 155–76, which shows the evolution of the Gajabāhu story from a matter-of-fact account within the chronicles to an elaborate myth in the *Pūjāvaliya* in the reign

of Parākramabāhu II (1236–70 CE) and especially in the *Rājāvaliya* four centuries later, an evolution providing major evidence of a dynamic ritualistic process at work in which South Indian and Sinhalese elements on the one hand and diverse religious and mythic ingredients on the other were gradually amalgamated; (4) H. L. Seneviratne, "The Āsala Perahāra in Kandy," *Ceylon Journal of Historical and Social Studies* 6, no. 2 (July–December 1963): 169–80, and also his book *Rituals of the Kandyan State* (Cambridge: Cambridge University Press, 1978), both of which depict the subsuming of Hindu gods and the provincial chiefs to the centralizing process at work in Kandyan Buddhism and Kandyan political administration; and (5) Paul Wirz, *Kataragama: The Holiest Place in Ceylon,* 2nd ed. (Colombo: Lake House Investments, 1972), which examines briefly what has become the most popular pilgrimage place for Buddhists, Hindus, and Muslims in Sri Lanka, resulting in a fusing of pietistic beliefs and practices on the folk level (alongside deliberate attempts at retaining distinctions) centered on the god Kataragama (Kārttikeya, Subrahmanya, Skanda, Murukan).

30. Obeyesekere, "Social Change and the Deities," 41. See also Kitsiri Malalgoda, "Millennialism in Relation to Buddhism," *Comparative Studies in Society and History* 12, no. 4 (October 1970): 424–41, which examines the way millennial expectations emerge with the rise of frustrations when a community's image of its identity clashes with the actual reality it faces in periods of self-confusion and rapidly increasing pluralism. The relevance of this phenomenon to Sinhalese Buddhism's long-term stress on its guardian deities is of great importance. The essay by Obeyesekere on the Gajabāhu synchronism, mentioned in note 28, is very much to the point here.
31. Gananath Obeyesekere, "Theodicy, Sin and Salvation in a Sociology of Buddhism," in *Dialectic in Practical Religion,* ed. E. R. Leach (Cambridge: Cambridge University Press, 1968), 7–40.
32. Michael M. Ames, "Magical-Animism and Buddhism: A Structural Analysis of the Sinhalese Religious System," in "Aspects of Religion in South Asia," *Journal of Asian Studies* 23 (1964): 47.
33. Obeyesekere, "The Pataha Ritual," 294. See also John Halverson, "Dynamics of Exorcism: The Sinhalese Sanniyakuma," *History of Religions* 10, no. 4 (May 1971): 334–59, which describes at length how the demonic (specifically here the *sanniyaku* or demons of ill health) is assimilated in ritualistic fashion and is thereby domesticated. The process is one that combines the need for integration and individuation, a process having psychic, communal, and cosmic dimensions.
34. Frank E. Reynolds, "Dhammadīpa: A Study of Indianization and Buddhism in Sri Lanka," *Ohio Journal of Religion* 2, no. 1 (April 1974): 63–78. See also Lowell W. Bloss, "The Buddha and the Nāga: A Study in Buddhist Folk Religiosity," *History of Religions* 13, no. 1 (August 1973): 36–53, which shows how Buddhism relates to other religious phenomena not simply by a process of accretion or assimilation but often by a kind of dialectic or tension whereby it accepts and at the same time rejects elements of popular belief and practice, in different ways and at different times.
35. Diran K. Dohanian, "The Wata-dā-ge in Ceylon: The Circular-Relic-House of

Polonnaruwa and Its Antecedents," *Archives of Asian Art* 23 (1969–70): 37. For an extensive treatment of this subject, see his doctoral dissertation (Harvard University, 1964), entitled "The Mahāyāna Buddhist Sculpture of Ceylon." See note 16 above for a similar judgment on Mahayana's impact.

36. Senarat Paranavitana, "The Significance of Sinhalese 'Moonstones,'" *Artibus Asiae* 17 (1954): 197–231.
37. I am indebted to Eric Voegelin's discussion of the relationship between the symbolic and the nonsymbolic. See his *Order and History (*Baton Rouge: Louisiana State University Press, 1956), 1–11.
38. Paul Mus, "Bouddhisme et monde occidental: Pour une nouvelle méthode," in *Présence du Bouddhisme,* ed. Rene Berval (Saigon: France-Asie, 1959), 187–200. Without question, the most comprehensive and perceptive study of this entire subject is Paul Mus, *Barabudur: Esquisse d'une histoire du Bouddhisme fondée sur la critique archeologique des textes,* 2 vols. (Hanoi: Imprimerie d'Extrême-Orient, 1935).
39. H. A. L. Fisher, *A History of Europe* (London: Edward Arnold, 1936), v.

4. The Pursuit of Equilibrium

1. Paul Wheatley, *The Pivot of the Four Quarters* (Chicago: Aldine, 1971), 225–26. For shorter treatments of related topics, see Shils, "Centre and Periphery," 117–30; S. N. Eisenstadt, "Some Observations on the Dynamic of Traditions," *Comparative Studies in Society and History: An International Quarterly* 2 (1969): 451–75; and Robert Redfield and Milton Singer, "The Cultural Role of Cities," *Economic Development and Cultural Change* 3, no. 1 (1954): 53–72.
2. Because of the thematic approach to this subject a variety of materials have been used to formulate the problems and explore their several dimensions. Basic to the study are primary materials such as the *Cūlavaṃsa, Nikāya Sangrahāwa, Rājāvaliya, Hatthavanagallavihāravaṃsa,* the first two of the *Sāsana Katikāvatas* in the Polonnaruva period, and, for historical perspective, the *Dīpavamsa, Mahāvaṃsa, Dāthāvaṃsa, Thūpavaṃsa,* and the *Saddhamma-Sangaha.* Portions of other pertinent materials from Pāli and Sinhalese literature, as well as Sanskrit, have been consulted. Also of major importance is the standard University of Ceylon *History of Ceylon,* vol. l, parts 1 and 2, edited by H. C. Ray, which covers in detail the political and cultural history of this age and of the Anurādhapura period. Beyond these are a number of basic monographs covering shorter periods of time or specialized subjects. While several have been published, some that are of equal importance appear only in doctoral dissertation form. Finally, the relevant journals have also been important to this study, including those that discuss inscriptional materials. Beyond these more obvious sources, because of the nature of the topic, use has been made of other materials that help to illuminate aspects of the pluralism that thrived during this period. These fall essentially into two categories: anthropological and archeological. While the latter can be used with considerably more precision in understanding various developments during this period, the former, if used with caution, provide insight into the dynamics that have constituted Sinhalese Buddhism's

relation to folk religious elements, Brahmanism and bhakti forms of Hinduism, and the continuing waves of Mahayana Buddhism that influenced the essentially Theravada tradition in Sri Lanka. There is no lack of historic evidence in the documents, inscriptions, and archeological remains about these several influences, but they are provided considerable perspective by the anthropological studies of scholars such as Obeyesekere, Leach, H. L. Seneviratne, Yalman, Tambiah, Gombrich, Evers, Ames, and others.

3. In his article "The Capital of Ceylon during the Ninth and Tenth Centuries," *Ceylon Journal of Science* (Section C. Anthropology) 2 (1930): 141–47, Paranavitana makes a reasonable case for Anurādhapura's remaining the capital, however precarious its hold during those two centuries.
4. This essay was written as a counterpart to another one, in which primary and secondary materials for examining the theme of identity and pluralism in tension in this period are examined extensively. See Bardwell L. Smith, "The Polonnaruva Period (ca. 993–1293 A.D.): A Thematic Bibliographic Essay," in *Religion and Legitimation of Power in Sri Lanka*, ed. Smith, 119–54 (Chambersburg, PA: Anima, 1978.)
5. This may be compared with the policy of monarchs who fostered the interdependence of these regions, with Rājarattha remaining the *primus inter pares*. For example, see the stance of Sena I (833–53 CE) as described in the *Cūlavaṃsa*, 50: 51–60, trans. 1, 143–43, and the response of Udaya II (885–96 CE), whenever someone tries to upset the political balance among the three kingdoms (*Cūlavaṃsa*, 51:94:–136, trans. 1, 157–60). To be fair to Parākramabāhu I, the beginning of the end of the tripartite policy was visible in the post–Vijayabāhu I era. See *Cūlavaṃsa*, chap. 60, trans. 1, 214–24. Even in Vijayabāhu's time there was "the inauguration of a policy of administrative centralization which did away with the large degree of autonomy which the provinces, particularly Rohana, had previously enjoyed" (Ray, *History of Ceylon*, vol. 1, part 2, 428).
6. B. J. Perera, "Some Political Trends in the Late Anuradhapura and Polonnaruwa Period," *Ceylon Historical Journal* 10, nos. 1–4 (1961): 60–76. See also S. Pathmanathan, "Social and Religious Conditions under Cola Rule in Sri Lanka (A.D. 993–1070)," *Ceylon Studies Seminar* (1975 series) no. 1, serial no. 53.
7. K. A. Nilakanta Sastri, "Vijayabāhu I, the Liberator of Lanka," *Journal of the Royal Asiatic Society* (Ceylon Branch), n.s., 5 (1954): 45–71.
8. *Cūlavaṃsa*, 61:53, trans. 1, 229–30.
9. Keith Taylor, "The Devolution of Kingship in Twelfth Century Ceylon," in *Explorations in Early Southeast Asian History: The Origins of Southeast Asian Statecraft*, ed. Kenneth R. Hall and John K. Whitmore (Ann Arbor: Center for South and Southeast Asian Studies, University of Michigan, 1975), 57.
10. Taylor, "The Devolution of Kingship in Twelfth Century Ceylon," 257–58, respectively.
11. Taylor, "The Devolution of Kingship in Twelfth Century Ceylon," 265.
12. Liyanagamage, *The Decline of Polonnaruwa and the Rise of Dambadeniya (circa 1180–1270 A.D.)*. See also two chapters in Ray, *History of Ceylon*, vol.1, part 2,

namely, Wickramasinghe, "Successors of Parākramabāhu I," 507–28, and Paranavitana, "The Dambadeni Dynasty," 613–35.

13. Indrapala, *The Collapse of the Rājarata Civilization in Ceylon and the Drift to the South-West* (Peradeniya: Ceylon Studies Seminar, University of Ceylon, 1971).
14. C. V. Nicolas, "A Short Account of the History of Irrigation Works Up to the 11th Century," *Journal of the Royal Asiatic Society* (Ceylon Branch), n.s., 7 (1959): 43–69.
15. Senarat Paranavitana, "Some Regulations Concerning Village Irrigation Works in Ancient Ceylon," *Ceylon Journal of Historical and Social Studies* 1 (1958): 1–7.
16. C. W. Nicolas, "The Irrigation Works of Parākramabāhu I," special issue, *Ceylon Historical Journal* 4, nos. 1–4 (1954–55): 52–68.
17. R. A. L. H. Gunawardana, "Irrigation and Hydraulic Society in Medieval Ceylon," *Past and Present: A Journal of Scientific History* 53 (1971): 3–27.
18. For a more extensive treatment of this subject, see Gunawardana's doctoral dissertation submitted to the University of London (1965), entitled "The History of the Buddhist 'Saṅgha' in Ceylon from the Reign of Sena I (833–53 CE) to the Invasion of Māgha (1215)," and the published version of this, entitled *Robe and Plough: Monasticism and Economic Interest in Early Medieval Sri Lanka.* For an article on different aspects of the same topic, see Leach, " Hydraulic Society in Ceylon," which tests Karl Wittfogel's thesis—see his *Oriental Despotism: A Comparative Study of Total Power* (New Haven, CT: Yale University Press, 1957)—about hydraulic societies and Asian despotism with respect to Sri Lanka and concludes that the hydraulic societies of India and Sri Lanka are cellular, not centralized in structure.
19. W. I. Siriweera, "Land Tenure and Revenue in Mediaeval Ceylon (A.D. 1000–1500)," *Ceylon Journal of Historical and Social Studies,* n.s., 2, no. 1 (January–June 1972): 1–49. For further bibliographical references, see my essay cited above, note 4.
20. Again, the essay by Keith Taylor "The Devolution of Kingship in Twelfth Century Ceylon," is recommended. Also, the following are important: (1) the special issue entitled "The Polonnaruva Period" in the *Ceylon Historical Journal* 4, nos. 1–4 (July 1954 through April 1955); and (2) Sirima Wickramasinghe, "The Age of Parākramabāhu I," PhD diss., University of London, 1958.
21. Three essays by Balkrishna Govind Gokhale are helpful in understanding the formative years of Buddhism's relationship to the state in India: "Dhamma as a Political Concept in Early Buddhism," *Journal of Indian History* 46 (April 1968): 249–61; "The Early Buddhist View of the State," *Journal of American Oriental Society* 89, no. 4 (1969): 731–38; and "Early Buddhist Kingship." Frank Reynolds examines early Buddhism's combining of soteriological goals with a concern for establishing and maintaining proper order in the world in "The Two Wheels of Dhamma: A Study of Early Buddhism," in *Essays on the Theravada Tradition in India and Ceylon,* ed. by Bardwell L. Smith, 6–30 (Chambersburg, PA: American Academy of Religion, 1972).
22. *Cūlavaṃsa* 44:36, trans. 1, 141.
23. Among the vast literature on Indian political theory the following are important examples: J. Gonda, *Ancient Indian Kingship from the Religious Point of View;* Charles Drekmeier, *Kingship and Community in Early India* (Stanford, CA: Stanford Univer-

sity Press, 1962); Spellman, *Political Theory of Ancient India; Kautilya's Arthashastra,* trans. R. Shamasastry, 8th ed. (Mysore: Mysore Printing and Publishing House, 1967); Thomas R. Trautmann, *Kautilya and the Arthaśāstra* (Leiden: E. J. Brill, 1971); U.N. Ghoshal, *A History of Indian Political Ideas* (London: Oxford University Press, 1966); R. P. Kangle, *The Kautilīya Arthashastra* (Bombay: Bombay University, 1965). As for the influence of Kautilya in Sri Lanka, it was Wilhelm Geiger who discovered and first discussed it: Wilhelm Geiger, "Kenntnis der indischen Nitiliteratur in Ceylon," *Beiträge zur Literaturwissenschaft und Geistesgeschichte Indiens, Festgabe für Hermann Jacobi, edited by Willibald Kirfel* (Bonn: Klopp, 1926), 418–21. Earlier authors had misread the relevant passages of the *Cülavamsa (kocallādisu niīlisu* instead of *kotallādisu nītisu* as conjectured by Geiger). The medieval Sinhalese used the alternative form of Kautilya's name, viz., *Kautalya,* as seen in the Pāli *Kotalla.*

24. *Cūlavaṃsa,* 58:1–3, trans. 1, 201. See also Geiger's note 2 on the same page.
25. For discussions of the classical Hindu tension between priestly and political orders, see the works of Louis Dumont. His essay "The Conception of Kingship in Ancient India," *Contributions to Indian Society* 6 (December 1962): 48–77 (reprinted in his book *Religion, Politics and History in India: Collected Papers in Indian Sociology* [Paris: Mouton, 1970], chapter 4) has proven to be a stimulating and frequently debated article. A symposium on Dumont's work was published in the *Journal of Asian Studies* 35, no. 4 (August 1976).
26. For discussion of this in the Pāli canon, see the *Lakkhana Suttanta (Dīgha Nikāya),* sutta 30, PTS ed. 3:142–79, trans. in *Dialogues of the Buddha,* sutta 30, 3:132–67).
27. *Cūlavaṃsa,* 57:50, trans. 1, 197.
28. *Cūlavaṃsa,* 59:37–39, trans. 1, 212.
29. *Cūlavaṃsa,* 62:49, trans. 1, 236.
30. For an extended discussion of this topic, see Smith, *Religion and Legitimation of Power in Sri Lanka.* See also the article by Obeyesekere on the persistent ideological underpinnings of Sinhalese nationalism, "Dutthagāminī and the Buddhist Conscience."
31. *Cūlavaṃsa,* 61:48–73, trans. 1, 229–31.
32. *Cūlavaṃsa,* 68:11, trans. 1, 277.
33. Tambiah, *World Renouncer and World Conqueror: A Study of Buddhism and Polity in Thailand against a Hisotrical Background* (Cambridge, UK: Cambridge University Press, 1976), 50. See also the *Aṅguttara Nikāya* 4.7.70 (PTS ed. 2:74–75), trans. *The Book of Gradual Sayings (Aṅguttara Nikāya)* or *More-Numbered Suttas,* trans. F. L. Woodward (London: Pāli Text Society, 1933) 85–86.
34. *Cūlavaṃsa,* 60:85, trans. 1, 223.
35. *Cūlavaṃsa,* 73:8, trans. 2, 1.
36. *Cūlavaṃsa,* 74:242–43, trans. 2, 48.
37. This subject is of considerable importance and can only be reviewed in passing here. For a few of the many treatments of this theme, one may consult the following: John W. Spellman, "The Symbolic Significance of the Number Twelve in Ancient India," *Journal of Asian Studies* 22, no. 1 (November 1962): 79–88; Senarat Paranavitana, *The Shrine of Upulvan at Devundara, Memoirs of the Archaeological Survey of Ceylon;*

Paranavitana, "The Sculpture of Man and Horse Near Tisāvava at Anurādhapura, Ceylon," *Artibus Asiae* 16 (1953): 167–90; Paranavitana, "Sīgiri, the Abode of a God-King," *Journal of the Royal Asiatic Society* (Ceylon Branch), n.s., 1 (1950): 129–83, which includes an extensive discussion of this article by various scholars; Gananath Obeyesekere, "The Pataha Ritual"; Obeyesekere, "Gajābāhu and the Gajabāhu Synchronism"; D. T. Devendra, "The Symbol of the Sinhalese Guardstone," *Artibus Asiae* 21 (1958): 259–68; Wheatley, *The Pivot of the Four Quarters,* 304–5, 311, 479; and Deborah Winslow, "A Political Geography of Deities: Space and the Pantheon in Sinhalese Buddhism," *Journal of Asian Studies* 43, no. 2 (February 1984): 273–91.

38. Geiger, *Culture of Ceylon in Mediaeval Times,* 205.
39. See Ratnapala, *The Katikāvatas.* See also Heinz Bechert, "Theravāda Buddhist Sangha: Some General Observations on Historical and Political Factors in Its Development," *Journal of Asian Studies* 29, no. 4 (August 1970): 761–78.
40. This was introduced in chapter 3.
41. An excellent perspective on this for the Polonnaruva period may be seen in the doctoral dissertation by Gunawardana and in his book mentioned above in note 18.
42. Note 30 lists two works on the theme of religion and the legitimation of power in Sri Lanka. For a companion volume to my *Religion and the Legitimation of Power in Sri Lanka,* see Smith, *Religion and Legitimation of Power in Thailand, Laos, and Burma.*
43. *Cūlavaṃsa,* 74:1–14, trans. 2, 21–22. Here the reasons for the continued reverencing of Anurādhapura are given: because of the belief that the Buddha had visited this site, because of the sacred Bodhi Tree, and because various relics are enshrined there.
44. Wheatley, *The Pivot of the Four Quarters,* 398.
45. Wheatley, *The Pivot of the Four Quarters,* 416–17.
46. Wheatley, *The Pivot of the Four Quarters,* 434. See Redfield and Singer, "The Cultural Role of Cities," 69, in which the point is made about "the necessity for an enlarged cultural consciousness" whenever there is a rapid change or great diversity. Often, this is the context out of which "civil religion" emerges. Also, the discussion of this theme by Robert Heine-Geldern is well known, namely, the parallelism between the macrocosmos and the microcosmos and the capital as the magic center of the empire, a miniature Mount Meru at the heart of the universe. See his "Conceptions of State and Kingship in Southeast Asia," data paper 18, Southeast Asia Program (Ithaca, NY: Cornell University, 1956), 1–3. One of the more interesting discussions of this is by S. J. Tambiah in a chapter on the "galactic polity" within Theravada Buddhist societies, in Sri Lanka as well as Southeast Asia; see Tambiah, *World Renouncer and World Conqueror,* 102–131.
47. *Cūlavaṃsa,* 79:85, trans. 2, 123.
48. *Cūlavaṃsa,* 88:121, trans. 2, 191.
49. Wheatley, *The Pivot of the Four Quarters,* 315.
50. Paranavitana, "Sīgiri, the Abode of a God-King."
51. *Cūlavaṃsa,* 72:329, trans. 1, 348.
52. *Cūlavaṃsa* 72:59, trans. 1, 324.
53. *Cūlavaṃsa,* 81:40–57, trans. 2, 139–40; 81:51–80, trans. 2, 140–42.

54. The reader is referred to the study by Amaradasa Liyanagamage, cited in note 12, on this period of history. This provides an excellent analysis of the forces at work.
55. *Cūlavaṃsa,* 86:18–36, trans. 2, 172–74. Vijayabāhu I was similarly interested (*Cūlavaṃsa* 60:64–66, trans. 1, 220–21). For a stimulating but speculative discussion of this site, see Paranavitana, *The God of Adam's Peak.*
56. *Cūlavaṃsa,* 85:85–89, trans. 2, 167. Also see the volume by Paranavitana, *The Shrine of Upulvan at Devundara.* It was only later, perhaps the fifteenth century, that Hindus in Sri Lanka identified this god as Vishnu, not Varuna. See John Clifford Holt, "Pilgrimage and the Structure of Sinhalese Buddhism," *Journal of the International Association of Buddhist Studies* 5, no. 2 (1982): 23–40.
57. *Cūlavaṃsa,* 82:15–27, trans. 2, 144–45.
58. Bardwell L. Smith, "The Ideal Social Order as Portrayed in the Chronicles of Ceylon, in *Religion and Legitimation of Power in Sri Lanka,* ed. Smith (Chambersburg, PA: Anima, 1978), 48–72.
59. *Cūlavaṃsa,* 72:153, trans. 1, 334.
60. *Cūlavaṃsa,* 67:72–73, trans. 1, 273.
61. See, respectively, *Majjhima Nikāya* suttas 11–12 (PTS ed. 1:63–83, trans. *Middle Length Sayings,* 1:85–110); and *Dīgha Nikāya* sutta 28 (PTS ed. 3:99–116, trans. *Dialogues of the Buddha,* 3:95–110).
62. See Victor Turner, *The Ritual Process: Structure and Anti-Structure* (Chicago: Aldine Publishing, 1969), 125–30.
63. Jonathan Z. Smith, "Earth and Gods," *Journal of Religion* 49 (1969): 119.
64. *Cūlavaṃsa,* 51:81, trans. 1, 155.
65. *Cūlavaṃsa,* 87:1–13, trans. 2, 177–78.
66. H. L. Seneviratne, "The Sacred and the Profane in a Buddhist Rite," *University of Ceylon, Ceylon Studies Seminar* (series no. 7, 1969–70): 1–31. This article discusses the rite of ordination along similar lines.
67. Giuseppe Tucci, *The Theory and Practice of the Mandala* (New York: Samuel Weiser, 1971), 16.

5. Sinhalese Buddhism and Its Modern Quests for Identity

1. Geiger, *Culture of Ceylon in Mediaeval Times,* 176.
2. Donald Eugene Smith, *Religion and Political Development* (Boston: Little, Brown, 1970), 201.
3. D. E. Smith, *Religion and Political Development,* 1. See Lucian W. Pye, *Politics, Personality, and Nation Building* (New Haven, CT: Yale University Press, 1962), in which he identifies this process as the diffusion of a world culture whose ingredients include "the secular state and the industrialized organization of human activities, the reliance upon rational and conscious choice and a faith in impartial justice, and the acceptance of the virtue of merit and of rewards according to skill" (xv).
4. Drekmeier, *Kingship and Community in Early India,* 6.
5. Drekmeier, *Kingship and Community in Early India,* 252–53. See also p. 10: "Hindu political thought never escapes from this dilemma of royal power [*danda*] and

priestly authority. The *rājadharma,* the dharma of the king, exists as guarantor of the whole social structure. Danda is thus means, dharma the end."

6. Bechert, "Theravāda Buddhist Sangha," 766. This statement by Bechert is appropriately qualified by a comment of B. G. Gokhale on the differences between early Buddhist political thinking and the concepts of Kautilya. See Gokhale, "Early Buddhist Kingship."
7. Gokhale, "Early Buddhist Kingship," 15. Gokhale adds: "In this line of reasoning, then, the state is never an end in itself but rather a means to an end. As an instrument, it is possessed of total power that encompasses within its jurisdiction all areas of human activity. It is an awesome power and it is per se neither moral nor immoral. But it cannot exist outside of human beings for it is not just an abstraction or a thought-construct; it can be exercised only through human agencies. It is this association of total power with human beings that creates the dilemma of power. Orderly human existence is not possible without power but power is easily misused and often is misused. The Buddhists set themselves to find an answer to this problem of total power" (20).
8. See also Drekmeier, *Kingship and Community in Early India:* "The king's chief duty was, of course, to protect his subjects. But this involved more than law enforcement. By the fourth century B.C. there had been a notable increase in the welfare functions of the state in India. . . . If the sacred tradition was upheld, the country would prosper; this idea had the effect of making the king accountable for the general prosperity of the people as well as for their security" (225).
9. Sarkisyanz, *Buddhist Background of the Burmese Revolution,* 56.
10. Sarkisyanz, *Buddhist Background of the Burmese Revolution,* 36–37.
11. N. A. Nikam and Richard McKeon, ed. and trans., *The Edicts of Aśoka* (Chicago: University of Chicago Press, 1959), 65.
12. Rahula, *History of Buddhism in Ceylon.* "The influence of the Sangha over the masses was so great that rulers were careful to win the hearts of the bhikkhus for the sake of peaceful and successful government. To obtain the approval of the Sangha was to ensure public support" (70). See also Gokhale, "The Early Buddhist View of the State," 737–38. Also Arasaratnam, *Ceylon,* 78–81. See also Geiger, *Culture of Ceylon in Mediaeval Times,* 203–15; Rahula, *History of Buddhism in Ceylon;* and Richard A. Gard, "Buddhism and Political Authority," in *The Ethic of Power: The Interplay of Religion, Philosophy, and Politics,* ed. Harold D. Lasswell and Harlan Cleveland (New York: Harper and Brothers, 1962), 43–48, 55–58.
13. See *Mahāvaṃsa* 34:82–94, trans. 245 for a typical passage.
14. D. E. Smith, *Religion and Political Development,* 10.
15. Frantz Fanon, *The Wretched of the Earth* (New York: Grove, 1964), 175.
16. Pye, *Politics, Personality, and Nation Building,* 12.
17. Soedjatmoko, "Cultural Motivations to Progress: The 'Exterior' and the 'Interior' Views," in *Religion and Progress in Modern Asia,* ed. Robert N. Bellah (New York: Free Press, 1965), 5.
18. Bechert, "Theravāda Buddhist Sangha." See also Richard H. Robinson, *The Buddhist Religion: A Historical Introduction* (Belmont, CA: Dickenson, 1970): "Everywhere,

Buddhists have been staunch nationalists, have taken part in anticolonial movements, have claimed to be custodians of the national culture, and have longed to reestablish the old symbiosis between Sangha and state. In a secular age, this dream is not going to come true, but nationalist sentiment will undoubtedly maintain Buddhism wherever freedom of religion prevails. However, the Dharma is presently too weak, and the Sangha, too dependent, to exercise moral authority and restrain political excesses. Most citizens are nationalists first, and Buddhists second, if at all" (115).

19. Arasaratnam, *Ceylon*, 60.
20. Pye, *Politics, Personality, and Nation Building*, xv.
21. Pye, *Politics, Personality, and Nation Building*, 106. See also 139–41.
22. Heinz Bechert, *Buddhismus, Staat und Gesellschaft in den Ländern des Theravada-Buddhismus* (Frankfurt am Main: Alfred Metzner Verlag, 1966), 1:112–14.
23. *Mahāvaṃsa*, 25:108, trans. 178. This assurance confirmed the faith of Dutthagāmanī who earlier had gone forth to battle with the cry "not for the kingdom but for the doctrine [Buddhism]." See Rahula, *History of Buddhism in Ceylon*, 228–29, for the incongruous endorsement of violence by arahants.
24. For example, the consecrating of Vijaya, the arrival of the relics, the coming of the Bodhi Tree, the enshrining of the relics, and other events. As W. Howard Wriggins notes in his book *Ceylon: Dilemmas of a New Nation* (Princeton, NJ: Princeton University Press, 1960), "Despite this cultural heritage many Sinhalese are keenly sensitive to the ebb and flow in their own creative energies. More than five centuries separated the late Polonnaruwa period from its predecessors and another hundred years intervened before the Kandyan kingdom put its stamp on the culture of the central highlands. The coming of the Europeans, it is felt, all but destroyed many aspects of indigenous culture. Many Sinhalese, therefore, consider their culture fragile, requiring unusual defenses if it is to survive in proximity to the vigorous Tamil culture and in the face of insistent European influences" (239–40).
25. Pye, *Politics, Personality, and Nation Building*, 287.
26. D. E. Smith, *Religion and Politics in Burma* (Princeton, NJ: Princeton University Press, 1965), 327.
27. C. D. S. Siriwardene, "Buddhist Reorganization in Ceylon," in *South Asian Politics and Religion*, ed. Donald E. Smith (Princeton, NJ: Princeton University Press, 1966), 545. He continues: "It was to undertake the traditional functions of the Buddhist king in promoting the general welfare of Buddhism and also take upon itself the functions appropriate to a religious organization in modern society."
28. See Bechert, *Buddhismus*, 1:267–85; Wriggins, *Ceylon*, 195–201; D. E. Smith, *South Asian Politics and Religion*, 460–67, 500–509. See also Smith's analysis of somewhat comparable problems in Myanmar in *Religion and Politics in Burma*, 186–229. See also Rahula's account of sectarian developments in ancient Sri Lanka, in *History of Buddhism in Ceylon*, 194–97, inter alia.
29. Nikam and McKeon, *The Edicts of Asoka*: "The monk or nun who disrupts the Sangha shall be required to put on white robes [instead of the customary yellow]

and to live in non-residence (*anabasasi*). It is my desire that the Sangha be united and endure forever" (67–68).

30. Bechert, "Theravāda Buddhist Sangha," 777–78. This article is a helpful portrayal of Sāsana reform historically and in different Theravada settings. It also deals with the issue of structure in relationship to this.
31. As he says, a critical study of the *Vinaya Pitaka* shows "how the original rules were modified by supplementary regulations to meet new situations." See Rahula, *History of Buddhism in Ceylon,* 153–154. Technically, the rules were not changed, only reinterpreted, but in practice they amounted to changes. See also Robinson, *The Buddhist Religion,* 42–45. While these interpretations would not be shared by most bhikkhus today, they seem not inconsistent with the counsel and practice of the Buddha.
32. The single most influential example of this overemphasis is probably Wijewardena, *The Revolt in the Temple,* which sees Buddhism primarily as a social gospel. Heinz Bechert's treatment of Buddhist modernism analyzes several of the same tendencies during the past hundred years in Sri Lanka and elsewhere. See *Buddhismus,* 1:36–108. While the modernist movement has many emphases (e.g., rationality, accord with scientific principles, support of lay activity, countercolonialism, organizational restructuring of Buddhism, participation in the international Buddhist movement, scholarship in Buddhist materials, general educational improvement), one of its purposes was the creation of an effective social ethic. For Buddhism to relate significantly to the modern world this will be necessary; on the other hand, it cannot be seen as the primary substance of Buddhism.
33. *Dhammapada* 26:24 (406) and 26:22 (404), respectively, trans., *The Dhammapada,* translated by Sarvepalli Radhakrishnan (London: Oxford University Press, 1966), 183. For a description of the attitude of people in ancient Sri Lanka toward impurity within the Sangha, see Rahula, *History of Buddhism in Ceylon,* 259.
34. Siriwardene, "Buddhist Reorganization in Ceylon," 544.
35. Wriggins, *Ceylon,* 191–92. See Bechert, *Buddhismus,* 1:225–44, for a thorough description of this situation. See also his "Theravāda Buddhist Sangha," in which he discusses an instance of successful Sāsana reform in East Bengal, whereby the monks are "in a certain sense under the control of laymen" (772) and where reform was successful "not in spite of the poverty, but on account of the poverty of their monastic institutions" (778).
36. Rahula, *History of Buddhism in Ceylon,* 252. See 251–62 for further description of monk-lay attitudes toward each other. Also, Robinson, *The Buddhist Religion,* 47–49.
37. Rahula, *History of Buddhism in Ceylon,* 194.
38. See Donald K. Swearer, "Lay Buddhism and the Buddhist Revival in Ceylon," *Journal of the American Academy of Religion* 38 (1970): 255–75; and Gananath Obeyesekere, "Religious Symbolism and Political Change in Ceylon," *Modern Ceylon Studies* 1 (1970): 43–63. The latter has an interesting section on Anagarika Dharmapala (1864–1933) in which the author stresses the meaning of the *anagarika* role that

Dharmapala assumed and that his new name "Anagarika" means "homeless" and symbolizes the combination of monastic renunciation with worldly involvement, a kind of this-worldly asceticism in the Calvinist sense, fitting neither the pattern of the typical monk nor of the typical layperson. Dharmapala was neither one nor the other, yet he sought to combine the advantages of each in a way that was unprecedented within Sinhalese Buddhism.

39. D. E. Smith, *Religion and Politics in Burma,* 120.
40. See Nash, *Anthropological Studies in Theravada Buddhism.* See also Ediriweera R. Sarachandra, "Traditional Values and the Modernization of a Buddhist Society: The Case of Ceylon," in Bellah, *Religion and Progress in Modern Asia,* for a sensitive plea for Sinhalese Buddhism to integrate folk culture with the higher culture of the traditional elite.
41. R. W. J. H. Donoughmore, *Government of Ceylon: Report of the Special Commission of the Ceylon Constitution* (London: H.M.Stationery Office, 1928), 31. See Wriggins, *Ceylon,* 211–70, for an excellent chapter entitled "The Problem of National Unity."
42. Bellah, *Religion and Progress in Modern Asia,* 219. See also D. E. Smith, *Religion and Political Development,* 10–12, 241–45, for a discussion of the movement toward a functional-valuational pluralism.
43. Wriggins, *Ceylon,* 50.
44. D. E. Smith, *Religion and Political Development,* 203–204.
45. Selig S. Harrison, "Hindu Society and the State," in *Expectant Peoples: Nationalism and Development,* ed. K. H. Silvert (New York: Random House, 1963), 99. Harrison's phrase was "Hindu glory with Muslim humiliation."
46. Joseph M. Kitagawa, "The Buddhist Transformation in Japan," *History of Religions* 4 (1965): 336.
47. Nikam and McKeon, *The Edicts of Asoka,* 51–52.
48. Gokhale, "Early Buddhist Kingship": "The theory of the two domains is well expressed by a putative statement of Ajatasattu (circa 493–63 BCE) at the commencement of the First Buddhist Council held at Rājagaha when he said to the assembled monks, 'Yours is the authority of the spirit as mine is of power (*dhammacakka* and *anacakka*)'" (22).
49. Gokhale, "The Early Buddhist View of the State," 732–33.
50. Gokhale, "The Theravāda-Buddhist View of History," 356.
51. Gokhale, "The Theravāda-Buddhist View of History," 357.
52. Conze, "Dharma as a Spiritual, Social and Cosmic Force," 240.
53. Robinson, *The Buddhist Religion,* 51. The Hindu term *sanātana dharma* (eternal or cosmic law which continually needs to be reinterpreted) is suggestive here as well.
54. Robinson, *The Buddhist Religion,* 52–53.
55. Robinson, *The Buddhist Religion,* 22.
56. Soedjatmoko, "Cultural Motivations to Progress," 2.
57. Clifford Geertz, "Modernization in a Muslim Society: The Indonesian Case," in Bellah, *Religion and Progress in Modern Asia,* 166–67.
58. American Cassinese Congregation of Benedictine Monasteries, *Renew and Create,*

36th General Chapter of the American Cassinese Congregation (Benedictines), June 1969.

59. D. E. Smith, *Religion and Political Development,* 198.
60. Wilfred Cantwell Smith, "Traditional Religions and Modern Culture," unpublished address presented at the 11th Congress of the International Association for the History of Religions, Claremont, California, September 9, 1965, 5–6.
61. D. E. Smith, *Religion and Political Development,* 33. See also 201–2.
62. Pye, *Politics, Personality, and Nation Building,* xiii.
63. Wriggins, *Ceylon,* 469.
64. *Renew and Create,* 24. Compare this with the attitude toward change in ancient India or Sri Lanka, where it was regarded as only a sign of degeneration. See Rahula, *History of Buddhism in Ceylon,* 199–205.
65. Robert N. Bellah, "Epilogue: Religion and Progress in Modern Asia," in Bellah, *Religion and Progress in Modern Asia,* 202.

6. Identity Issues of Sinhalas and Tamils

1. Bartholomeusz and de Silva, *Buddhist Fundamentalism and Minority Identities in Sri Lanka* (Albany, NY: State University of New York Press, 1998). This collection is a constructively critical contribution to understanding the causes of ethnic tension in this country, beginning in the late nineteenth century and becoming increasingly explosive in the late twentieth century. The essays are scholarly, nonpartisan, and informative. This publication looks at less explored areas with a common theme in mind, namely, how the phenomenon termed *Sinhala-Buddhist fundamentalism* has stimulated and shaped the identities of non-Buddhist ethnic and religious minorities in Sri Lanka over the past century.
2. John Clifford Holt, "The Persistence of Political Buddhism," in Bartholomeusz and de Silva, *Buddhist Fundamentalism and Minority Identities in Sri Lanka,* 189.
3. Holt, "The Persistence of Political Buddhism," 189.
4. These are, respectively, "The Plurality of Buddhist Fundamentalism: An Inquiry into Views among Buddhist Monks in Sri Lanka" and "Buddhist Burghers and Sinhala-Buddhist Fundamentalism."
5. Tessa Bartholomeusz, "In Defense of Dharma: Just-War Ideology in Buddhist Sri Lanka," *Journal of Buddhist Ethics* 6 (1999): 2. The subject of Sinhala-Buddhist attitudes toward the use of violence, whether expressed by members of the Sangha or by influential laypersons, is obviously a complex one that requires extensive study.
6. Chandra R. de Silva, "The Plurality of Buddhist Fundamentalism: An Inquiry into Views among Buddhist Monks in Sri Lanka," in Bartholomeusz and de Silva, *Buddhist Fundamentalism and Minority Identities in Sri Lanka,* 53–73.
7. Holt, "The Persistence of Political Buddhism," 189.
8. Holt, "The Persistence of Political Buddhism," 194.
9. Thapar, *Aśoka and the Decline of the Mauryas* (Oxford: Oxford University Press, 1961), 165.

10. Thapar, *Aśoka and the Decline of the Mauryas,* 3.
11. Cited in Thapar, *Aśoka and the Decline of the Mauryas,* 255.

Epilogue

1. Richard A. Gardner, "Asian Rural Institute: Living Together with the Earth," *euodoo: Journal of Rural Future Study* 1 (2017): 43–44.

SELECTED BIBLIOGRAPHY

Primary Sources in Translation

[*Aṅguttara Nikāya*] *The Book of Gradual Sayings (Aṅguttara Nikāya) or More-Numbered Suttas.* Translated by F. L. Woodward. 5 vols. London: Pāli Text Society, 1933.

The Chronicle of the Thūpa and the Thūpavaṃsa. Edited and translated by N. A. Jayawickrama. London: Luzac, 1971. [Reprinted as *The History of the Buddha's Relic Shrine,* translated by Stephan C. Berkwitz. New York: Oxford University Press, 2007.]

Cūlavaṃsa: Being the More Recent Part of the Mahāvaṃsa. 2 parts. Edited and translated from the Pāli by Wilhelm Geiger, and from German into English by C. Mabel Rickmers. Colombo: Ceylon Government Information Department, 1953. [Geiger's translation was first published in 1929 by Oxford University Press.]

The Dāthāvaṃsa: A History of the Tooth-Relic of the Buddha. Edited and translated by Bimala Charn, Law. Lahore: Motilal Banarsidas, 1925.

The Dhammapada. Translated by Sarvepalli Radhakrishnan. London: Oxford University Press, 1966.

[*Dīgha Nikāya*] *Dialogues of the Buddha, Translated from the Pāli of the Dīgha Nikāya.* Translated by T. W. and C. A. F. Rhys Davids. 3 vols. London: Oxford University Press, 1910.

Dīpavaṃsa (Chronicle of the Island of Ceylon). Introduction, text, and translation by B. C. Law. Mahāragama. Ceylon: Saman, 1959.

Hatthavanagallavihāravaṃsa. Edited by C. E. Godakumbura. Translated by James d'Alwis. Pāli Text Society text series, 55. London: Luzac, 1956.

The Katikāvatas: Laws of the Buddhist Order of Ceylon from the 12th to the 18th Century. Translated and edited by Nandasena Ratnapala. Munich: Kitzinger, 1971.

Kautilya's Arthashastra. 8th ed, translated by R. Shamasastry. Mysore: Mysore Printing and Publishing House R., 1967.

The Laws of Manu (Manusmṛti). Translated by George Buhler. Sacred Books of the East, 25. Oxford: Clarendon Press, 1886.

Mahāvaṃsa: The Great Chronicle of Ceylon. Translated by Wilhelm Geiger. Assisted by Mabel Haynes Bode. London: Luzac, 1964. [Originally published: London: Pāli Text Society, 1912.]

[*Majjhima Nikāya*] *The Book of Middle Length Sayings (Majjhima Nikāya).* Translated by I. B. Horner. 3 vols. Bristol, UK: Pali Text Society, 1954–59.

A Manual of Buddhist Historical Literature (Saddhamma-Samgaha). Translated by Bimala Churn Law. Calcutta: University of Calcutta, 1941. [Republished as *A Manual of Buddhist Historical Traditions.* New Delhi: Asian Educational Services, 1999.]

The Minor Anthologies of the Pāli Canon. Part 2, *Udāna: Verses of Uplift and Itivuttaka: As It Was Said* translated by F. W. Woodward. London: Geoffrey Cumberlege, 1948.

The Nikāya Sangrahāwa: Being a History of Buddhism in India and Ceylon. [By Dhammakitti.] Edited by W. F. Gunawardhana. Translated by C. M. Fernando. Colombo: H. C. Cottle, Acting Government Printer, Ceylon, 1908.

The Rámáyana of Válmíki, Translated into English Verse. Translated by Ralph T. H. Griffith. London: Trübner, 1870–74.

The Sutra of Golden Light. [Suvarṇaprabhāsa Sūtra]. Translated by R. E. Emmerick. London: Luzac, 1970.

Secondary Sources

Abeysekara, Ananda. *Colors of the Robe: Religion, Identity, and Difference.* Columbia: University of South Carolina Press, 2002.

Adikaram, E. W. *Early History of Buddhism in Ceylon.* Colombo: M. D., 1946.

Allen, Douglas, ed. *Religion and Political Conflict in South Asia: India, Pakistan, and Sri Lanka.* Westport, CT: Greenwood, 1992.

American Cassinese Congregation of Benedictine Monasteries. *Renew and Create.* 36th General Chapter of the American Cassinese Congregation (Benedictines), June 1969.

Ames, Michael M. "Buddha and the Dancing Goblins: A Theory of Magic and Religion." *American Anthropologist* 66 (1964): 75–82.

———. "Magical-Animism and Buddhism: A Structural Analysis of the Sinhalese Religious System." *Journal of Asian Studies* 23 (1964): 21–52.

———. "Ritual Prestations and the Structure of the Sinhalese Pantheon." In *Anthropological Studies in Theravada Buddhism,* edited by Manning Nash, 27–50. New Haven, CT: Yale University Southeast Asia Studies, 1966.

Arasaratnam, S. *Ceylon.* Hoboken, NJ: Spectrum/Prentice-Hall, 1964.

Ariyapala, M. B. *Society in Mediaeval Ceylon: The State of Society in Ceylon as Depicted in the Saddharmaratnavaliya and Other Literature of the Thirteenth Century.* Colombo: Department of Cultural Affairs, 1956.

Ariyaratne, A. T. *Buddhism and Sarvodaya: Sri Lankan Experience.* Delhi: Indian Books Centre, Sri Satguru Publications, 1996.

Arunachalam, Sir P. "Polonnaruwa Bronzes and Siva Worship and Symbolism." *Journal of the Royal Asiatic Society (Ceylon Branch)* 24, no. 68 (1915–16): 189–222.

Balakrishna. "The Evolution of the State." *Indian Historical Quarterly* 3 (1927): 315–35.

Bartholomeusz, Tessa. "Buddhist Burghers and Sinhala-Buddhist Fundamentalism." In *Buddhist Fundamentalism and Minority Identities in Sri Lanka,* edited by Tessa Bartholomeusz and Chandra R. de Silva, 167–85. Albany: State University of New York Press, 1998.

———. "In Defense of Dharma: Just-War Ideology in Buddhist Sri Lanka." *Journal of Buddhist Ethics* 6 (1999): 1–16.

———. *In Defense of Dharma: Just-War Ideology in Buddhist Sri Lanka.* London: Routledge, 2002.

Bartholomeusz, Tessa, and Chandra R. de Silva, eds. *Buddhist Fundamentalism and Minority Identities in Sri Lanka.* Albany: State University of New York Press, 1998.

Basham, A. L., ed. *A Cultural History of India.* Oxford: Clarendon, 1975.

Bechert, Heinz. "The Beginnings of Buddhist Historiography: Mahāvaṃsa and Political Thinking." In *Religion and Legitimation of Power in Sri Lanka,* edited by Bardwell L. Smith, 1–12. Chambersburg, PA: Anima, 1978.

———. *Buddhismus, Staat und Gesellschaft in den Ländern des Theravāda-Buddhismus.* 3 vols. Frankfurt: Alfred Metzner, 1966.

———. "Contradictions in Sinhalese Buddhism." In *Religion and Legitimation of Power in Sri Lanka,* edited by Bardwell L. Smith, 188–98. Chambersburg, PA: Anima, 1978. [First published in *Tradition and Change in Theravada Buddhism: Essays on Ceylon and Thailand in the 19th and 20th Centuries,* edited by Bardwell L. Smith, 7–17. Contributions to Asian Studies 4. Leiden: E. J. Brill, 1973.]

———. "Eine alte Gottheit in Ceylon and Südindien." *Beitraäge zur Geistesgeschichte Indiens, Wiener Zeitschrift für die Kunde Süd- und Ostasiens* 12–13 (1968–69): 33–34.

———. "Notes on the Formation of Buddhist Sects and the Origins of Mahāyāna." In *German Scholars on India: Contributions to Indian Studies,* vol. 1. Edited by Annemarie Schimmel, 6–18. Varanasi: Chowkhamba Sanskrit Series Office, 1973.

———. "On the Popular Religion of the Sinhalese." In *Buddhism in Ceylon and Studies on Religious Syncretism Countries: Report on a Symposium in Gottingen,* edited by Heinz Bechert, 217–33. Gottingen: Vandenhoeck and Ruptrecht, 1978.

———. "Theravāda Buddhist Sangha: Some General Observations on Historical and Political Factors in Its Development." *Journal of Asian Studies* 23 (1970): 761–78.

Bellah, Robert N. "Epilogue: Religion and Progress in Modern Asia." In *Religion and Progress in Modern Asia,* edited by Bellah, 168–229. New York: Free Press, 1965.

———, ed. *Religion and Progress in Modern Asia.* New York: Free Press, 1965.

Berger, Peter L. *The Sacred Canopy: Elements of a Sociological Theory of Religion.* New York: Anchor Books, 1990.

Bloss, Lowell W. "The Buddha and the Nāga: A Study in Buddhist Folk Religiosity." *History of Religions* 13, no. 1 (August 1973): 36–53.

Bond, George D. *Buddhism at Work: Community Development and the Sarvodaya Movement.* Bloomfield, CT: Kumarian, 2004.

———. *The Buddhist Revival in Sri Lanka: Religious Tradition, Reinterpretation and Response.* Columbia: University of South Carolina Press, 1988.

Carrithers, Michael. *The Forest Monks of Sri Lanka: An Anthropological and Historical Study.* Delhi: Oxford University Press, 1983.

Conze, Edward. "Dharma as a Spiritual, Social and Cosmic Force." In *Further Buddhist Studies: Selected Essays,* 1–14. London: Bruno Cassirer, 1975.

Coomaraswamy, Ananda K. *Yaksas.* New Delhi: Munshiram Manoharlal, 1971.

Deegalle, Mahinda, ed. *Buddhism, Conflict and Violence in Modern Sri Lanka.* London: Routledge, 2006.

de Silva, Chandra R. "The Plurality of Buddhist Fundamentalism: An Inquiry into Views among Buddhist Monks in Sri Lanka." In *Buddhist Fundamentalism and Minority Identities in Sri Lanka,* edited by Tessa Bartholomeusz and Chandra R. de Silva, 53–73. Albany: State University of New York Press, 1998.

de Silva, K. M. *Reaping the Whirlwind: Ethnic Conflict, Ethnic Politics in Sri Lanka.* New Delhi: Penguin, 1998.

Devendra, D. T. "The Symbol of the Sinhalese Guardstone." *Artibus Asiae* 21 (1958): 259–68.

Dohanian, Dirian. "The Mahāyāna Buddhist Sculpture of Ceylon." Ph.D. diss., Harvard University, 1964.

———. "Prolegomena to the Study of the Mahayana in Ancient Ceylon." In *India's Contribution to World Thought and Culture,* edited by Lokesh Chandra, 424–37. Vivekananda Commemoration Volume. New Delhi: Archaeological Survey of India, 1970.

———. "The Wata-dā-ge in Ceylon: The Circular-Relic-House of Polonnaruwa and Its Antecedents." *Archives of Asian Art* 23 (1969–70): 119–122.

Donoughmore, R. W. J. H. *Government of Ceylon: Report of the Special Commission of the Ceylon Constitution.* London: H. M. Stationery Office, 1928.

Drekmeier, Charles. *Kingship and Community in Early India.* Stanford, CA: Stanford University Press, 1962.

Dumont, Louis. "The Conception of Kingship in Ancient India." *Contributions to Indian Society* 6 (December 1962): 48–77. [Reprinted in Louis Dumont, *Religion, Politics and History in India: Collected Papers in Indian Sociology.* Paris: Mouton, 1970, chapter 4.]

Dutt, Sukumar. *The Buddha and the Five After-Centuries.* London: Luzac, 1957.

Eisenstadt, S. N. "Some Observations on the Dynamic of Traditions." *Comparative Studies in Society and History: An International Quarterly* 2 (1969): 451–75.

Ellawala, H. *Social History of Early Ceylon.* Colombo: Department of Cultural Affairs, 1969.

Evers, Hans-Dieter. *Monks, Priests and Peasants: A Study of Buddhism and Social Structure in Central Ceylon.* Leiden: E. J. Brill, 1970.

Fanon, Frantz. *The Wretched of the Earth.* New York: Grove, 1964.

Fernando, P. E. E. "Tantric Influence on the Sculptures at Gal Vihāra, Polonnaruva." *University of Ceylon Review* 18 (1960): 50–66.

Fisher, H. A. L. *A History of Europe.* London: Edward Arnold, 1936.

Gard, Richard A. "Buddhism and Political Authority." In *The Ethic of Power: The Interplay of Religion, Philosophy, and Politics,* edited by Harold D. Lasswell and Harlan Cleveland, 39–70. New York: Harper and Brothers, 1962.

Gardner, Richard A. "Asian Rural Institute: Living Together with the Earth." *Euodoō: Journal of Rural Future Study* 1 (2017): 43–44.

Geertz, Clifford. "Modernization in a Muslim Society: The Indonesian Case." In *Religion and Progress in Modern Asia,* edited by Robert N. Bellah, 93–108. New York: Free Press, 1965.

Geiger, Wilhelm. *Culture of Ceylon in Mediaeval Times.* Wiesbaden: O. Harrassowitz, 1960.

———. "Kenntnis der indischen Nitiliteratur in Ceylon." In *Beiträge zur Literaturwissenschaft und Geistesgeschichte Indiens, Festgabe für Hermann Jacobi,* edited by Willibald Kirfel, 418–21. Bonn: Klopp, 1926.

Ghoshal, U. N. "An Aspect of State Administration in the Pre-Maurya Period-Influence of Public Opinion on Kingly Governments." *Journal of Indian History* 40 (1962): 551–55.

———. *A History of Indian Political Ideas.* London: Oxford University Press, 1966.

———. "Principle of the King's Righteousness." *Indian Historical Quarterly* 32 (1956): 304–12.

Godakumbura, C. E. *Sinhalese Literature.* Colombo: Colombo Apothecaries, 1955.

Gokhale, B. G. "Dhamma as a Political Concept in Early Buddhism." *Journal of Indian History* 46 (April 1968): 249–61.

———. "Early Buddhist Kingship." *Journal of Asian Studies* 22, no. 1 (1966): 15–22.

———. "The Early Buddhist View of the State." *Journal of American Oriental Society* 89, no. 4 (1969): 731–38.

———. "The Theravāda-Buddhist View of History." *Journal of the American Oriental Society* 85, no. 3 (1965): 354–60.

Gombrich, Richard F. "The Consecration of a Buddhist Image." *Journal of Asian Studies* 26, no. 1 (November 1966): 23–36.

———. *Precept and Practice: Traditional Buddhism in the Rural Highlands of Ceylon.* Oxford: Clarendon, 1971.

Gombrich, Richard, and Gananath Obeyesekere. *Buddhism Transformed: Religious Change in Sri Lanka.* Princeton, NJ: Princeton University Press, 1988.

Gonda, J. *Ancient Indian Kingship from the Religious Point of View.* Leiden: E. J. Brill, 1969.

Goonetileke, H. A. I. "The Sri Lanka Insurrection of 1971: A Select Bibliographical Commentary." In *Religion and the Legitimation of Power in South Asia,* edited by Bardwell L. Smith, 134–83. Leiden: E. J. Brill, 1978.

Gunawardana, R. A. L. H. "Before the State: An Early Phase in the Evolution of Political Institutions in Ancient Sri Lanka." *Studies in History* 4, no. 2 (1982): 197–236.

———. "Buddhist Nikāyas in Medieval Ceylon." *Ceylon Journal of Historical and Social Studies* 9, no. 1 (1966): 55–66.

———. "The History of the Buddhist 'Saṅgha' in Ceylon from the Reign of Sena I (833–53) to the Invasion of Māgha (1215)." PhD diss., University of London, 1968.

———. "Irrigation and Hydraulic Society in Medieval Ceylon." *Past and Present: A Journal of Scientific History* 53 (1971): 3–27.

———. *Robe and Plough: Monasticism and Economic Interest in Early Medieval Sri Lanka.* Tucson: University of Arizona Press, 1979.

Halverson, John. "Dynamics of Exorcism: The Sinhalese Sanniyakuma." *History of Religions* 10, no. 4 (May 1971): 334–59.

Harris, Elizabeth J. "Pilgrimage and Interreligious Understanding: A Case Study of Sri Pada Mountain in Sri Lanka." *Dharma World: For Living Buddhism and Interfaith Dialogue* 39 (January–March 2012): 16–19.

Harrison, Selig S. "Hindu Society and the State." In *Expectant Peoples: Nationalism and Development,* edited by K. H. Silvert, 267–99. New York: Random House, 1963.

Heine-Geldern, Robert. "Conceptions of State and Kingship in Southeast Asia." Data paper 18, Southeast Asia Program. Ithaca, NY: Cornell University, 1956.

Hettiarachchy, Tilak. *History of Kingship in Ceylon Up to the Fourth Century A.D.* Colombo: Lake House Investments, 1972.

Ho, Ping-ti, and Tang Tsou, eds., *China in Crisis.* Vol. 1, *China's Heritage and the Communist Political System.* Chicago: University of Chicago Press, 1968.

Hocart, A. M. *Polonnaruva. Memoirs of the Archaeological Survey of Ceylon. Vol. 2.* Colombo: Ceylon Government Press, 1924.

———. *The Temple of the Tooth in Kandy. Memoirs of the Archeological Survey of Ceylon. Vol. 4.* Colombo: Ceylon Government Press, 1931.

Holt, John Clifford. *Buddha in the Crown: Avalokiteśvara in the Buddhist Traditions of Sri Lanka.* New York: Oxford University Press, 1991.

———. *Buddhist Extremists and Muslim Minorities: Religious Conflict in Contemporary Sri Lanka.* New York: Oxford University Press, 2016.

———. "Hindu Influences on Medieval Sri Lankan Buddhist Culture." In *Buddhism, Conflict and Violence in Modern Sri Lanka,* edited by Mahinda Deegalle, 38–66. London: Routledge, 2006.

———. "The Persistence of Political Buddhism." In *Buddhist Fundamentalism and Minority Identities in Sri Lanka,* edited by Tessa Bartholomeusz and Chandra R. de Silva, 186–95. Albany, NY: State University of New York Press, 1998.

———. "Pilgrimage and the Structure of Sinhalese Buddhism." *Journal of the International Association of Buddhist Studies* 5, no. 2 (1982): 23–40.

———. *The Sri Lanka Reader: History, Culture, Politics.* Durham, NC: Duke University Press, 2011.

———. *The Religious World of Kīrti Śrī: Buddhism, Art and Politics in Late Medieval Sri Lanka.* New York: Oxford University Press, 1990.

Indrapala, Karthigesu, ed. *The Collapse of the Rajarata Civilization in Ceylon and the Drift to the South-West.* Peradeniya: Ceylon Studies Seminar, 1971.

Iyer, P. Sarvesvara. "Puranic Saivism in Ceylon during the Polonnaruwa Period." In *Proceedings of the 1st Conference-Seminar of Tamil Studies, University of Malaya, Kuala Lumpur. International Association of Tamil Research* 1 (1968): 462–74.

Jayasekera, U. D. *Early History of Education in Ceylon.* Colombo: Department of Government Affairs, Government of Ceylon, 1969.

Kangle, R. P. *The Kautilīya Arthashastra.* Bombay: Bombay University, 1965.

Kemper, Steven E. G. "Buddhism without Bhikkhus: The Sri Lanka Vinaya Vardena Society." In *Religion and Legitimation of Power in Sri Lanka,* edited by Bardwell L. Smith, 212–35. Chambersburg, PA: Anima Books, 1978.

———. *The Presence of the Past: Chronicles, Politics, and Culture in Sinhala Life.* Ithaca, NY: Cornell University Press, 1992.

Kiribamune, Sirima. "Some Reflections on Professor Paranavitana's Contribution to History." *Ceylon Journal of the Humanities* 1, no. 1 (1970): 76–92.

Kitagawa, Joseph M. "The Buddhist Transformation in Japan." *History of Religions* 4 (1965): 336.

Law, B. C. *On the Chronicles of Ceylon.* Calcutta: Journal of the Royal Asiatic Society of Bengal, 1947.

Leach, Edmund R. "Hydraulic Society in Ceylon." *Past and Present: A Journal of Scientific History* 15 (1959): 2–26.

———. "Pulleyar and the Lord Buddha: An Aspect of Religious Syncretism in Ceylon." *Psychoanalysis and the Psychoanalytical Review* 49 (1962): 80–102.

Liyanagamage, Amaradasa. *The Decline of Polonnaruwa and the Rise of Dambadeniya (circa 1180–1270 A.D.)*. Colombo: Department of Cultural Affairs, Government Press, 1968.

Malalasekera, G. P. *The Pali Literature of Ceylon*. London: Royal Asiatic Society of Great Britain and Ireland, 1928.

Malalgoda, Kitsiri. "Millennialism in Relation to Buddhism." *Comparative Studies in Society and History* 12, no. 4 (October 1970): 424–41.

Mudiyanse, Nandasena. *Mahāyāna Monuments in Ceylon*. Colombo: M. D. Gunasena, 1967.

Mus, Paul. *Barabadur: Esquisse d'une Histoire du Bouddhisme fondée sur la critique archéologique des textes*. Hanoi: Imprimerie d'Extrême-Orient, 1935.

———. "Bouddhisme et monde occidental: Pour une nouvelle méthode." In *Présence du Bouddhisme*, edited by Rene Berval, 187–200. Saigon: France-Asie, 1959. [Unpublished translation by George O. Totten.]

Nash, Manning, ed. *Anthropological Studies in Theravada Buddhism*. Cultural Report Series 13, Southeast Asia Studies. New Haven, CT: Yale University Press, 1966.

Nicolas, C. V. "A Short Account of the History of Irrigation Works Up to the 11th Century." *Journal of the Royal Asiatic Society (Ceylon Branch)*, n.s., 7 (1959): 43–69

Niebuhr, H. Richard. *Christ and Culture*. New York: Harper and Brothers, 1951.

Nikam, N. A., and Richard McKeon, eds. and trans. *The Edicts of Asoka*. Chicago: University of Chicago Press, 1959.

Nilakanta Sastri, K. A. *The Colas*. Rev. ed., 2 vols. Madras: University of Madras, 1955.

———. *The Pandyan Kingdom: From the Earliest Times to the 16th Century*. London: Luzac, 1925.

———. "Vijayabāhu I, the Liberator of Lanka." *Journal of the Royal Asiatic Society (Ceylon Branch)* 5 (1954): 45–71.

Obeyesekere, Gananath. "The Buddhist Pantheon in Ceylon and Its Extensions." In *Anthropological Studies in Theravada Buddhism*, edited by Manning Nash, 1–26. Cultural Report Series 13, Southeast Asia Studies. New Haven, CT: Yale University Press, 1996.

———. "Duṭṭhagāmaṇī and the Buddhist Conscience." In *Religion and Political Conflict in South Asia: India, Pakistan, and Sri Lanka*, edited by Douglas Allen, 135–60. Westport, CT: Greenwood, 1992.

———. "Gajabāhu and the Gajabāhu Synchronism: An Inquiry into the Relationship between Myth and History." *Ceylon Journal of the Humanities* 1, no. 1 (January 1970): 25–56. [Reprinted in *Religion and the Legitimation of Power in Sri Lanka*, edited by Bardwell L. Smith, 155–76. Chambersburg, PA: Anima Books, 1978.]

———. "The Great Tradition and the Little in the Perspective of Sinhalese Buddhism." *Journal of Asian Studies* 22, no. 2 (February 1963): 139–53.

———. "The Pataha Ritual: Genesis and Function." *Spolia Zeylanica* 30, part 2 (1965): 279–96.

———. "Religious Symbolism and Political Change in Ceylon." *Modern Ceylon Studies* 1 (1970): 43–63.

———. "Social Change and the Deities: The Rise and Fall of Deities in the Sinhalese Buddhist Pantheon." Unpublished manuscript, read at a symposium held at Swarthmore College, April 1972.

———. "Theodicy, Sin and Salvation in a Sociology of Buddhism." In *Dialectic in Practical Religion*, edited by E. R. Leach, 7–40. Cambridge: Cambridge University Press, 1968.

Panditha, Vincent. "Buddhism during the Polonnaruva Period." In *The Polonnaruva Period*, edited by S. D. Suparamadu. *Ceylon Historical Journal* 4 (special number, July 1954–April 1955): 113–29.

Paranavitana, Senarat. "The Art and Architecture of the Polonnaruva Period." In *The Polonnaruva Period*, edited by S. D. Suparamadu. *Ceylon Historical Journal* 4 (special number, July 1954–April 1955): 69–90.

———. "The Capital of Ceylon during the Ninth and Tenth Centuries." *Ceylon Journal of Science* (Section C. Anthropology) 2 (1930): 141–47.

———. *Ceylon and Malaysia.* Colombo: Lake House Investments, 1966.

———. "Civilisation of the Polonnaru Period: Religion, Literature and Art." In *History of Ceylon*, edited by H. C. Ray, vol. 1, *From the Earliest Times to 1505*, part 2, 563–612. Colombo: Ceylon University Press, 1959.

———. "The Dambadeni Dynasty." *History of Ceylon.* Vol. 1, *From the Earliest Times to 1505*, part 1, *Up to the End of the Anuradhapura Period*, edited by H. C. Ray, 613–35. Colombo: Ceylon University Press, 1959.

———. *The God of Adam's Peak.* Ascona, Switzerland: Artibus Asiae, 1958.

———. "Mahayanism in Ceylon." *Ceylon Journal of Science* 2 (1928): 35–71.

———. "Pre-Buddhist Religious Beliefs in Ceylon." *Journal of the Royal Asiatic Society (Ceylon Branch)* 31, no. 82 (1929): 302–27.

———. "The Sculpture of Man and Horse Near Tisāvava at Anurādhapura, Ceylon." *Artibus Asiae* 16 (1953): 167–90.

———. *The Shrine of Upulvan at Devundara. Memoirs of the Archeological Survey of Ceylon. Vol. 6.* Colombo, Sri Lanka: Ceylon Government Press, 1953.

———. "Sīgiri, the Abode of a God-King." *Journal of the Royal Asiatic Society (Ceylon Branch)*, n.s., 1 (1950): 129–83.

———. "The Significance of Sinhalese 'Moonstones.'" *Artibus Asiae* 17 (1954): 197–231.

———. "Some Regulations Concerning Village Irrigation Works in Ancient Ceylon." *Ceylon Journal of Historical and Social Studies* 1 (1958): 1–7.

———. *The Story of Sigiri.* Colombo: Lake House Investments, 1972.

———, ed. *The University of Ceylon History of Ceylon*, vol. 1, part 1. Colombo: Ceylon University Press Board, 1959.

Pathmanathan, S. "Social and Religious Conditions under Cola Rule in Sri Lanka (A.D. 993–1070)," *Ceylon Studies Seminar* (1975 series) no. 1, serial no. 53.

Perera, A. D. T. E. "Buddha on the Sacred Seat of Brahma." *World Buddhism* 21 (May 1973).

Perera, B. J. "Some Political Trends in the Late Anuradhapura and Polonnaruwa Period." *Ceylon Historical Journal* 10, nos. 1–4 (1961): 60–76.

The Polonnaruva Period. Edited by S. D. Suparamadu. *Ceylon Historical Journal* 4 (special number, July 1954–April 1955).

Pye, Lucian W. *Politics, Personality, and Nation Building.* New Haven, CT: Yale University Press, 1962.

Rahula, Walpola. *History of Buddhism in Ceylon.* 2nd ed. Colombo: M. D. Gunasena, 1966.

Ray, H. C., ed. *History of Ceylon.* Vol. 1, *From the Earliest Times to 1505,* part 1, *Up to the End of the Anuradhapura Period.* Colombo: Ceylon University Press, 1959.

Redfield, Robert, and Milton Singer. "The Cultural Role of Cities." *Economic Development and Cultural Change* 3, no. 1 (1954): 53–72.

Reynolds, Frank E. "Dhammadīpa: A Study of Indianization and Buddhism in Sri Lanka." *Ohio Journal of Religion* 2, no. 1 (April 1974): 63–78.

———. "The Two Wheels of Dhamma: A Study of Early Buddhism." In *Essays on the Theravada Tradition in India and Ceylon,* edited by Bardwell L. Smith, 6–30. Chambersburg, PA: American Academy of Religion, 1972.

Robinson, Richard H. *The Buddhist Religion: A Historical Introduction.* Belmont, CA: Dickenson, 1970.

Sarachandra, Ediriweera R. "Traditional Values and the Modernization of a Buddhist Society: The Case of Ceylon." In *Religion and Progress in Modern Asia,* edited by Robert N. Bellah, 109–23. New York: Free Press, 1965.

Sarkar, Himansu Bhusan. "The Evolution of Śiva-Buddha Cult in Java." *Journal of Indian History* 45 (1969): 637–46.

Sarkisyanz, E. *Buddhist Backgrounds of the Burmese Revolution.* The Hague: Martinus Nijhoff, 1965.

Scheible, Kristin. *Reading the "Mahāvaṃsa": The Literary Aims of a Theravāda Buddhist History.* New York: Columbia University Press, 2016.

Seneviratne, H. L. "The Āsala Perahāra in Kandy." *Ceylon Journal of Historical and Social Studies* 6, no. 2 (July–December 1963): 169–80.

———. "The Sacred and the Profane in a Buddhist Rite," *University of Ceylon, Ceylon Studies Seminar* (series no. 7, 1969–70): 1–31

———. *Rituals of the Kandyan State.* Cambridge: Cambridge University Press, 1978.

———. *The Work of Kings: The New Buddhism in Sri Lanka.* Chicago: University of Chicago Press, 1999.

Seneviratne, Sudharshan. "'Peripheral Regions' and 'Marginal Communities': Towards an Alternative Explanation of Early Iron Age Material and Social Formations in Sri Lanka." In *Tradition, Dissent and Ideology: Essays in Honour of Romila Thapar,* edited by R. Champakalakshmi and S. Goyal, 264–75. Delhi: Oxford University Press, 1996.

Shils, Edward. "Centre and Periphery." In *The Logic of Personal Knowledge: Essays Presented to Michael Polanyi on His Seventieth Birthday,* edited by Polanyi Festschrift Committee, 117–30. London: Routledge and Kegan Paul, 1961.

Sinha, B. P. "The King in the Kautilyan State." *Journal of the Bihar Research Society* 40 (1954): 291–308.

Sirisena, W. M. *Sri Lanka and South-East Asia: Political, Religious and Cultural Relations from A.D. c. 1000 to c. 1500.* Leiden: E. J. Brill, 1978.

Siriwardene, C. D. S. "Buddhist Reorganization in Ceylon." In *South Asian Politics and Religion.* edited by Donald E. Smith, 531–46. Princeton, NJ: Princeton University Press, 1966.

Siriweera, W. I. "Land Tenure and Revenue in Mediaeval Ceylon (A.D. 1000–1500)." *Ceylon Journal of Historical and Social Studies,* n.s., 2, no. 1 (January–June 1972): 1–49.

Smith, Bardwell L. "Casting Stones for Peace: Talismans of Hope in War-Torn Sri Lanka." In *Excursions and Explorations: Cultural Encounters between Sri Lanka and the United States,* edited by Tissa Jayatilaka, 133–67. Nugegoda, Sri Lanka: The United States–Sri Lanka Fulbright Commission, 2002.

———. "The Ideal Social Order as Portrayed in the Chronicles of Ceylon." In *Religion and Legitimation of Power in Sri Lanka,* edited by Bardwell L. Smith, 48–72. Chambersburg, PA: Anima, 1978.

———. "Identity Issues of Sinhalas and Tamils." In *Buddhism, Conflict and Violence in Modern Sri Lanka,* edited by Mahinda Deegalle, 163–76. London: Routledge, 2006.

———. "In Pursuit of Equilibrium: Polonnaruva as a Ceremonial Center." In *The City as a Sacred Center: Essays on Six Asian Contexts,* edited by Bardwell L. Smith and Holly Reynolds, 60–87. Leiden: E. J. Brill, 1987. [Also published in the *Journal of Developing Societies* 2 (1986): 208–35.]

———. "Kingship, the Sangha, and the Process of Legitimation in Anurādhapura Ceylon: An Interpretive Essay." In *Religion and Legitimation of Power in Sri Lanka,* edited by Bardwell L. Smith, 73–95. Chambersburg, PA: Anima, 1978.

———. "The Pagān Period (1044–1287): A Bibliographic Note." *Contributions to Asian Studies* 16 (1981): 112–30.

———. "Polonnaruva as a Ceremonial Complex: Sinhalese Cultural Identity and the Dilemmas of Pluralism." In *History of Buddhism,* edited by A. K. Narain, 295–320. New Delhi: B. R. Publishing, 1980.

———. "The Polonnaruva Period (ca. 993–1293 A.D.): A Thematic Bibliographic Essay." In *Religion and Legitimation of Power in Sri Lanka,* edited by Bardwell L. Smith, 119–54. Chambersburg, PA: Anima, 1978.

———. "Religion and Art in the Gupta Age: A Bibliographic Essay." In *Essays on Gupta Culture,* edited by Bardwell L. Smith, 307–40. Delhi: Motilal Banarsidass, 1983.

———, ed. *Religion and Legitimation of Power in Sri Lanka.* Chambersburg, PA: Anima, 1978.

———, ed. *Religion and Legitimation of Power in Thailand, Laos, and Burma.* Chambersburg, PA: Anima, 1978.

———. "Religion, Social Conflict and the Problem of Identity in South Asia: An Interpretive Introduction." In *Religion and Social Conflict in South Asia,* edited by Bardwell L. Smith, 1–12. Leiden: E. J. Brill, 1976.

———. "Religious Assimilation in Early Medieval Sinhalese Society." In *Studies in Pali and Buddhism,* edited by A. K. Narain, 347–68. New Delhi: B. R. Publishing, 1979.

———. "Sinhalese Buddhism and the Dilemmas of Reinterpretation." In Bardwell L. Smith, Frank Reynolds, and Gananath Obeyesekere, *The Two Wheels of Dhamma: Essays on the Theravada Tradition in India and Sri Lanka,* 79–106, AAR Studies in Religion 3. Chambersburg, PA: American Academy of Religion, 1972.

———. "Talismans of Hope in Worn-Torn Sri Lanka." *Dharma World: For Living Buddhism and Interfaith Dialogue* 29 (November/December 2002): 21–25.

———, ed. *Tradition and Change in Theravada Buddhism: Essays on Ceylon and Thailand in the 19th and 20th Centuries.* In *Contributions to Asian Studies,* 4. Leiden: E. J. Brill, 1973.

———. "Varieties of Religious Assimilation in Early Medieval Sri Lanka." In *Buddhist Philosophy and Culture: Essays in Honour of Nicholas J. Jayawickreme,* edited by David J. Kalupahana and W. G. Weeraratne, 259–78. Kelaniya: Vidyalankara University, 1987.

Smith, Donald Eugene. *Religion and Political Development: An Analytical Study.* Boston: Little, Brown, 1970.

———. *Religion and Politics in Burma.* Princeton, NJ: Princeton University Press, 1965.

Smith, Jonathan Z. "Earth and Gods." *Journal of Religion* 49 (1969): 103–27.

Smith, Wilfred Cantwell. "Traditional Religions and Modern Culture." Unpublished address presented at the 11th Congress of the International Association for the History of Religions, Claremont, California, September 9, 1965.

Soedjatmoko. "Cultural Motivations to Progress: The 'Exterior' and the 'Interior' Views." In *Religion and Progress in Modern Asia,* edited by Robert N. Bellah, 1–14. New York: Free Press, 1965.

Spellman, John W. *Political Theory of Ancient India: A Study of Kingship from the Earliest Times to circa A.D 300.* Oxford: Clarendon, 1964.

———. "The Symbolic Significance of the Number Twelve in Ancient India." *Journal of Asian Studies* 22, no. 1 (November 1962): 79–88.

Spencer, George W. "The Politics of Plunder: The Cholas in Eleventh-Century Ceylon." *Journal of Asian Studies* 35, no. 3 (1976): 405–19.

Spencer, Jonathan, ed. *Sri Lanka: History and the Roots of Conflict.* London: Routledge, 1990.

Strong, John S. *The Legend of King Aśoka: A Study and Translation of the "Aśokāvadāna."* Princeton, NJ: Princeton University Press, 1983.

Subramanian, Samanth. *This Divided Island: Life, Death, and the Sri Lankan War.* New York: Thomas Dunne Books, 2015.

Suparamadu, S. D., ed. *The Polonnaruva Period. Ceylon Historical Journal* 4, nos. 1–4 (special number, July 1954–April 1955).

Swearer, Donald K. "Lay Buddhism and the Buddhist Revival in Ceylon." *Journal of the American Academy of Religion* 38 (1970): 255–75.

Tambiah, Stanley Jeyaraja. "The Galactic Polity in Southeast Asia." *HAU: Journal of Ethnographic Theory* 3, no. 3 (2013): 503–34.

———. "The Ideology of Merit and the Social Correlates of Buddhism in a Thai Village." In *Dialectic in Practical Religion,* edited by E. R. Leach, 41–121. Cambridge, UK: University of Cambridge Press, 1968.

———. *World Conqueror and World Renouncer: A Study of Buddhism and Polity in Thailand against a Historical Background.* Cambridge, UK: Cambridge University Press, 1976.

Taylor, Keith. "The Devolution of Kingship in Twelfth Century Ceylon." In *Explorations in Early Southeast Asian History,* edited by Kenneth R. Hall and John K. Whitmore, 257–302. Ann Arbor: Center for South and Southeast Asian Studies, University of Michigan, 1976.

Thapar, Romila. *Aśoka and the Decline of the Mauryas.* Oxford: Oxford University Press, 1961.

Trautmann, Thomas R. *Kautilya and the Arthaśāstra.* Leiden: E. J. Brill, 1971.

Tucci, Giuseppe. *The Theory and Practice of the Mandala.* New York: Samuel Weiser, 1971.

Turner, Victor. *The Ritual Process: Structure and Anti-Structure.* Chicago: Aldine, 1969.

Twitchett, Denis C. "Varied Patterns of Provincial Autonomy in the T'ang Dynasty." In *Essays on T'ang Society: The Interplay of Social, Political and Economic Forces,* edited by Bardwell L. Smith and John Curtis Perry, 90–109. Leiden: E. J. Brill, 1976.

Voegelin, Eric. *Order and History.* Baton Rouge: Louisiana State University Press, 1956.

Wheatley, Paul. *The Pivot of the Four Quarters.* Chicago: Aldine, 1971.

Wickramasinghe, Sirima. "The Age of Parakramabahu I." Ph.D. thesis, University of London, 1958.

———. "Successors of Parākramabāhu I: Downfall of the Polonnaru Kingdom." In *History of Ceylon,* vol. 1, *From the Earliest Times to 1505,* edited by H. C. Ray, vol. 1, part 2, 507–28. Colombo: Ceylon University Press, 1959.

Wijesekera, Nandadeva. *Early Sinhalese Sculpture.* Colombo: M. D. Gunasena, 1962.

Wijesekera, O. H. de A. "Sanskrit Civilization among the Ancient Sinhalese." *Ceylon Historical Journal* 1, no. 1 (1951): 23–29.

Wijewardena, D. G. *The Revolt in the Temple, Dharma-Vijaya (Triumph of Righteousness).* Colombo: Sinha, 1953.

Winslow, Deborah. "A Political Geography of Deities: Space and the Pantheon in Sinhalese Buddhism." *Journal of Asian Studies* 43, no. 2 (February 1984): 273–91.

Wirz, Paul. *Kataragama: The Holiest Place in Ceylon,* 2nd ed. Colombo: Lake House Investments, 1972.

Wittfogel, Karl. *Oriental Despotism: A Comparative Study of Total Power.* New Haven, CT: Yale University Press, 1957.

Wriggins, W. Howard. *Ceylon: Dilemmas of a New Nation.* Princeton, NJ: Princeton University Press, 1960.

Yalman, Nur. "The Structure of Sinhalese Healing Rituals." *Journal of Asian Studies* 23 (June 1964): 115–50.

INDEX

Abhayagirivihāra, 53, 58, 59, 64, 81, 88
abhiśeka or "anointing," 17
Acariyavāda (heterodox) movement, 10
Adam's Peak (Sumanala Kanda), footprint on, xii–xiii, 12, 65, 96
adhamma (chaos), 68, 88, 90, 99, 108
Adikaram, E. W., 140n20, 141n42
Aganna Sutta of the Dīgha Nikāya, 32
Aggabodhi I, 42
Aggabodhi VII, 26–27
agricultural gentry, emergence of, 79
Ālakamandā, 38, 94
Alms Bowl of the Buddha, 48, 65, 89, 95
Ames, Michael, 66, 69
Aṅgulimāla Sutta, 33
Anguttara-Nikāya, 42
anicca (impermanence), 21–22
"anointing" or *abhiśeka,* 17
antistructure, concept of, 99
Anurādhapura: as ceremonial complex, 92–93; Polonnaruva compared, 94; rise and collapse of, 76–77, 80, 85, 92–93. *See also* ideal social order; legitimation
arahants, 16, 108, 139n11, 160n23
ārannika (forest-dwelling monks), 59, 68, 69
Aransaratnam, Sinnappah, 139n9
ARI (Asian Rural Institute), Japan, 4, 135–37
Ariyavaṃsa, 46
Arthaśāstra (Kautilya), 9, 41, 88, 103
Asian Rural Institute (ARI), Japan, 4, 135–37
Aśoka: bhikkhu community, regulation of, 91; conversion of, 17; cruelty and piety combined in, vii–viii, 12–13, 15, 104; *Devānampiya* honorific, use of, 140n28; edicts of, vii–viii, xii, 20, 21, 91, 133, 160–61n29; ideal social order, in early concepts of, 7, 10–13, 16–19, 22, 142n60; India, continuity of tradition with, 109; legitimation and, 32, 35, 38, 40, 46, 47, 91; Parākramabāhu I the Great compared, 61, 62; religious tolerance of, 7, 59, 118, 130, 133, 134; on ritual and ceremony, 47; state's right to reform and purify community under, 111; welfare provisions of, 104, 122
Aśoka and the Decline of the Mauryas (Thapar), vii–viii
Aśokāvadāna, 12
assimilation. *See* religious assimilation
authority. *See* kingship and political order; legitimation
Avalokiteśvara (Nātha), x, 67, 150n17

Bandaranaike, W. R. D., assassination of (1959), 108
Bartholomeusz, Tessa, 128, 129, 131
Bechert, Heinz, 103, 106, 110, 146n38, 151n29, 159n6, 159–60n18, 161n35
Bellah, Robert, 122–23
Berger, Peter, 34–35, 39, 49
bhakti (devotion) tradition, 63–65, 90
bhikkhus (monks): Abhayagirivihāra, 53, 58, 64, 81, 88; forest-dwellers (*ārannika*), 59, 68, 69; ideal social order and, 9, 10, 12, 16–18, 25, 27, 140n20, 142n53; Jetavāna, 59; killed in Tamil Tiger attack on Śri Mahā Bodhi, xii; laypersons, relationship to, 113–14, 117, 159n12, 161n35; legitimation and, 33, 36, 40–45, 47, 51, 89, 90, 91, 147n50, 148n60; modernization process in Sri Lanka and, 110–15; Pamsukulin sect, 81; political activity, involvement in, 112, 120, 129; Polonnaruva period, pursuit of equilibrium in, 81, 89, 90, 91, 95; purity of Sangha, role in, 45; religious assimilation and, 53, 58–59, 61, 63–65, 67–69; Tamils, variety of responses to, 129–31; Vaitulyavādins (Vetulla School), 58, 59; village-dwellers (*gāmavāsī*), 59, 68; vow of poverty conflicting with monastic wealth, 112–13. *See also* Mahāvihāra

Bhuvanekabāhu V, 91
Bible, early chronicles compared to, 6, 14, 16, 144n98
Bimbisāra, 17, 38
Bodhisattas (Bodhisattvas): emergence and influence of concept of, 24–25, 144n94; king's role as, 24, 27, 28, 46, 119; Mahāyāna Buddhism, Bodhisattva cult in, 69, 150n17; religious assimilation and, 63, 64, 67, 69; Theravada Buddhism, Metteyya as only current Bodhisatta recognized by, 29
Bodhi Tree, x–xi, 8, 10, 23, 29–30, 36, 47, 48, 63, 157n43, 160n24
Brahmā, Buddha on sacred seat of, 35, 37, 39
brāhmanavaggo (Way of the Brahmin), 112
Brahmanism, 7–9, 50, 53, 62, 66, 71, 87–90, 101, 103, 109, 141n34, 150n23, 154n2
British colonialism, 60, 105, 109, 115
Buddha: Aśoka and, 12; demonic forms, encounters with, 33; distinctive marks on infant Siddhartha, 9; enthronement on sacred seat of Brahmā, 35, 37, 39; establishment in Sri Lanka, 5, 9–11; evil/disordered aspect of world and, 13, 14, 33; footprint of, on Adam's Peak, xii–xiii, 65, 96; in Hindu pantheon, 8, 9, 66–67, 145–46n25, 151–52n29; incomprehensibility of, 24; India, continuity of Sinhalese tradition with, 109; last will and testament of, 33; lineage of, 7, 9; on model bhikkhu, 112; Parākramabāhu I and, 88, 97; *parinibbāna* of, 8, 144n5; pilgrimage to places visited by, 96; relics of, 8, 10–11, 23, 24, 28–30, 36–37, 47, 48, 63, 89, 90, 157n43, 160n24 (*see also specific relics*); reverence shown toward, 27; as supreme monarch, 28–29, 35–39, 119
Buddha Sāsana Commission, 1959 report of, 110, 111
Buddhadāsa, 25, 34
Buddha Sāsana Mandalaya, 110
Buddhaghosa, 109, 140n29
Buddharākkhita, 108
Buddhism: canonical and traditional Buddhism, balancing, 110, 114–15; China, persecutions in, 60; conciliar movement in, 10; First Council, 162n48; fundamentalism, moving beyond, 128–34; international/ecumenical, 118; Mantryana, 53, 55, 57, 69; primary goals of, 123–24, 132; social and economic welfare concerns, 25, 33, 41, 48, 85, 102–4, 120, 123–24, 159n8, 161n32; Tantrayana, 50, 53. *See also* Mahāyāna Buddhism; Sinhalese Buddhism and history of Sri Lanka; Theravada Buddhism
Buddhist community. *See* Sangha
Buddhist Fundamentalism and Minority Identities in Sri Lanka (Bartholomeusz and de Silva), 128–29, 163n1
Burma. *See* Myanmar

Cakkavatti, 12, 19, 24, 25, 26, 27, 29, 38, 88, 119
Cakkavatti-Sīhanāda Sutta, 13
Cambodia, 70
canonical and traditional Buddhism, balancing, 110, 114–15
CARITAS Japan, 136
Catholicism, xii, 108
center-periphery tensions: equilibrium, pursuit of, in Polonnaruva period, 75–78, 83–84; religious assimilation and, 55–56
ceremony. *See* ritual and ceremony
change and continuity, balancing, 122–23
change and progress, attitudes toward, 121–22, 163n64
Charles (Prince of Wales), ix
China: persecutions of Buddhism in, 60; T'ang in, 75
Cholas, viii, 7, 60, 65, 76, 77, 79–82, 84, 95
Christianity, xii, 108, 113, 116, 117, 128, 131, 133, 135, 136
cities, cultural role of, 157n46
City of Righteousness, 7, 13, 21, 29–30
civil religion, 56, 60–62, 65, 73, 157n46
Colebrook Reforms (1832–34), 113
Collapse of the Rājarata Civilization in Ceylon and the Drift to the Southwest, The (ed. Indrapala), 83
colonialism/postcolonialism, 60, 105, 106, 108, 109, 114, 115, 128, 160n24

community. *See* Sangha
conciliar movement in Buddhism, 10
continuity and change, balancing, 122–23
continuity of tradition, in ideal Sri Lankan social order, 6, 7–12
Conze, Edward, 48–49, 119–20, 143n65, 145n9
counterkarma, 69
Cūlavaṃsa: idea social order in, 25, 26, 30, 142n56, 143n89; legitimation and, 41, 85, 87, 88; pursuit of equilibrium in Polonnaruva period and, 81, 85, 87, 88, 94, 95, 97, 154n5; on religious assimilation, 58, 61, 64, 150n21

Dakkhinadesa, 76, 77, 79, 80, 86
Dālada Māligāwa (Temple of the Tooth), Kandy, ix–x
Damilas, 34, 96
Dasaka, 9
Dāthāsiva, 42
Dāthāvaṃsa, 64, 96
democracy and Sinhalese Buddhism, 123
de Silva, Chandra, 128, 129, 131
de Silva, Kingsley, vii, 1
Devanagara (Devundara), 96
Devānampiya Tissa, 10, 11, 15, 22, 34, 36, 38, 40, 46, 85, 93
devas, 22, 35
devatās, 36, 95, 145n19
Dhamma: Aśoka on conquest by, viii, 133, 134; equilibrium, pursuit of (in Polonnaruva period), 85, 86, 88, 90, 91, 95, 97; ideal social order and, 6, 8–10, 13, 15–19, 21, 23, 24, 30; king's role as protector of, 45–46; legitimation and, 33–37, 40, 42, 43, 45–47; modernization process and, 104, 107, 108, 112, 119; religious assimilation and, 53, 58, 67–70, 72
dhamma-danda tension, 30, 85
Dhammadhātu, 58
dhammadīpa, Sri Lanka as, 2, 78, 84–85, 108, 129, 130
Dhammakitti, 91, 95
Dhammapada, 161n33
Dharma, 7, 20, 42, 42n60, 47, 49, 104, 118, 120, 145n9, 158–59n5, 159–60n18
Dharmapala, Anagarika, 161–62n38
Dharma-vijaya, 7, 13, 21, 24, 28, 30, 104
Dhātusena, 9, 34, 38, 41, 146n38
Dhaulī, Aśoka's 13th Rock Edict at, vii–viii, xii
Dīgha Nikāya, 38, 157n48
Dīpavaṃsa: ideal social order in, 1, 5, 9, 15, 17; on legitimation, 33, 46; religious assimilation and, 63
disorder, threat of. *See* precariousness of order
diversity. *See* pluralism
divine kingship theory, 69, 146n30
Dohanian, Dirian K., 64, 71
Donoughmore Constitution (1931), 115–16
Drekmeier, Charles, 102–3, 158–59n5, 159n8
Dumont, Louis, 156n25
Dutthagāmanī: faith of, 160n23; ideal social order and, 7, 10, 12, 16, 23, 27–28, 141–42n46; legitimation and, 34, 36, 46, 147n55; Mahāthūpa constructed by, 96; Parākramabāhu I compared, 88, 96; religious assimilation and, 64; Sinhalese identity and, 108

economic and social welfare concerns, 25, 33, 41, 48, 85, 102–4, 120, 123–24, 159n8, 161n32
economic segregation of Tamils and Sinhalese, 117
Edicts of Aśoka, vii–viii, xii, 20, 21, 91, 133, 160–61n29
Eelam, 125
Eisenstadt, S. N., 56
Elara the Tamil, 23, 108
equilibrium, pursuit of (in Polonnaruva period), 2–3, 75–100; center-periphery tensions, 75–78, 83–84; civil religion in, 61; dating of period, 77; descriptions of Polonnaruva, 94; Hindu migration and influences during, viii; legitimation and, 77, 85–92; mercantile class and agricultural gentry, emergence of, 79, 82; pluralism and, 3, 74, 75–78, 80, 83–85, 88, 92, 95, 98–100; political and socioeconomic developments, 77, 78–85; religious assimilation in, 63–64; rise and collapse of Polonnaruva, 76–77, 80; ritual and ceremony, use of, 78, 92–98,

equilibrium (*continued*)
99; sources for, 153–54n2; threat of disorder and, 85–92; transformation from orthogenetic to heterogenetic society, 77; writing down of canon, 95
Esala Perahera festival, ix
eschatology/millennialism, 21, 152n30
Evers, Hans-Dieter, 50, 65
exile, as metaphor, 99

Fa Hsien, 64
Federal Party, Sri Lanka, 117
First Council, 162n48
Fisher, H. A. L., 73
fishes, law of the (*mātsya-nyāya*), 32, 144n2
footprint, Adam's Peak, xii, 65
forest chieftains (*vanni*), 79, 96
forest-dwelling monks (*ārannika*), 59, 68, 69
Four Noble Truths, 14
fundamentalism, moving beyond, 128–34

Gajabāhu, 152n29
Gajabāhu II, 41
gāmavāsī (village-dwelling monks), 59, 68
Ganesha, 151n27
Geertz, Clifford, 120–21
Geiger, Wilhelm, 8, 22, 25, 26, 35, 41, 42, 64–65, 90, 101, 140n14, 142n53, 147n55, 155–56n23
Ghoshal, U. N., 42
Gokhale, Balkrishna Govind, 19, 103–4, 119, 140n14, 155n21, 159nn6–7, 162n48
Gombrich, Richard E., 15–151n23
Gotama. *See* Buddha
Gothābhaya, 42, 96
Great Thūpa, 36
Gunawardana, R. A. L. H., 59, 83–84
Gunawardhana, W. F., 59

Hair Relic of the Buddha, 48
Hatthavanagalla, 96
Hatthavanagallavihāravaṃsa, 96, 150n21
Heine-Geldern, Robert, 157n46
heterodoxy/heresy, Sinhalese Buddhist concern over, 9–10, 50, 53–54. *See also* religious assimilation
Hettiarachchy, Tilak, 43–44, 147n45
Hinduism: Adam's Peak and, xii; adoption of Buddha into pantheon of, 8, 9, 66–67, 145–46n25, 151–52n29; Buddhist monasteries, Hindu shrines inside, 65; continuity of tradition with/Buddhist tolerance of, 7–9, 37, 50, 101, 109; legitimation and, 35, 37, 50, 87, 88; nationalism and, 118; Polonnaruva period, migration and influences during, viii, 87; priestly and political orders, tension between, 156n25; religious assimilation and, 53, 62–66, 69, 73; sacro-political authority and, 102–3; *saṃdhyā* in, xiii; Tooth of the Buddha in, ix. *See also* Brahmanism
historical consciousness, modern heightening of, 121
history of Sri Lanka. *See* Sinhalese Buddhism and history of Sri Lanka
Holt, John, 130–31
Hurlbutt, Jerri, 135

ideal social order (in early chronicles), 1–2, 5–30; awareness of evil and threat of disorder, 6, 12–15; continuity of tradition in, 6, 7–12; ecclesiastical and political order, relationship between, 11–12; king and community, relationship between, 7, 13, 16–20, 142n53; legitimation and, 30, 31; reciprocity, centrality of, 19, 23, 27; society and cosmos, relationship between, 7, 21–30; source material for, 5–6, 139n1
identity, 3, 125–34; fundamentalism, moving beyond, 128–34; inclusive identity, practicing vision of, 4, 130–31, 136; modernization process in Sri Lanka and, 100, 101, 102, 106–9; personal, communal, and national, 125–27; preservation of, Sinhalese concern with, 131; problem of, 100, 126; as religious issue, 126–27; Tamils and Sinhalese identity, 107, 108, 109, 160n24; transformation from orthogenetic to heterogenetic society and, 77
India: advance of Islam into, 60; continuity of Sinhalese tradition with, 6, 7–9, 50, 101, 109; ideal king, model of, 40;

migration/invasion from, viii, 7, 63, 81; nationalist sentiment in, 118; ontological perceptions of authority in, 35; sacro-political authority in, 102–3; Tamil migration/invasion/influence from, viii, 7, 63, 83, 100, 101, 133
Indra (Sakka), 8, 15, 17, 33, 39, 94, 101, 109, 140n13, 144n5
Indrapala, K., 93
Intercollegiate Sri Lanka Education (ISLE) program, vii, ix
international/ecumenical Buddhism, 118
irrigation system, 83–84
Islam and Muslims, xii, 60, 113, 117, 133, 136, 152n30, 162n45
ISLE (Intercollegiate Sri Lanka Education) program, vii, ix
Itihāsa tales, 88

Jains, viii, 146n30
Jātakas, 6, 88
Jāvakas, 82
Jayasekera, U. D., 42
Jetavāna, 59
Jetthatissa, 42

Kailāsa, 37, 38, 94, 145–46n25
Kāka Jātaka, 28
Kālāśoka, 33
Kāliṅgas, viii, 13, 77, 79, 80, 81, 87
kamma, 20, 22, 45, 61, 66
Kandyan Convention (1815), 105
Karens, Myanmar, 117
karma and counterkarma, 69, 119
karunā (compassion), 22
Kassapa I, 38, 94
Kassapa V, 41, 81, 86, 146n38
Kataragama, 151–52nn28–29
Kautilya, 9, 20, 41, 88, 103, 155–56n23, 159n6
Kingship and Community in Early India (Drekmeier), 102–3, 158–59n5, 159n8
kingship and political order: Bodhisatta, king's role as, 24, 27, 28, 46, 119; Brahmanical influences on, 8–9, 109; Buddha, as supreme monarch, 28–29, 35–39, 119; community, relationship to, 7, 13, 16–20, 142n53; continuity, political, 11–12; cosmos-society, role in relationship between, 23–28; Dhamma, king as protector of, 45–46; divine kingship theory, 69, 146n30; ecclesiastical order and, 11–12, 34, 38, 109–11; ideal king, epithets for, 140n28, 140–41n33; modernization process and sacro-political authority, 102–5; in Polonnaruva period, 79–85; religious assimilation and, 61–62, 69; secular and sacred, balancing, 118–19; total power, problem of, 159n7. *See also specific entries at* legitimation; *specific rulers*
Kitagawa, Joseph M., 118, 142n60
Kubera (Kuvera), 39, 94
Kumaratunga, x, 130

Lakkana Sutta, 38
land tenure, 83, 84
Lankatilaka Temple, 65
Law, B. C., 6
law of the fishes (*mātsya-nyāya*), 32, 144n2
legitimation (in Anurādhapura period), 2, 31–52; continuity of tradition and, 9, 11; extent, balancing, and exercise of power, 31, 39–44, 146n41; ideal social order and, 30, 31; nurturing, 31, 44–49; ontological status of legitimated authority, 31, 34–39; pluralism and, 2, 30, 31, 44, 49–52; precariousness of order and, 31, 32–34; religious assimilation and, 51–52; ritual and ceremony, role of, 44–45, 47–49, 148n60; Sāsana, importance of royal support for, 34
legitimation (in Polonnaruva period), 77, 85–92
Liberation Tigers of Tamil Eelam (LTTE), vii, x, xi, 129–30, 134
"lion's roar" of Parākramabāhu I, 97–98
Liyanagamage, Amaradasa, 82
lokapālas, 67, 94
lokka-nibbāna (Nibbāna in this world), 20
Lotus Sutra, 118
LTTE (Liberation Tigers of Tamil Eelam), vii, x, xi, 129–30, 134
Ludowyk, E. F. C., 6, 12

Maga Brāhmana, 38
Māgha, 51, 60, 77, 82–84, 95, 98

Mahābharata, 88
Mahāsammata, 9, 88
Mahāsaṅghikas, 111
Mahāsena, 42, 47
Mahāsudassana Sutta, 38
Mahā-Sudassana Sutta, 28–29
Mahāthūpa, 63, 64, 96
Mahāvaṃsa: Buddhism and Brahmanism, close relationship of, 101; Buddhist fundamentalism and, 128–29, 130; ideal social order in, 1, 5, 8–11, 13–14, 16, 21–24, 30, 142n52; on legitimation, 33, 35, 36, 47, 90; Polonnaruva period, pursuit of equilibrium in, 78, 90; on religious assimilation, 58, 63; on sacro-political authority, 105
Mahāvihāra: Buddhist fundamentalism and, 128, 130, 131; ideal social order and, 6, 9, 10, 18, 23; legitimation and, 34, 36, 42; Polonnaruva period, pursuit of equilibrium in, 93, 97; religious assimilation and, 53–54, 57, 59, 63–64, 69
Mahāyāna Buddhism: Bodhisattva cult in, 69, 150n17; change within, 50; enlightenment in, 70–71; ideal social order, early concepts of, 10, 21, 24, 28; influence on Sinhalese Buddhism, 36–37, 53; religious assimilation and, 53, 55, 57, 58, 60, 63–64, 66, 69–71, 150n17; sovereignty, different concepts of, 119; unity out of diversity, cultivation of, 118
Mahinda (purported bhikkhu son of Aśoka), 9, 10, 11, 15, 23, 33–34, 36, 40, 46, 85, 109, 142n54
Mahinda II, 62
Majjhima Nikāya, 33
Malalasekera, G. P., 10, 147n55
Maṅgala-Sutta, 18
Mantryana Buddhism, 53, 55, 57, 69
Manusmriti, 33, 39
mātsya-nyāya (law of the fishes), 32, 144n2
May 1958 riots between Sinhalese and Tamils, 107
Megha (the Cloud), 38
mercantile class, emergence of, 79, 82
mercenaries, use of, in Polonnaruva period, 81
Metteyya (Maitreya, the future Buddha), 9, 29, 141n34
millennialism/eschatology, 21, 152n30
modernization process in Sri Lanka, 3, 101–24; canonical and traditional Buddhism, balancing, 110, 114–15; colonialism/postcolonialism and, 105, 106, 108, 109, 114, 115, 160n24; continuity and change, balancing, 122–23; contributions of religion to, 101–2; definition of modernization, 102, 158–59n3; dynamic modernity versus static traditionalism, assumptions regarding, 121; historical consciousness, heightening of, 121; identity and, 100, 101, 102, 106–9; nationalist sentiment and, 106–7, 114, 116, 118, 159–60n18; pluralism and, 101–2, 116–17, 119, 120; primary goal of Buddhism and, 124; progress and change, attitudes toward, 121–22, 163n64; sacro-political authority and, 102–5; Sangha and, 102, 109–15; secular and sacred, balancing, 102, 118–21; unity in diversity, search for, 102, 115–18
Moggaliputa Thera, 18, 46
Moggallāna, 38, 142n56
monarchy. *See* kingship and political order
monks. *See* bhikkhus
moonstones, 37, 63, 71
Mudiyanse, N., 63
Murga (Skanda), 67, 151nn27–28
Mus, Paul, 9, 28, 72, 104, 144n94, 153n38
Muslims and Islam, xii, 60, 113, 117, 133, 136, 152n30, 162n45
Myanmar (Burma): ideal social order and, 29; identity issues, 135; legitimation in, 44; modernization process in, 107–9, 111, 114–17, 120, 123, 161n28; religious assimilation and, 62, 66, 70

nāgas, 22, 33, 37, 145n9, 145n19
Nātha (Avalokiteśvara), x, 67, 150n17
National Christian Council, Japan, 136
nationalist sentiment, 106–7, 114, 116, 118, 159–60n18
Ne Win, 117
Nibbāna (Nirvana), 7, 8, 15, 19–20, 45, 47, 66, 113, 120, 123, 143n89

Niebuhr, H. Richard, 149n6
Nigrodha, 17
Nikāya Sangrahāwa (Dhammakitti), 58, 59, 91
nuns, xi, 46, 114, 160–61n29

Obeyesekere, Gananath, 66–67, 68–69, 141–42n46, 151–52nn28–29, 152n30
orthodoxy, Sinhalese Buddhist concern over, 9–10, 50, 53–54. *See also* religious assimilation

Pāli and Sanskrit terms, 139n8
Pamsukulin sect, 81
Panditha, Vincent, 62
Pāndyas, 7, 79, 81, 82, 86
Parākramabāhu I the Great: ideal social order and, 12, 23; "lion's roar" of, 97–98; pursuit of equilibrium in Polonnaruva period and, 76, 79–84, 87–91, 94–98, 154n5; religious assimilation and, 59, 61–62, 63, 71
Parākramabāhu II, 61, 64, 65, 76, 82, 91, 95–96, 99, 150n21, 152n29
Parākramabāhu III, 77
pāramitā (perfections), theory of, 63
Paranavitana, Senarat, 37, 38, 65, 71, 94, 146n30, 150n17, 154n3
parinibbāna, 8, 144n5
paritta and *Parittas* (Protection Suttas), 48, 99, 141n42
Pasenadi of Kosala, 33
pataha ritual, 69, 151n29
paticca-samuppāda (dependent origination), 21–22
Pattinī, x, 67
Perera, B. J., 80
Perera, D. T. F., 37
Pivot of the Four Corners, The (Wheatley), 75–76, 92
plausibility structures, 49–50
pluralism: equilibrium, pursuit of, in Polonnaruva period, 3, 74, 75–78, 80, 83–85, 88, 92, 95, 98–100; identity and, 3; legitimation and, 2, 30, 31, 44, 49–52; modernization process and, 101–2, 116–17, 119, 120; Polonnaruva period, pursuit of equilibrium in, 3, 74; problematic multicentricity, 76–77; realization of pluralistic community, 4, 135–37; religious assimilation and, 56, 71; secularization and, 116; Sir Lanka's capacity to become model of, 132; unity in diversity, search for, 102, 115–18
political order. *See* kingship and political order
Polonnaruva period. *See* equilibrium, pursuit of
Portuguese colonization, 105
power, legitimation of. *See* legitimation
precariousness of order: discontinuities in social order, 8, 77, 93, 139n7; ideal social order, awareness of evil and threat of disorder to, 6, 12–15; legitimation and, 31, 32–34; pursuit of equilibrium in Polonnaruva period and, 85–92; religious assimilation and tension between traditional/dominant values and behavior, 67–70
Priyadarśī, 21, 118
problematic multicentricity, 76–77
progress and change, attitudes toward, 121–22, 163n64
Pūjāvaliya, 152n29
Pulatthinagara (Polonnaruva). *See* equilibrium, pursuit of
purohita, 8, 42, 87, 88
Pye, Lucian, 107, 109

Questions of King Milinda, The, 13

Rahula, Walpola, 6, 28, 104, 139n1, 140n28, 161n31
Rājarattha, 41, 51, 76, 79, 80, 82, 85, 86, 99, 154n5
Rājāvaliya, 152n29
Rāmāyana, 88, 144n2
Ratanāvalī, 87–88
Ray, H. C., 153n2
reciprocity, centrality of, 19, 23, 27, 44
Redfield, Robert, 157n46
relics of the Buddha, 8, 10–11, 23, 24, 28–30, 36–37, 47, 48, 63, 89, 90, 157n43, 160n24. *See also specific relics*

religious assimilation (in early Medieval Sri Lanka), 2, 53–74; accommodation of/proneness to, 60–62; center-periphery tensions in, 55–56; civil religion and, 56, 60–62, 65, 73; defined, 55; Eisenstadt's typology of, 56; evidence for, 54; future areas of study in, 73; as hierarchical relationship, 66–67; legitimation and, 51–52; Niebuhr's typology of, 149n6; orthodoxy/heterodoxy, Buddhist concern over, 9–10, 50, 53–54; pluralism and, 56, 71; resistance/opposition to, 58–60; spectrum of positions within Sinhalese Buddhism regarding, 56–57; syncretism/synthesis/incorporation, 62–66; tension between traditional and dominant values/behavior, 67–70; theoretical approach to, 54–55; transformative approach to, 70–72
religious tolerance: of Aśoka, 7, 59, 118, 130, 133, 134; Hinduism, continuity of tradition with/Buddhist tolerance of, 7–9, 37, 50, 101, 109; restoration of ability to engage in and promote, 131–32
Reynolds, Frank, 69, 152n34, 155n21
Rissho-Kosei-kai, 136
ritual and ceremony: legitimation, as means of, 44–45, 47–49, 148n60; in pursuit of equilibrium (in Polonnaruva period), 78, 92–98, 99
Robe and Plough (Gunawardana), 59
Robinson, Richard, 120
Rohana, 43, 65, 76, 79–82, 86, 88, 154n5
Roman Catholicism, xii, 108

sacramental terms, envisioning universe in, 35–36
Saddhamma-Saṅgaha (Dhammakitti), 95
Śaivism/Shaivism, viii, 57, 62, 63
Sakka (Indra), 8, 15, 17, 33, 39, 94, 101, 109, 140n13, 144n5
Saman/Samantabhadra (Sumana), xii, 65, 67, 96, 150n17
saṃdhyā, xiii
Samghamitta, x, 42, 142n54
Sampasādaniya Sutta, 98
samsāra, 24, 119
sanātana dharma, 162n53
Sangha (Buddhist community): discipline, issues of, 111, 160–61n29; ideal social order of (*see* ideal social order); king and community, relationship between, 7, 13, 16–20, 142n53; laypersons and religious, relationship between, 113–14, 117, 159n12, 161n35; modernization process in Sri Lanka and, 102, 109–15; organizational structure and reform of, 110–11; purity, importance of, 45–46; traditional and canonical Buddhism, balancing, 110, 114–15
sanniyaku, 152n33
Sanskrit and Pāli terms, 139n8
Sāriputta, 98
Sarkisyanz, Emanuel, 28, 29, 104, 144n94
Sastri, K. A. Nilakanta, 81
sāvaka-saṅgha. *See* ideal social order
Second Council, 10, 33, 111
secularism: pluralism and, 116; sacred and secular, balancing, 102, 118–21
Sena I, 76, 86, 99, 154n5
Sena II, 26, 59, 62, 86
Seneviratne, H. L., 152n29
Shaivism/Śaivism, viii, 57, 62, 63
Shils, Edward, 55–56
Shiva, viii–ix, xii, 145n25, 151n27
Siam Nikāya, 113
Siddhartha. *See* Buddha
Sigālovāda Sutta, 19, 27, 147n48
Sīhanāda Sutta, 98
Silākāla, 48, 58
sinānāpūjā (bathing the holy tree), 48
Singer, Milton, 157n46
Sinhalese Buddhism and history of Sri Lanka, 1–4; classical period in (3rd century BCE–1029 CE), 1–2, 5; equilibrium, pursuit of, Polonnaruva period, 2–3, 75–100 (*see also* equilibrium, pursuit of); ethnic conflict of twentieth and twenty-first centuries, vii–xiv, 1; ideal social order, early concepts of, 1–2, 5–30 (*see also* ideal social order); identity issues, 3, 125–34 (*see also* identity); legitimation in Anurādhapura period, 2, 31–52 (*see also* legitimation); modern-

ization process in, 3, 101–24 (*see also* modernization process in Sri Lanka); pluralistic community, realization of, 4 (*see also* pluralism); religious assimilation, in early Medieval period, 2, 53–74 (*see also* religious assimilation); stones of reconciliation, author's placement of, vii–xiii, 3–4
Sirimeghavanna, 64
Sirisamghabodhi, 25, 96, 150n21
Siriwardene, C. D. S., 112, 113, 160n27
Siriweera, W. I., 84
Skanda (Murga), 67, 151nn27–28
Smith, Bardwell L.: at ARI (Asian Rural Institute), Japan, 4, 135–37; stones of reconciliation, placement of, vii–xiii, 3–4
Smith, Charlotte, vii, 135, 136
Smith, Donald, 109–10, 114, 117, 121, 158–59n3
Smith, Jonathan, 99
Smith, Wilfred Cantwell, 121
social and economic welfare concerns, 25, 33, 41, 48, 85, 102–4, 120, 123–24, 159n8, 161n32
Soedjatmoko, 106
Sri Ekambaranātha Temple, Kānchipuram (Conjeeveram), Tamil Nadu, viii–ix
Sri Lanka. *See* Sinhalese Buddhism and history of Sri Lanka
Sri Lanka Vinaya Vardena Society, 59
Śri Mahā Bodhi, Anurādhapura, x–xiii
state, the. *See* kingship and political order
stones of reconciliation, author's placement of, vii–xiii, 3–4
Strong, John, 12
stūpas, 24, 36–37, 47–49, 72
Sukranīti, 39
Sumana (Saman/Samantabhadra), xii, 65, 67, 96, 150n17
Sumanala Kanda (Adam's Peak), footprint on, xii–xiii, 12, 65, 96
Swearer, Donald K., 161–62n38

Takami, Toshihiro, 135
Tambiah, S. J., 45, 89, 148n60, 157n46
Tamils: economic segregation of, 117; historical antipathy between Sinhalese and, 107, 116, 117; identity concerns of, as minority group, 117, 125, 132–33; LTTE (Liberation Tigers of Tamil Eelam), vii, x, xi, 129–30, 134; migration/invasion/influence from India, viii, 7, 63, 83, 100, 101, 133; self-determination goals of, 125, 132; Sinhalese identity and, 107, 108, 109, 125, 129–31, 160n24
T'ang, China, 75
Tantrayana Buddhism, 50, 53
Tathāgata, the, 9, 10, 17, 37, 49, 72, 90
Taylor, Keith, 81–82, 84
Temple Land Registration Act (1856), 113
Temple of the Tooth (Dālada Māligāwa), Kandy, ix–x
Thailand, 19, 44, 62, 66, 70, 109, 111, 115, 135
Thapar, Romila, vii–viii, 132
Theravada Buddhism: bhikkhus' role in purity of Sangha, 45; change within, 50; continuity of tradition and, 8, 9, 12; enlightenment in, 70–71; "galactic polity" within, 157n46; ideal social order in, 21; last thoughts before dying in, 69; Metteyya as only current Bodhisatta recognized by, 29; national identity of Sinhalese Buddhists and, 106; religious assimilation and, 55, 56, 60, 63, 65, 69–71; ritual and ceremony in, 44–45, 47–49; sacred and secular, balancing, 118–19; sacro-political authority in, 103; social ethic of, 19; unity out of diversity, cultivation of, 118
Thomas, Saint (apostle), xii
threat of disorder. *See* precariousness of order
Three Gems/Jewels, 17, 21
Thūpavaṃsa, 64, 96
Tibet, 60
Tipitaka, 59
Tiruchelvam, Neelan, assassination of, xiii
tolerance. *See* religious tolerance
Tooth of the Buddha: *bhakti* tradition and, 64, 65; *Dāthāvaṃsa* and cult of, 96; festival of, ix, 47–48, 90, 96; legitimizing power of, 89, 90, 95; miracle of, 150n21; Temple of the Tooth (Dālada Māligāwa), Kandy, ix–x
total power, problem of, 159n7

traditional and canonical Buddhism, balancing, 110, 114–15
transliteration practices, xvii
Tucci, Giuseppe, 100
Turner, Victor, 99

Udaya II, 26, 154n5
umbrella, as symbol of sovereignty, 37, 87–89, 142n56
U Nu, 114, 117
Upāli, 9, 109
Upatissa I, 25, 34
upekkhā (tranquility or equanimity), 20
Uppalavanna (Upulvan), 66
Urbuddhismus, 54, 102, 110, 115

Vaiśālī, 10, 111
Vaishnavism, 57, 63
Vaitulyavādins (Vetulla School), 58, 59
Vajrayana, 50
Varma, Vishwanath Prasad, 144n2
Varuna, 39, 66, 90, 94, 96, 158n56
Vasabha, 41
Vattagāmanī, 34
Vāyu, 39
Veddās, 14
Vedism, xiii, 42, 90
Vēlaikkāras, 81
Vibhīsana, 67
Vijaya, 5, 8, 15, 109, 144n5, 160n24
Vijayabāhu I, 34, 65, 81–82, 87–89, 93, 95, 154n5, 158n55
Vijayabāhu III, 82, 95
Vijayabāhu IV, 65, 94
Vikkamabāhu I, 49
village-dwelling monks (*gāmavāsī*), 59, 68
Vinaya, 19, 45, 53, 58, 59, 111–12
Vinaya Pitaka, 161n31
violence, Sinhala-Buddhist attitudes toward, 163n5
Vishnu, 8, 63, 66, 96, 140n13, 144n5, 145n25, 158n56
Vohārika Tissa, 46, 50, 58

Wata-dā-ge, Polonnaruva, 71, 153n35
Weber, Max, 104
welfare, economic and social, 25, 33, 41, 48, 85, 102–4, 120, 123–24, 159n8, 161n32
Wheatley, Paul, 75–76, 78, 92, 93–94
wheel of power, 88–89
wheel of righteousness, 88–89
wheel of suffering, 66
Wheel of the Law, 24, 35, 47
Wijeskera, O. H. de A., 104
Wijewardena, D. G., 139n3, 161n32
Wirz, Paul, 152n29
Wriggins, W. Howard, 116, 160n24
written canon, creation of, 95

yakkhas, 14, 33, 86, 88–89, 94, 141n41, 144n7, 145n9
Yalman, Nur, 66
Yama, 39, 94

RECENT BOOKS IN THE SERIES

Studies in Religion and Culture

Precarious Balance: Sinhala Buddhism and the Forces of Pluralism
Bardwell L. Smith

Words Made Flesh: Formations of the Postsecular in British Romanticism
Sean Dempsey

A Language of Things: Emanuel Swedenborg and the American Environmental Imagination
Devin P. Zuber

The Pragmatist Turn: Religion, the Enlightenment, and the Formation of American Literature
Giles Gunn

Rethinking Sincerity and Authenticity: The Ethics of Theatricality in Kant, Kierkegaard, and Levinas
Howard Pickett

The Newark Earthworks: Enduring Monuments, Contested Meanings
Lindsay Jones and Richard D. Shiels, editors

Ideas to Live For: Toward a Global Ethics
Giles Gunn

The Pagan Writes Back: When World Religion Meets World Literature
Zhange Ni

Freud and Augustine in Dialogue: Psychoanalysis, Mysticism, and the Culture of Modern Spirituality
William B. Parsons

Vigilant Faith: Passionate Agnosticism in a Secular World
Daniel Boscaljon

Postmodernism and the Revolution in Religious Theory: Toward a Semiotics of the Event
Carl Raschke

Textual Intimacy: Autobiography and Religious Identities
Wesley A. Kort

When the Sun Danced: Myth, Miracles, and Modernity in Early Twentieth-Century Portugal
Jeffrey S. Bennett

Encountering the Secular: Philosophical Endeavors in Religion and Culture
J. Heath Atchley

Religion after Postmodernism: Retheorizing Myth and Literature
Victor E. Taylor

Mourning Religion
William B. Parsons, Diane Jonte-Pace, and Susan E. Henking, editors

Praise of the Secular
Gabriel Vahanian

Doing Justice to Mercy: Religion, Law, and Criminal Justice
Jonathan Rothchild, Matthew Myer Boulton, and Kevin Jung, editors

Bewildered Travel: The Sacred Quest for Confusion
Frederick J. Ruf

Sacred Claims: Repatriation and Living Tradition
Greg Johnson

Religion and Violence in a Secular World: Toward a New Political Theology
Clayton Crockett, editor

John Ruskin and the Ethics of Consumption
David M. Craig

Pontius Pilate
Roger Caillois

The Value of Solitude: The Ethics and Spirituality of Aloneness in Autobiography
John D. Barbour

Meditation and the Martial Arts
Michael L. Raposa

Between Faith and Thought: An Essay on the Ontotheological Condition
Jeffrey W. Robbins

Exhibiting Religion: Colonialism and Spectacle at International Expositions, 1851–1893
John P. Burris

Taking Responsibility: Comparative Perspectives
Winston Davis, editor

Symbolic Loss: The Ambiguity of Mourning and Memory at Century's End
Peter Homans, editor

Boredom and the Religious Imagination
Michael L. Raposa

www.ingramcontent.com/pod-product-compliance
Lightning Source LLC
Chambersburg PA
CBHW021731220426
43662CB00008B/801

* 9 7 8 0 8 1 3 9 4 5 3 8 5 *